The Graying of America

Retirement and Why You Can't Afford It

by James Jorgensen

McGraw-Hill Book Company

New York   St. Louis   San Francisco   Bogotá
Guatemala   Hamburg   Lisbon   Madrid   Mexico
Montreal   Panama   Paris   San Juan   São Paulo
Tokyo   Toronto

To my wife, Pat

Copyright © 1980 by James Jorgensen

1234567890FGFG87654321

Reprinted by arrangement with The Dial Press

First McGraw-Hill Paperback Edition, 1981

Library of Congress Cataloging in Publication Data

Jorgensen, James A.
  The graying of America.

  1. Retirement—Economic aspects—United States.
2. Retirement income—United States.   3.   Old age
pensions—United States.   4.   Civil service pension
—United States.   I.   Title.
HQ1062.J67   1981   646.7′9   81-8313
ISBN 0-07-033027-1 (pbk.)   AACR2

Preface

This book is written in simple-to-understand, nontechnical language and covers in a general way the subject of retirement plans, both private and government. By its nature it cannot cover every subject in great depth, nor is it intended as a reference book in this field.

Questions you have about your own retirement plan should be directed to those advisors best suited to serve you: your attorney, plan trustee, accountant, and financial advisor.

Part of this book deals with events that may occur in the future. The author makes no guarantees, implied or otherwise, that these events and/or predictions will actually occur. The reader is free to draw whatever conclusions seem most appropriate.

James Jorgensen

Contents

Contents

The Graying of America

Introduction

Over the years, as a practitioner in the world of pensions and financial planning, I have come to the inescapable conclusion that most Americans really do not understand the staggering problems facing our nation's retirement plans. What's more, just as I had realized earlier as a stockbroker that most investors really did not understand the market, I now find that most people do not understand how their basic retirement plans work.

As I searched for a book I could give my clients, I kept running up against basic textbooks—long out of date—or lengthy books dealing only with fragments of our national retirement program. What was needed, I believed, was a straightforward book on America's entire retirement system, why we have what we have and why it is no longer working.

In today's changing world our financial security seems, as our government tiptoes from crisis to crisis, to be crumbling about our feet; and all the while you and I are relentlessly growing older: We are all part of the graying of America.

By the time this book appears, some of the material may be out of date. I have tried to keep the book as current as possible, fully recognizing that our nation's entire retirement system is resting on a sea of shifting sand and that I might fail in this attempt. I make no claim to infallibility. In addition I have purposely left out much of the detailed material that supports many of the conclusions made in this book.

I believe that principles and ideas expressed in this book should be easy to understand so that you may not only discover what is happening today but also visualize how these developments may affect the future. Since the beginning of our nation's retirement system over one hundred years ago, little has changed in the basic way we operate our retirement plans. Unless all of us become better informed about the colossal mess we and our bumbling politicians have created, there is little hope that things will be straightened out in the future.

I am writing this book because I am concerned that our failure to adapt to new fiscal realities has now clearly pushed my retirement security to the brink of disaster. You are reading this book because you are observant enough to sense that you have been ripped off by a financial-security system that has become dishonest and inequitable.

You are not alone. Millions of Americans are growing uneasy about the future. We are earning more money, but keeping less. The institutions we have trusted for years to solve our problems are now themselves in deep trouble. With double-digit inflation loose in our land, the value of our dollar is shrinking fast. And there is growing concern that whatever we save for our retirement might not, in the end, keep us from falling below the poverty level.

This book is not intended as a "doom and gloom" recital of all that is wrong with our national retirement system. We have not created insoluble problems, nor have we reached the point of total despair. My purpose is to make people see that time is no longer on our side, that this may be the last chance we all have to save our retirement security system, not only for ourselves, but for our children and our grandchildren as well.

What you will read in the following chapters will be shocking and, frankly, a little scary. It will make some of you angry. It is my hope that it will make you want to change the system for the better. And to do so while there is still time.

In *Maxims for Revolutionists* George Bernard Shaw wrote, "The reasonable man adapts himself to the world: the unreasonable one persists in trying to adapt the world to himself. Therefore all progress depends upon the unreasonable man."

affect our lives and it has devised ways to change the system.

You and I, the average American worker, will need to increase our knowledge of the strengths and weaknesses of existing institutions geared to taking proper care of people in old age. Equally important, we must draw on courage and character to face our future. I hope we are successful, in part because I will have to share that future with you.

These concluding lines sum up the message of this book— it is a time of hope for all America.

Dean at work
883 — 2884

Catalog

**If you are interested in a list of fine Paperback
books, covering a wide range of subjects
and interests, send your name and address,
requesting your free catalog, to:**

**McGraw-Hill Paperbacks
1221 Avenue of Americas
New York, N.Y. 10020**

After reading this book, maybe you will become unreasonable. Maybe, working together, we can create the progress that will insure a financially secure future. The stakes are high, not only for ourselves and our families, but for the millions of Americans who have already retired into a world of crippling inflation and shaky pension plans.

The first chapter is a synopsis of the entire book. Hopefully it will help you visualize better how the parts make up the whole. For, in fact, the several components of our national retirement system are interrelated, since most of us will depend on Social Security, our company pension, and our individual savings as the basis for our retirement security.

Many of you may not agree with every conclusion I reach. The future is cloudy at best; but consider this: If I am wrong, nothing in this book will hurt you. If I am right, we all may be headed for a financial smashup at retirement.

Books are rarely written alone. I would like to thank Paul Gillette, an author of numerous best-sellers, but, more importantly, a man who unselfishly offered help and inspiration when it was needed most. My material was carefully reviewed by Virgil Salera, Professor of Business and Economics at California State University, Hayward, and by Mark Lipton, Esq., of Lipton & Lipton, San Jose, California. Their suggestions and ideas proved to be of immense help. I would also like to thank my secretary, Rhonda Baker, who has struggled under insistent and often unreasonable demands and has typed every word of the manuscript.

Most of all, I would like to dedicate this book to my wife, Pat, and our two children, Richard and Nancy. The children are about to graduate from college and make their own way in our marvelous country, surrounded by all the freedoms we hold so dear. As they begin to build their own lives, I am concerned about the economic problems I see coming. My children will have to live in a world beset by those problems, many of them of my making. I hope and pray that the legacy I leave my children will not include economic problems that I created but failed to solve. I know America will survive.

1 The View from the Top

The storm came up suddenly. Yesterday our national retirement system seemed benevolent and indestructible. But it has turned into a demon, creating a ten-trillion-dollar scandal so appalling that our public leaders have thus far chosen to suppress awareness of it. Congress must bear the main responsibility, for it is Congress that has ingenuously transformed our entire national pension system into a giant iceberg in search of the *Titanic*.

The decades-long swindle committed against the American worker by his own publicly elected officials can no longer be concealed: Inflation has brought it into the open. The basic pension plan, as conceived long before inflation disrupted our lives, required that money be set aside in our account over the years, growing with the magic of compound interest, so that at our retirement the promised monthly benefits could be paid in full. But today, each time our paycheck rises in an attempt to meet the cost of living, our expected monthly pension must also increase. This, in turn, requires more and more money so that the ever-higher pensions can be paid at retirement. When all of the required money is not set aside each year, the plan is termed "underfunded," and for all practical purposes the money is missing from the pension plan. It is this constantly mounting race for dollars to pay for these skyrocketing future benefits, and the fact that they have, for the most part, not been paid, that will tear apart our once sound retirement system. The catastrophe of underfunding that now threatens our pension system is of such magnitude that many retirement plans today are merely an exercise in futility.

According to a recent White House study, thirty-five million Americans—an incredible forty percent of the work force —now collect a pension from either government or industry. Total payments for these pension benefits have leaped three hundred percent over the last ten years, to an estimated $133 billion, with an even bigger increase expected in the future. The problem with our pension plans is not inflation alone, although that accounts for today's sharply higher pension benefits, but also the changing population mix. This is a major problem whose time is yet to come.

The world is now facing an old-age population explosion. In 1970 there were about three hundred million people over sixty years of age. Only two decades from now, by the year 2000, the number of over-sixties will more than double to about six hundred million. The graying of America will not be far behind. By the year 2000, only twenty years from now, the estimated number of Americans age sixty or older will jump thirty-five percent, reaching over forty-five million, up from only thirty-three million today. This sudden change will place a huge new burden on the working population to support those about to retire.

But who will carry this burden? Birth control has been an increasingly effective answer to excessive population growth. Unfortunately it has also greatly reduced the number of younger workers who have traditionally supported our nation's retirement system. So much so that today only six active workers support each retired citizen, down from something like an eight-to-one ratio as recently as 1970, and about a twenty-to-one ratio when pension plans were developed for widespread use immediately after the Second World War. By the year 2000 it is now estimated that the graying of America will have reached such proportions that, in combination with the falling birthrate, it will have pushed the burden for each retired person squarely on the pocketbooks of only three active workers.

It has already become apparent to anyone familiar with the growth of pension benefits that a concerted effort must now be made to increase the financial funding of old-age pensions if they are to avoid complete collapse under the burden of the demand for money to be paid out to an increasing number of retired workers. Future pension contributions by wage earners and their employers *must* be increased between two and three times their current rate if the nation's retirement system is to survive and keep pace with inflation. This can only result in our nation's pension plans undergoing substantial changes that will drastically affect the way Americans are paid during their retirement years.

As we all scramble for a place under the same tent, each of us may wonder who will pay for these future benefits when the cash is missing. The whole pension program, from Social Security to our employer plan, is so muddled up that a suspicion is gaining ground that no one is paying.

The President and Congress seem totally unable to solve any but the most superficial retirement problems as they wallow in the mounting number of federal programs that already jam the paper gears of government. Admittedly, with the amount of money already missing as large as it is, we as a nation are rapidly approaching the last opportunity we may have to save our pension system as a meaningful form of old-age security. Consider this: Our government will collect about $500 billion this year in taxes. This is only one twentieth of the $10 trillion currently estimated to be missing from our national pension plans.

For years average Americans never questioned nor, for the most part, understood the mechanics of retirement plans. After all, whether coverage was provided under a union, employer, or Social Security plan, they were caught in a tradition which precluded any active participation in the design or operation of the plan. In fact they rarely knew where their contributions were squirreled away, how effectively the funds were being used, and until recently they were even denied the basic right of inspecting the operations of the private employer plan. With a veil of secrecy continuing to shroud our retirement plans, there is considerable evidence in fact that the entire pension system is being managed by a headless bureaucracy, which in turn is responsible to no one.

A look at the federal Employee Retirement Program illustrates a classic example of a Congress gone mad, creating, one after another, retirement benefits much more luxurious than anything found in private enterprise. By various estimates the pension debt for the Civil Service Retirement System has spiraled to $204 billion. With 2.8 million federal employees, the government's own retirement plan has created a staggering unpaid future pension debt amounting to $72,860 for each active employee!

The meager figures available illustrate the politicians' unwillingness to look beyond the next election, for they have now succeeded in mortgaging much of our future tax money to pay for a bloated federal retirement plan. Only Uncle Sam, with an apparently inexaustible supply of taxpayers' money at his command coupled with an unrivaled borrowing potential, could mortgage our future on such a grand scale. But then, only Uncle Sam could devise a retirement system that would keep federal employees out of Social Security and allow them to escape the crushing tax burden the rest of us Americans face, for only he has the political clout. Congress has had repeated opportunities to make Social Security apply to federal workers as well as to themselves, but, this year again, they failed to act. So the American middle class continues ruefully to examine the toothmarks in its purse.

The explosive growth of federal, state, and local government employment over the last twenty-five years, much of it fueled by those same federal programs that created the expanding work force in the first place, has been a major cause of runaway costs for public pensions. The fact is that, excluding the military, public employment has climbed from 9.8 percent of the total work force in 1950 to a crushing 14.3 percent in 1976. Much of this explosive growth occurred at the state and local level, with this work force increasing an incredible 281 percent compared to a 34 percent increase in the private work force for the same period. There is no question that much of the money going to state and local payrolls is used unproductively and is simply swallowed up in the bureaucracy. Since almost fifty cents out of every dollar paid out in salary must be set aside for current and future fringe benefits, every unnecessary employee is a tremendous burden on a public retirement system that has been described as a national disaster waiting to happen.

Many Americans may feel uneasy about the colossal public

9

debt run up by the federal employees' pension plan, but the state and city pension plans are not far behind. Their claim to the future taxes of residents is estimated to run at least another $1 trillion.

The city of Los Angeles, whose retirees, like those in every major city, are struggling to get by on fixed incomes, now uses half of all the property taxes it collects to pay for the pensions of city employees. Even with one of the highest property tax rates in the nation, the city revealed that in 1975 it had an unbelievable $1.6 billion missing from its pension plan. The disaster is not limited to Los Angeles. Cities and states throughout the nation are faced with public debt which has yet to fall due. The city of Boston, with a population only one fourth the size of Los Angeles, succeeded recently in running up an unpaid pension debt almost as high, totaling $1.1 billion. Massachusetts kept pace with its largest city; with a population of six million, it had accumulated unpaid pension debts of $13 billion. This already amounts to a future tax bill of $2,166 for each resident of the commonwealth.

To make matters worse for cities like Los Angeles and Boston, a genuine taxpayers' revolt is emerging across America. In some eighty thousand tax districts the biggest source of income is the property tax, which usually tops the list as the most disliked and unfair tax. In 1978 the California voters approved, by an almost two-to-one margin, the Jarvis-Gann tax initiative to amend the State's constitution. "Proposition 13," as it is more commonly known (it was the thirteenth and last proposition on the ballot), has slashed property taxes to one percent of market value, as of 1975, and limited future increases to two percent per year. This has resulted in a reduction of California homeowner property taxes by as much as sixty percent below what would otherwise have been paid, and slashed the money flowing into local government coffers.

With cities across America straining simply to pay for pensions for those employees already retired, the loss of a major share of their income could have a significant impact on an already mounting pension debt. The harried local taxpayers are clearly demanding less government, less spending, and fewer employees from their city, county, and state elected officials. Unfortunately for the struggling pension plan, the rules of the game require that the newer, and usually younger, relatively low-salaried employees receive the "pink slip" first, while the higher-paid older employees, most of whom will probably soon retire at local government expense, must be retained. This means that despite tax-reduction measures like Proposition 13, the pension drain will continue, not merely unabated, but at an accelerated pace. In other words, we have a patient with cancer and our solution is to reduce his medical treatment.

But you say that you do not work for the government; let them work out their own problems. Okay, suppose you work for one of the nation's larger industrial companies. Now you are faced with an even more depressing situation, without the government behind you to raise taxes continually to pay for the future pension costs. It is well known that many of the larger private pension plans are in serious trouble with already promised retirement benefits creating a major drag on profits. Many of our larger companies have found it all but impossible to set aside even a small amount of the money that will be needed if their pension plans are to be fully funded and the future benefits paid in full.

Lockheed Corporation, admittedly not one of the most profitable companies the past few years, has allowed its liability for vested pension benefits—the amount an employee has earned and could take with him if he left the company today —to soar to $404 million, equal to one hundred sixty percent *more* than the company's total net worth. Lockheed has, for all practical purposes, become a giant pension plan that makes missiles to the moon on the side. Many other major companies are struggling with mounting pension costs, and are plainly losing the battle. Uniroyal Corporation has $560 million of vested pension benefits missing from its pension assets, or an incredible forty percent of its net worth. Bethlehem Steel has $1.3 billion missing from its account, or fifty-three percent of its net worth. What's more, International Harvester will need a powerful tractor to pull its load of $676 million back into its pension account, which represents forty-three percent of its total net worth. These are the figures available through the end of 1977 and only the amounts that were admitted as missing and made a public record at that time. As disquieting as this news may be, these unfunded vested pension liabilities merely consist of the money the employees have already earned, not the full costs should a majority of the employees actually begin drawing monthly retirement checks. What we do know is that pension costs have been skyrocketing during the seventies, with annual company contributions to pension funds already running at about twice the rate of increasing profits normally used to pay for these plans, without any apparent effect on the huge pension debt. Unless something is done soon, the pension trusts of many of America's largest companies may actually succeed in taking over the hand that feeds them.

Some hope has been held out to the approximately forty-two million workers who are covered by private pension plans so that they may have some assurance that their benefits will actually be received. The protection, too long in coming, will not cover many workers already caught up in the recent tragedy of pension-plan bankruptcies. For workers yet to retire into a less than full retirement plan, a provision of the Employee Retirement Income Security Act of 1974, better known to millions as ERISA, will provide the protection as best the government can without becoming directly involved in the pension dilemma.

Under the terms of ERISA, which only our amazing bureaucracy in Washington could have devised, every company with a defined benefit pension plan must now stand ready to bail out the employees of any other company that defaults on retirement benefits, either promised or earned. This could be one of the few successful ideas to come out of Washington, or it could turn out to be the world's biggest domino game.

It seems we have no choice but to turn to our once-trusted and long-endured friend, Social Security. Since nearly every working American has paid into the system for years, it is almost impossible to believe that Congress would allow the Social Security System to go broke. Congress has, however, drastically changed the actual retirement benefits and the conditions under which they are received. Much of the publicity associated with the passage of the 1977 Social Security bill was centered on the endlessly rising payroll taxes, which will increase over three hundred percent during the next ten years, and not on the across-the-board reduction in benefits for both current and future retirees. Social Security, which was established as a pension plan—providing for definite benefit levels at retirement—has in fact never been a pension plan. The once glorious concept of social legislation to prevent old-age dependency has been reduced to a simple "pay-as-you-go" scheme in which there is absolutely no intention of setting aside any money for future retirees. Furthermore, the benefits are not guaranteed, and they never have been. Sure enough, if you look at a copy of the first wall poster printed by the then Social Security Board in 1937, it clearly states that *There is no guarantee that the funds thus collected will ever be returned to you.* What's more, the next sentence can make quicksand out of any promises made by Social Security: *What happens to the money is up to Congress.*

By the government's own estimate, as of September 30, 1979, Social Security is in debt $4.225 trillion. Many experts believe the debt is closer to $5 trillion. As a matter of fact, with something this large, no one really knows for sure. In any event, the amount of money currently missing from Social Security is so huge that if every American working today, all ninety million of us covered by Social Security, were to pay our equal share of the debt, we would each need to bring to Washington a bag of money totaling over $47,000! But consider this, if you will. In 1972 the *total* government debt, including Social Security, was only $1.4 trillion. How did we transform our national retirement system into Social Insecurity, you ask? Easily. By giving money away to virtually anyone who could demonstrate a need to Congress. The list of "eligible recipients" has been stretched so wide that a torrent of money has been gushing out to provide benefits to those widowed, divorced, disabled, sick, dependent, or retired. In most cases Congress has been inspired to conceive laws that allow newly approved benefits to be paid almost before the ink is dry on the new legislation!

The classic case of "instant eligibility" under the system may have been when Ida Fuller, a legal secretary who retired on January 1, 1940, became the first American to retire under Social Security. She had contributed the princely sum of $22.54 in payroll taxes before she retired. By the time she died, she had succeeded in collecting over $21,000, most of which were big dollars, not eroded by the effects of inflation.

If you think Ms. Fuller did handsomely, consider the case of the first person to retire under the self-employment plan established in 1950. Under the instant eligibility feature, Social Security could have collected payroll taxes totaling $121.50 for which pension benefits would have amounted to over $43,000 by the end of 1977. Not a bad return, even by casino odds, but the best is yet to come: The entire $43,000 was paid income-tax free!

Social Security has emerged as a program incredibly generous to older workers about to retire, and immensely unfair to middle-aged and younger workers joining the system. This is because until recently payroll taxes have been relatively low. A twenty-five-year-old man, when the program began in 1937, could have retired in 1977 at age sixty-five, into a pot of gold. His maximum payroll taxes during this period would have totaled $7,705, but retiring with his wife, his first-year benefit checks could have amounted to $8,000, more than the entire amount he had contributed over the last forty years!

Everyone seems to come up a winner in the game of Social Security. "Something for nothing," as the saying goes, can only last so long and now our romance with the world's greatest giveaway program has suddenly come to a crashing halt. It is the younger worker whom the system has coerced into carrying the empty sack. He is at the bottom of the retirement pile, with a mounting tax burden as the only alternative to a complete breakdown of the current employee/employer-financed program.

What are his future prospects? Harvard economists Martin Feldstein and Anthony Pellechio believe that young wage earners can expect to pay more in taxes than they will ever receive in benefits. "If the current relation between benefits and taxes were to remain unchanged," they said, "each new generation would find its initial net Social Security wealth was negative." In other words, you cannot take out nearly as much as you pay in, not even in inflated dollars. But older people, who have already made the system work for them, have a positive figure, "because they are close to receiving benefits and have fewer taxpaying years left."

As it now is turning out, the young are not the only ones

NOTICE
Deductions from Pay
Start Jan. 1

Beginning January 1, 1937, your employer will be compelled by law to deduct a certain amount from your wages every payday. This is in compliance with the terms of the Social Security Act, sponsored and signed by President Roosevelt, August 14, 1935.

The deduction begins with 1%, and increases until it reaches 3%.

There is no guarantee that the fund thus collected will ever be returned to you. What happens to the money is up to each congress. No benefits of any kind before 1942.

This is NOT a voluntary plan. Your employer MUST make this deduction. Regulations are published by the Social Security Board, Washington, D.C.

who face an uphill battle; "soaking the successful" has emerged as yet another gimmick for bailing out the system. One reason the Social Security payroll tax bite is beginning to hurt so much is that it comes after you pay your income taxes. Obviously, the more successful you become the more you pay in income tax; however, with inflation pushing up your salary each year, you may already have discovered that you have become successful only as measured by the income tax tables.

Over the last forty years the benefits from Social Security have been roughly proportional to the money paid into the system. The new law exchanges the equality of the past for a future benefit formula that, by 1987, will allow a worker earning a maximum salary to expect a monthly benefit of $779, compared to $610 for those who earn only an average salary during this same period. Not much difference in the benefits, but what is going to cause massive discontent for many working Americans is the realization that in order to collect a few more dollars at retirement, a sharply higher payroll tax will be required from maximum-salary workers over the eight-year period than will be required of workers in the middle-income bracket.

Let's face it, Social Security will never again be a bargain. A good many Americans have a stake in the success or failure of the system. They have every right to be concerned when a major share of their retirement security is based on a national program that might not be guaranteed, has been changed by almost every successive Congress, and will, according to projections, substantially increase cash payouts to a growing multitude of beneficiaries supported by fewer and fewer workers.

There is, however, great promise for the future in certain new programs known collectively as "alphabet soup"—retirement plans established under the initials TSA, IRA, and HR 10, in which the individual—who owns, controls, and manages them—reigns supreme. The gates to this promised land of self-funded retirement are controlled by Congress. It alone determines who may pass through and enjoy an extended reprieve from the taxman—for it is the *delay of income tax,* and this feature alone, that separates the alphabet soups from the regular passbook savings accounts. Qualifications, however, are so narrow that only about three million accounts have been opened—by salaried workers not covered under an employer-sponsored retirement, and by self-employed individuals. The overwhelming number of American taxpayers remain on the other side of the fence.

For those who are eligible, the delaying of income taxes can have a tremendous impact on any retirement plan. If $1,000 of salary were made available each year for both an individual retirement account and a regular passbook savings account, the alphabet-soup crowd would be runaway winners. For example, if interest were to be seven percent compounded annually over the twenty years and the income-tax rate thirty-five percent, the IRA account would have grown to $43,865 while the passbook savings account would total only $21,308. The American public has waxed more skeptical of honest pension reform in recent years, and Congress has proved them right again by permitting only a few to share the tax advantages that should be enjoyed by all. As we have already seen, most Americans now find themselves covered under an unsafe-at-any-year employer-sponsored retirement plan with absolutely no chance to save tax-free money for their own retirement.

With our national pension system near disaster, let's look again at inflation, the single strongest influence on our fixed-dollar pension plans. The continuing double-digit inflation poses a basic question to which we have yet to find a workable answer, and that is: How can any long-term commitment in absolute dollar terms be reached between employer and employee during a prolonged phase of wage-price spirals? The nation's initial response has been to ignore the real question and seek a scapegoat instead of an answer.

But scapegoats are becoming increasingly difficult to find. For example, the responsibility for raising the price of gasoline at the local service station may lie with the Arabs, or even with the President for not being able to enact a workable national energy program, but neither of these possibilities is entirely satisfactory. We can no longer expect to solve anything by pinning the blame on any particular individual or group. Inflation is happening to each of us. In our own private way we have been forced to come to terms with an unknown future. We have allowed inflation to erode our moral values in business and government to such a degree that Henry Wallich, one of the governors of the Federal Reserve Board, was prompted to observe, "Nothing that is stated about dollars and cents any longer means what it says. . . . Everybody makes contracts knowing perfectly well that they will not be kept in terms of constant values. . . . We do not know whether the most valuable part of the contract may turn out to be the paper it is written on. . . . Inflation is like a country where nobody speaks the truth."

For us as individuals, inflation's cruelest threat may be that it forces us to postpone our dreams—at worst, to live without the hope of a better tomorrow; or, as we have already learned, without the hope of a reasonable pension measured in tomorrow's dollars. Even as you read this book, inflation is shrinking tomorrow's pension benefits, widening the gap between our working salary and our actual retirement income.

Bill Johnson of Omaha, Nebraska, was one of the few who knew about the Social Security replacement-rate factor, and he stormed into the Social Security office mad as hell one day, shouting, "The more I make, the less I get! What kind of deal is that?" It's not that Bill Johnson had anything against the local office; he was just mad as hell at the way his already-paid-for retirement benefits were going to decline relative to his working wages over the next decade. Unfortunately for every American covered under Social Security, that is the way the pension experts, who have a marvelous ability to hide the facts in their native language of pensionese, have calculated the relationship between our final salary (usually an average of the last five years of earnings) and our Social Security benefit.

Suppose that your final salary was $18,000 and your annual Social Security retirement benefit was $5,400; then the replacement rate would be about thirty percent. In other words, after you retire at age sixty-five, Social Security would pay you each month about thirty percent of your final working salary. One way to ease the burden on our national retirement system would be simply to reduce the replacement rate. Assume we did reduce the replacement rate from thirty percent to twenty-five percent; then your annual Social Security benefit would fall from $5,400 to $4,500. This would substantially reduce the unfunded debt for the system, since the expected cost at retirement would be reduced about twenty percent with only a modest five percent reduction in the replacement rate. This may not come as a surprise to you when you learn that Social Security has seen the wisdom of winding down the replacement rate as one way to bail out the system. The current law, sold to the American public as a way to save the system from bankruptcy, is now scheduled to reduce the maximum earner's replacement rate from thirty-one percent of the wage base in 1978 to only twenty-three percent in 1987. The experts who protect the system from its own beneficiaries have designed an ingenious plan that will keep the maximum Social Security retirement benefit sliding downward in relation to the taxable wage base over the next five years, even when the effects of inflation could easily double our final annual salary.

The net effect will be that Americans retiring on Social Security can expect successively stronger financial jolts as the falling replacement rate widens the gap between what they receive and what that income will buy in the years to come. Should you be unhappy, as Bill Johnson was, that's all right, our planners reason. After all, a stronger, healthier retirement plan is clearly in the public's best interest.

"Your best interest, my eye," said Joan Thomas of San Jose, California, as she stormed into the personnel office where she worked. "Boy, talk about a big rip-off," she said. "You people are all alike when it comes to 'now you see it, now you don't.' Why, you have more fine print than an insurance policy." Waving a copy of the company's pension plan in the face of the personnel clerk, she shouted, "You never told me about this offset business."

Unfortunately, during the next decade millions of Americans may not be aware of how offset "nibbles" are fast eating up their expected retirement benefits in the effort to shore up many larger employer-sponsored pension plans. The offset method is just that. It offsets, or adjusts, the amount you would normally receive from Social Security to reduce the amount of your employer pension benefits. Suppose, again, that your final salary is $18,000 and your employer pension plan offers a benefit of fifty percent of your final salary at retirement. Under this example you would expect a pension of $9,000, but as Joan Thomas found out, the fifty percent offset can cut deeply into your final retirement income, eliminating most of the advantage from the contributions made to the Social Security System.

The impact of the offset technique can best be shown by its effect on both you and your employer's pension plan. In your case, total retirement income has shrunk from $14,400 per year ($9,000 or fifty percent of your salary from the private plan and $5,400 from Social Security) to only $10,350 per year ($5,400 from Social Security and approximately seventy-five percent of Social Security used as an adjustment, or $4,950 from the private pension plan). From your employer's standpoint, the offset method goes a long way to bolster the sagging fortunes of the plan and helps to reduce the unfunded debt, since the plan is now only responsible for paying you $4,950 per year, not the full $9,000 the benefit might otherwise require. If you think that is a rip-off, consider this: Each time Social Security increases its benefit, the amount of money such private plans need to pay future retirees is reduced.

The magical properties of the Social Security replacement rate, the carnivorous offset formulas that threaten to eat up much of your retirement income, are only two of the many developments affecting your retirement future that we will cover in this book. Since these factors interrelate with many others, the world of pension planning has come to seem inordinately complicated. One of the most valuable lessons you can learn from this book is that pension and retirement plans in general are not extremely complicated, though professional pension managers have a marvelous ability to make it sound as if they were. In fact the experts would have you believe that if you know a pension solution, you cannot possibly understand the problem. Recently, however, the tide has begun to turn, as more and more Americans have started asking hard questions about their retirement plans.

Neither I nor anyone else knows all the answers to our massive pension problems. Most experts agree that we cannot continue to follow the rules of the past—rules that have transformed our national pension system into a giant slot machine into which nickels and dimes are continually fed while our leaders hope against hope that we as a nation will not hit the jackpot.

But, just as being poor increases the risk of being hungry, being uninformed increases the risk of being cheated out of basic retirement benefits.

Therefore, to better understand the various factors that are grinding up the retirement benefits provided you by the government, your private employer, and your own individual plans, we will first examine how the whole idea of saving money for our retirement years was originally designed to work.

The startling fact that it is not working that way today and that we Americans are in growing danger of virtually complete dependence on government-controlled retirement incomes is what this book is all about.

2 The Tangled Mess from the Beginning

Dr. Martin J. Routh was president of Magdalen College, Oxford, England, for sixty-three years, from 1791 to 1854. A lover of old ways, he always clung to his wig and to the fashion of dress of his younger years. Dr. Routh was a man who refused to believe in many of the new ideas then appearing in the nineteenth century. Our sanity is best served, he reasoned, by simply denying bizarre and alarming facts. He steadfastly refused to believe in the existence of trains, and when one of his students arrived from London in only a few hours, he denounced both the student and the trains for conspiring against his sanity. His longevity—he lived to the age of one hundred—was proof for many of his followers that modern ideas could indeed be ignored.

The Industrial Revolution, however, became such a powerful force that by the end of the nineteenth century it had overtaken the Routhian adherents and had begun a chain reaction of inventions and ideas that has continued to this day.

As the Industrial Revolution steamrolled its way throughout America, one of the key drivers of this progress machine was labor. Never before had so many industrial workers been required for the successful operation of a modern society.

This explosive growth of the labor force continued well into the twentieth century with the basic understanding between management and labor that their entire contract rested on the simple notion of "a day's work for a day's pay."

Human values, as we know them today, were virtually nonexistent. The novel idea that an individual worker had value to society, or even to himself, after his working years, was simply denied and ignored.

It has now been well over one hundred years since a few daring businessmen sought to change the world we live in. Their simple yet revolutionary idea that income should continue to be received when no work was produced was met with disbelief by the masters of the Industrial Revolution.

Retirement planning began in 1875 when American Express Company, which was later known as Railway Express Company, established what is believed to be the first industrial pension plan in America. The second formal plan was established in 1880 by the Baltimore and Ohio Railroad Company. Along the steel rails that fanned out across America during the late nineteenth century spread the startling promise that retirement could mean more than a gold watch—that one could hope, in fact, for financial independence during old age. Not much, it is true; many of the early pension plans were more in the form of pension arrangements. The workers had no rights in the plan and none were ever intended. The plans were considered gratuities, not wages, and the business owners were free to turn the payments on and off like a faucet.

During the next twenty years, until 1900, the railroads dominated the pension field, which had grown to include one hundred private plans.

The major incentive for the railroad barons, when pension plans were first considered, was to replace older workers with younger, more active and productive employees. The railroads soon discovered that they could spread a very low annual cost over twenty-five or thirty-five years offering a very limited monthly pension, and at the same time hire younger workers at an exceedingly lower salary. It was just good business for the railroad, and what was good business for the railroad was good business for America.

Unfortunately, during the five decades that followed, the growth of pension plans traveled at handcar speed. In fact, it was not until after the Second World War that pension plans experienced a meaningful growth rate because of the very tight and competitive labor market coupled with the very high demand for consumer goods. Another important reason was that in 1949 the Supreme Court upheld a ruling by the National Labor Relations Board that pension plans were subject to collective bargaining between the employer and the union. With the unions now leading the way, by the 1950s the growth of private retirement plans finally got out of control, reaching almost ten million workers who were covered under some 13,000 plans.

By 1970 the number of private plans had mushroomed to about 230,000. Today the best estimate is that the number of plans has grown to about 350,000, covering about forty-five million Americans. At first glance this appears to be substantial progress, and it is. But the actual situation today is quite different. Roughly half of the private work force neither works for a company nor belongs to a union that has a pension plan.

Possibly half the people covered under private plans will not receive the full stated benefits, since they will change employers several times over their working years. What's more, according to a Brandeis University study of nearly a thousand private pension plans, which appeared in a recent issue of the *Monthly Labor Review,* a magazine published by the Department of Labor itself, few of the remaining half—comprising one in four working Americans—will be able to maintain their living standard because the pension benefits received by a typical worker are too low. It is generally agreed, say the authors of the study, that a couple should receive as a pension approximately seventy percent of their working income if they are to maintain the same life-style in retirement. In real life, the study concluded, the vast majority of working Americans are unable to reach anywhere near the seventy percent replacement rate relying solely on their pensions and Social Security.

The study revealed that an average worker who made $15,-000 in 1975 and retired after thirty years of service—highly uncommon in today's job-hopping market—received a $3,150 annual pension. This amounts to only twenty-one percent of preretirement pay. The median pension benefit for a man was only $2,720, or twenty-two percent of his preretirement income.

The facts of life today remain little changed from those of the past; for most working Americans covered by a private employer pension plan, a realistic pension benefit is far from being attained.

In the meantime, in order to support even the modest pension benefit payments forecast by the Brandeis University study, America's private pension plans have squirreled away an enormous pile of stocks, bonds, notes, and hard cash. It is an astonishing fact, when one considers those mere hundred pension plans of the turn of the century, that the amount of money resting in private retirement plans today has become so large as to dwarf any other privately held asset in America. The five hundred largest private retirement plans alone have combined assets greater than the gross national product of all but seven countries of the world! Estimates of the combined assets range in excess of $300 billion. The money managers for these private plans have an enormous impact on both the stock prices and the sales volume on the national stock exchanges and they have, with their decisions to buy or sell, a major impact on the money markets throughout the American economy.

This huge sum of money, increasing by several billions of dollars each year, still functions under essentially the same guidelines that were laid down during the late nineteenth century by the railroad barons who believed pensions were good business.

One of those guidelines, from the original retirement plans of the late 1880s, has now become a part of our American way of life. It established normal retirement at age sixty-five.

The selection of age sixty-five as the division between middle and old age was an arbitrary one, and many believe that the early pension plans were copied from the pioneering social legislation of German Chancellor Otto von Bismarck, who during the 1880s recognized the need for assistance by the state for citizens who were too old to continue to work. The adoption of sixty-five as the retirement age, however, assured that the early retirement benefits were more hope than substance. As late as 1900 our average life expectancy was only forty-seven years and the number of Americans who survived beyond age sixty-five totaled a mere four percent of the population.

The fact that workers seldom reached the advanced age of sixty-five made employer pension plans extremely profitable during the early part of this century. The graying of America, however, threatens to increase the cost well beyond the employers' ability to pay during the last part of this century. By 1977 there were some twenty-two million people age sixty-five or older and their number is growing faster than any other group in our population. Over ten million, or almost half this group, are over age seventy-three, with one million over age eighty-five. In fact, more than 106,000 Americans reported themselves as being over one hundred years of age. By a combination of improved public-health measures and better living conditions, we have increased our life expectancy to seventy-one years, up from only forty-seven years as recently as the start of this century. What concerns retirement planners most is the fact that over seventy percent of the present age-sixty-five-plus population has joined that group since 1959. Over ten thousand Americans turn age sixty-five each day. Today twenty-five million people are age sixty-five and over and it is projected by the Department of Commerce that by the turn of the century the graying of America will turn over thirty-two million potential retirees loose on our national retirement system.

To add to the increasing number of Americans reaching the established retirement age of sixty-five, a new phenomenon called "early retirement" has become widespread throughout the world. In 1978 the French passed legislation that permits employees to retire at age sixty. In Italy, where the retirement age for men has already been reduced to that age, the labor unions are pressing for fifty-five. In America the swing to early retirement has been accelerating. In 1966 only thirty-eight percent of the workers chose early retirement under Social Security. Ten years later, in 1976, over sixty-six percent elected to retire before age sixty-five.

No change of such magnitude happens by accident. Liberal pension plans created by private industry and government, when costs were relatively low, have been largely responsible for the decline of average retirement age nationwide from just over sixty-four to sixty-one, over the last twenty years. The federal government's own workers do even better. Congress has continued to protect them from the crushing burden of Social Security taxes and, in turn, has provided incredibly generous retirement benefits and opportunities for early retirement. By the General Accounting Office's own figures, the government workers lead the pack in cashing monthly retirement checks. Their average retirement age is only 57.7 years.

Former Secretary of Health, Education and Welfare Joseph Califano, Jr., told the Senate Special Committee on Aging that changes in America's retirement planning may require a reconsideration of the whole U.S. policy on work and retirement.

For whatever reason, as the number of retired workers below age sixty-five increases, you can look for either mounting costs for your employer plans, or a sharp drop-off in expected retirement benefits. Congress has already eased the employer's burden by allowing you to continue to work up to age seventy. This will not cost your employer nearly as much as actual retirement, since presumedly he will not be required to make contributions past a plan's designated retirement age.

Your employer's effort to delay actual retirement age is largely accounted for by an idea originally put forth before the turn of the century—that a retirement delayed is a retirement lost.

Just as there will be a lot of congressional talk about pushing forward Social Security's retirement age from sixty-five to sixty-eight, your employer will also be busy pushing and shoving back his plan's retirement age. The best guess is that because of the graying of America, the normal retirement age in the future will be somewhere between sixty-eight and seventy. After all, when pension plans were actually conceived, fewer than thirty percent of the workers were expected to live to retirement age. Today the number is around sixty percent.

The graying of America, dramatically increasing the number of benefit checks, has drawn attention to the pension problem the way a magnet draws steel. Pension plans are now fighting for their financial lives. One way to apply the brakes against this hemorrhaging flow of cash would be to delay actual benefit payments. Look for this as a change that could occur in the 1980s.

The next guideline that early pension planners established dealt with the length of time an employee would have to work for the company before he or she was entitled to receive monthly retirement checks. The idea was to increase productivity and lower employee turnover. Longtime employees who had mastered the duties of their jobs were good business, and from this the concept that continued employment would fund the retirement benefits began to take shape.

Early plans stipulated that benefits were to be contingent on the worker's spending virtually his entire lifetime with one employer, or at the least on twenty-five years of unbroken employment service.

Over the years millions of workers lost their expected pension benefits because they failed to meet the requirements implied in the seemingly harmless but powerful words "unbroken employment service."

Since the employer did not need to disclose what the odds were that a worker would ever collect a cent in pension benefits, the idea of a future retirement benefit has, over most of this century, been more myth than reality. In fact, most employees who were fired, laid off, or who simply changed employers for a better future unknowingly left behind their expected pension benefits.

Gradually a small measure of protection has been offered, allowing some employees to salvage part of their previously earned retirement benefits, but the rules continue to remain heavily tilted in favor of the retirement plan.

To illustrate how bizarre the rule of "unbroken service" has become, I only need to let you look at a 1979 case filed in the federal courts in San Francisco.

In this case Teamsters Union truck drivers had their work time credited to either the Western Conference of Teamsters pension plan or to the Teamsters Local 85 pension plan, depending on the type of driving performed. Dividing up the time between the two pension plans in this way could either result in a failure to qualify for coverage because of insufficient years of service, or, more importantly, violate the rule on unbroken employment. This problem came to light when a driver planned to retire and he was told that even though he met the requirements of twenty-five years of work under the Western Conference plan, he was not qualified in all respects, including in the matter of "unbroken service," and so was not entitled to receive any pension benefits. If he wanted to work three more years he might qualify for a pension benefit of only thirty-seven percent of what he had expected to receive.

As recently as early 1979 a case of lost pension benefits finally made its way to the U.S. Supreme Court. The decision seems confirmation that the pension plan's fine print will continue to thwart the long-suffering employee. The case involved a Teamster truck driver by the name of John B. Daniel. He had worked a full twenty-two and a half years before he was forced to retire due to failing eyesight. Unfortunately for John, thirteen years before his retirement he had been briefly (for four months) involuntarily laid off. Not an unusual event in itself, for it had happened, and probably will continue to happen, to many employees just like John.

But when he confidently applied for his Teamster pension, he was told that he did not qualify since his plan provided benefits only to those who had at least twenty "continuous" years of service.

John, like millions of other workers, had not only overlooked the fine print, but in this case had overlooked the giant killer of them all, the rule on "unbroken employment service."

What made the difference this time was that unlike many unhappy workers before him, John Daniel sued. He maintained that he had been misled and that if he had known how slight his chances were of ever collecting a pension, he would have changed to a job with a better retirement plan.

As the case went through the courts, a novel legal issue was raised, since Daniel's lawyer argued that when a worker joins a pension plan he is agreeing, in effect, to invest a portion of his wages in return for benefits when he retires.

The Supreme Court rejected this argument, finding that a worker's interest in a retirement plan is not an investment within the meaning of the securities laws.

In the decision Supreme Court Justice Lewis F. Powell wrote, "Looking at the economic realities, it seems clear that an employee is selling his labor to obtain a livelihood, not making an investment for the future."

What the Court did not say when they made their decision was that to rule in Daniel's favor would have been to overturn one of the first and firmest of pension guidelines. Chaos would have erupted in pension systems all over America. "Looking at the economic realities," the cost to change now to a pension plan on whose promised payment workers could actually rely would be phenomenal. It has been estimated that pension funds could be hit for as much as $40 billion if they had to make good on all the lost pension benefits similar to John Daniel's. The blunt assessment of the Court is that pension plans are risky. The original guidelines were intended to make them that way. Worse yet, some forty million workers covered under pension plans directly affected by the Daniel decision continue to remain unaware of the powerful rule of "unbroken service." Somehow a way must be found to inform them.

Yet another guideline established by early pension planners determined after what length of service and at what age an employee was to be allowed to join the retirement plan. This was called "eligibility."

Obviously, the longer a worker had to wait before joining the plan, the lower the employer's cost. Over the years this guideline began to resemble a carrot on a stick giving merely the appearance of a pension, holding the eligibility requirements tantalizingly close but never within the employee's grasp.

Once the employee was eligible to join the plan, but before he could grab that carrot, the plan was pulled away from him yet another time.

Early pension planners reasoned that if retirement benefits were for longtime employees (those with years of unbroken service), a waiting period for new workers would insure that only "permanent" employees entered the plan. For example, a plan could have been designed with a requirement that the worker be at least thirty-five years old and have at least seven years of prior employment with the company before retirement-plan coverage began.

The progress against these early guidelines, established more to exclude than benefit the workers, has been agonizingly slow. Today, more than half a century later, the employee must be at least age twenty-five with the maximum waiting period limited to three years of prior employment with the company.

Once a worker was covered by the plan, the early pension planners anticipated that benefits would be paid only at the retirement age of sixty-five, providing the employee survived to that advanced age and was fully employed prior to retirement. There were few, if any, benefits in the event of death, and usually nothing for the surviving spouse.

Since the annual contributions to the plan were paid by the employer, it was logical, the owners reasoned, that they should make the rules. After all, the worker was offered a retirement plan paid for by the company, and it was up to him to comply if he expected to collect the employer's paid-for benefits.

Incredible as it may seem, as late as 1979 Justice Powell of the Supreme Court appeared to concur. The employee is selling his labor, not making an investment for the future, he wrote.

But what about employees like John Daniel who had worked almost twenty-three years and failed to receive a retirement check? Under the terms of the pension plan, the company was required to make a contribution in their behalf each year.

Presumably there was a pile of cash in the plan that would no longer be needed. Ingeniously the owners reasoned that since the money was already in the pension plan, it could now be used to reduce future company contributions. This was a discovery that changed the course of pension planning. It now became profitable for the boss to deny, for whatever reason, earned retirement benefits. With even a moderate level of employee turnover, the contributions to the plan could now be used to fund the retirement benefits of several employees, not just one.

As the years went by, more and more workers began to realize that they would not be spending the greater part of their working lives with one employer. What they needed, the workers reasoned, was credit for the years spent with each employer. In that way, even though they might work for three or four employers over their working lives, they could still piece together realistic retirement benefits.

Now the battle was really on. Who would gain control of the money left behind when the employee was terminated from the plan prior to retirement? The employers were insistent.

They wanted the money to reduce substantially their future contributions. The workers wanted the money saved toward their eventual retirement so that successive changes of employment did not rob them of all that had previously been saved on their behalf.

What finally emerged was a compromise contained in a new word, *vesting*. For the first time the workers had tilted the scales the other way. It was a small victory at first, since the employers, as usual, made up the new rules. But at least the point had been made that the loss of a job need not necessarily result in the loss of all future retirement benefits.

In simple, nonpension language, vesting is your right to receive your employer's contribution when employment is terminated prior to retirement.

If you were one hundred percent vested, that would mean that if you left your employer, you would be entitled to receive all of the past contributions made on your behalf. The retirement plan would come up empty-handed.

It should not be surprising to learn that under the rules that evolved for vesting, business owners who were funding the retirement plans now set about to delay vesting as long as possible. Well into this century, some of the plans had schedules that did not permit the worker even to start vesting until five or ten years into the plan, and then only on a gradual scale over the next twenty or thirty years.

Under the vesting schedule that we find in our current retirement plans, a worker normally will now be one hundred percent vested after only fifteen years. In the early years he is allowed what is called *fractional vesting*. For example, after ten years in the plan a worker could be fifty percent vested. As with most everything related to private company-sponsored retirement plans, the employer still has several options regarding the vesting schedule, including one that permits no vesting at all for the first five years of coverage.

Since "job hopping" has become a way of life for millions of Americans, the chances today of ever collecting a full company-paid pension are almost as remote as they were for the Railway Express workers back in 1875.

Before our private pension plans can have any credibility, we must solve the vesting problem. Our system cries out for portability: the simple right to take the full amount of the pension account whenever a job change occurs.

Social Security works that way. No matter how many times you change your job, you receive full credit for each year you make a contribution. But not our private pension plans. With less than six years of employment (including a one-year waiting period) you could come up empty-handed upon termination. The employer keeps it all.

It should now be clear that the original guideline regarding vesting is a key part in any retirement plan. So key, in fact, that the scenario has remained virtually unchanged since 1875: If you change jobs over the years, only your vested benefits will be there when you retire.

You might want to check your own plan and determine when your employer's contributions will actually become your vested benefit.

This basic review of the retirement-plan guidelines, established by the turn of the century, brings clearly into focus the problems we all face in the 1980s. Times have changed but our nation's retirement plans have not.

The first guideline is in trouble because Americans, and for that matter the rest of the industrial world, no longer want to wait until age sixty-five to retire. The way our retirement systems have frozen in place makes a retirement date before age sixty-five today prohibitively expensive. Just to refresh your memory, pension planners, Social Security, and even our own government are currently pushing for a later retirement date, somewhere between ages sixty-eight and seventy. The public desire, in this case, is clearly running against the tide.

Some real progress has been made on the second guideline—eligibility—since workers now must be covered under a retirement plan after at most a three-year waiting period.

Unfortunately, as we have learned in the recent Supreme Court decision, a requirement in some plans of unbroken service of over twenty years with one employer still plagues the system. The idea of working that many years for one employer is no longer realistic. Americans today are changing jobs at such a frantic pace that company personnel offices are swamped in paperwork. Today it is widely believed that frequent job changes actually promote one's career. The old-fashioned idea that retirement plans should be provided only for very long-term employees is badly dated.

For the same reason, the third guideline, called "vesting," is also unrealistic. To give everyone full credit for each year they are covered under their employer's plan would, at this late date in retirement planning, increase the cost beyond the reach of many company-sponsored plans. Only Social Security can offer this equitable treatment, but then its plan does not face the burden of full funding now required of all privately sponsored plans.

Since it now appears unlikely that you and I can change our firmly established retirement system to meet our changing life-style, all of us who work for a living must accept the "shell game" for what it has been over the last century: merely an employer promise.

So much for the guidelines, those rules supposedly set in stone. Our world has not only changed, it seems to be falling apart altogether. Our beloved retirement plans now face yet another major problem so bizarre that the early pension planners never even considered it. The ugly word for this problem is "inflation." Had they considered its impact, or even dreamed of its devastating effect, the whole idea of pension plans would probably have been radically changed or even abandoned from the start. Since the end of World War II inflation has become so uncontrolled in its attack on our retirement plans that today it threatens to kill off the very possibility of a meaningful pension benefit.

I will cover the threat of inflation and how it is affecting our financial security more fully in Chapter 4.

For now, I would like to dig into the different retirement plans that have evolved over the years to form our private retirement system. There are only three different plans that you need to understand to become an expert in retirement planning.

Pension Plan

The first, and the one I will refer to most often in this book, is a pension plan. This is called a "defined-benefit plan"—simply because the retirement benefits are defined. If you are covered by a pension plan, your employer has promised you a defined benefit at retirement. Your plan, for example, might promise a retirement benefit of fifty percent of your final salary at age sixty-five. Some plans offer as much as seventy-five percent or even more of your final salary at retirement.

Pension plans became popular after the Second World War when costs were low and private employers were operating plants full-tilt to fill the public's long-pent-up demand for consumer goods. Today the costs have risen out of sight and pension plans are in deep trouble. The reason is simple. Your employer has promised a definite benefit, payable thirty or even forty years in the future, with virtually no way to control the runaway costs.

Inflation and the graying of America have changed the rules. The problem we face today is not that the idea of providing a pension was wrong, but that the idea of saving money over many years for a rapidly increasing and unknown monthly pension benefit is almost unworkable under the concept of retirement planning.

A quick look at the arithmetic can explain how inflation has forced us into this mess.

Suppose your pension plan was established on the basis that your retirement income would be $5,000 per year on a final salary of $10,000. The actuary—a person with special training in determining the cost of future benefits—would then calculate the amount of money your employer would need to set aside each year so that your benefit would be fully funded at retirement.

Let's say the amount needed at age sixty-five is $50,000. If you are now age thirty, then the pension plan has thirty-five years to save this money. Without considering the effects of interest, if your employer saved about $1,425 each year, the pension plan would then contain $50,000 at your age sixty-five. The guarantee of the pension plan could be met and you could retire fully confident that you would receive each month in your mailbox a check for fifty percent of your final salary.

That is the way the system was designed to work. Your employer was supposed to make adequate contributions each year, regardless of business conditions or profits.

Now let's look at the real world. Your final salary is no longer estimated to be $10,000, but $30,000 at retirement. You are now age fifty and fighting for your life against an avalanche of bills that even your huge salary cannot pay. But if you think you have problems, consider your pension plan. The $50,000 it was saving for your retirement benefit has mushroomed to $150,000. Worse yet, the number of years left to retirement has shrunk to only fifteen.

In order to accumulate $150,000 at your age sixty-five, the remaining fifteen years will now require that the annual pension contribution of $1,425 be increased to an astonishing $8,100.

This example clearly illustrates how inflation robs us of one of the most precious commodities we have in retirement planning: time. Most Americans, at one time or another, have used time-payment plans to purchase big-ticket items. In my case, I'm only too eager to flash my plastic card when the ready cash is not at hand.

Suppose I buy a TV set for $1,000 using a three-year time-payment plan. Again ignoring interest, I would expect to pay $27.78 each month under my time-purchase agreement. Time-purchase plans have worked well because the amount to be repaid remains constant.

Not so for pension plans. They are, in effect, promising us a TV set at retirement, regardless of its cost.

Now the bills are beginning to fall due for the TV sets, but the money in the till is coming up short. While the costs of pensions have increased, the money going into pension plans has not. The deficit is called, in pensionese, "unfunded pension liabilities." What that really means, in plain English, is that a good part of the money that will be needed to pay the pension promises is missing. Not small figures, but boxcar figures, hundreds of billions of dollars, with the amounts growing every day at an alarming rate.

Up to this point I've concerned myself with how a pension plan works and how incredibly difficult it has become to guarantee into the future a rapidly increasing retirement benefit. Now comes the groundswell of support from those Americans retired or about to retire for the indexing of pension benefits for inflation. This would mean that, after you retired, your monthly pension benefit would be increased each time the cost of living went up.

With inflation currently running in excess of fourteen percent, a fixed pension benefit could quickly pull the retiree below the poverty line. The very concept of a meaningful pension would be lost: to provide, as Robert J. Myers, former chief actuary of Social Security, has stated, "a retirement income that will enable the pensioner to maintain a certain relative standard of living."

Millions of Americans agree with Mr. Myers. But the facts are not encouraging. Government and private studies show that only a handful of private pension plans have automatic cost-of-living increases, and the few that do usually have a ceiling of only three percent a year.

The idea of indexing pension benefits to the cost of living was never a part of the original pension guidelines, and, in fact, was never even considered a problem until the 1970s.

You might ask that if inflation is watering down the value of a retiree's monthly pension benefit, why don't employers simply provide for cost-of-living adjustments now? The answer, at this late date in pension planning, is money. It would take a fortune to provide meaningful future pensions in the face of our rapidly increasing inflation.

Last year, on a flight home from a business trip, I found myself sitting next to an employee-benefit manager for one of America's largest companies. During the course of our conversation I asked him if his company offered pension benefits that were indexed for inflation. "Hell, no," he said, "we can't afford it. And what's more, I don't think any company can."

"How do you know?" I asked.

"Because I've seen the figures," he said. And then he turned to me and caught my eye. "Listen, the only people who can index pension benefits for inflation are those who can print money."

"Social Security?" I asked.

"Yes," he said.

My friend pointed out that Donald Grubbs, a former actuary with the Internal Revenue Service, has estimated that to include a four percent cost-of-living increase, the typical company over the years would have to increase its pension outlays by thirty-three percent. If inflation were running at eight percent, it would now be estimated to cost this same company at least seventy-seven percent more to finance its pension plan.

"That's grim news," I volunteered.

"Damn right," he said, "but what do you do with inflation today running over fourteen percent? It's going to eat every one of our retirees alive!"

My friend was right, of course. Saddled with fixed incomes, we all could become captives of runaway inflation. The failure to include the effects of inflation in our past pension planning has now forced us to the brink of disaster.

The entire responsibility for throwing pension guidelines into reverse should not fall on the employer alone. Jim Hacking of the American Association of Retired Persons put his finger on the mess we find ourselves in today when he said, "It's sort of like a rock and a hard place. If you mandate even within the limits of five or six percent a year, the costs are just tremendous and you're going to get employers dropping plans."

The only apparent solution to the problem caused by the already outmoded idea of guaranteeing a certain pension benefit and then increasing that benefit to keep pace with inflation is to substantially increase the contributions to the pension plan. But increasing the boss's contribution will further aggravate the balance between productivity and wages, pushing us relentlessly toward greater inflation with varying losses of business by firms who must now pass on these added costs to the consumers.

These additional pension-plan contributions providing cost-of-living increases for retired workers do not pay one penny toward wage hikes for current workers. The boss now must scramble for the extra cash to pay not only the current worker's increasing salary and retiree's increasing pension benefits, but to provide greater pension-plan contributions for current workers so *their* retirement benefits will also increase with the cost of living.

Today the employer's zooming pension costs clearly do put

him between a rock and a hard place. For unless we Americans can learn to control our runaway inflation, the sharply higher pension costs may become a shared responsibility, and the worker will be forced to make increasing personal contributions to save the pension plan.

For many employers the hassles associated with pension plans were just not worth the effort. It was the guarantees that ultimately made pensions so hard to live with. If it were not necessary to guarantee a certain benefit at retirement, costs could be controlled and the effects of inflation overcome.

Money Purchase Pension Plans

The happy solution for many of our employers was the money purchase pension plan. Instead of a defined benefit plan —pension—this was a defined contribution plan. That is, the amount of the annual contribution for each employee is established by a formula—usually a percentage of salary—and the only obligation of the company is the requirement that payments must be made into the plan each year. The money purchase pension plan is, in fact, called a "pension" because of the requirement that contributions be made each year. The actual retirement benefits are, just as the name of the plan implies, whatever the money in the account will purchase. If you are among the millions of workers who are covered under a money purchase pension plan, and you believe the word "pension" will assure you of a realistic retirement check, you are wrong. Your actual retirement benefits, adjusted for inflation, may be no more than five or ten percent of your final salary when you retire. That may sound like highway-robbery to you. Your employer, who is not guaranteeing any pension benefits, need not even tell you how little you may ultimately get.

The money purchase pension plan provides a classic example of why retirement benefits are fast becoming illusory.

Suppose you have been covered under a money purchase pension plan for ten years, you were age fifty when you started, and your salary has averaged $20,000. If your employer contributed ten percent of your salary each year, and if the plan could earn eight percent interest, your account would now hold $31,290. At first glance this may seem like a lot of money. But now you are sixty and let's look at your options. If you were to leave your job, you might save only half of that amount, or a little over $15,000, for your future retirement. That is because of "vesting," which was covered under pensions but applies equally to all retirement plans.

Suppose, on the other hand, that you decided to retire early and your retirement plan permitted this without a loss of benefits. The guaranteed retirement benefit has now been transferred from your employer—who would have to offer this under a pension plan—to you. The employer is off the hook. He no longer needs to keep retirement benefits up with inflation, you do.

Your retirement benefits under this plan would be whatever the money in your personal savings account would purchase.

Profit-Sharing Plan

For employers who are looking for a way out of the pension debacle, the profit-sharing plan has to be an answer to their prayers. All guarantees are out the window. If you are among the millions of workers covered by a profit-sharing plan, you are standing on quicksand.

The original idea behind this retirement plan was to reward the employees when and if their employer made a profit. Therefore, contributions to the plan normally could occur only if a profit has actually been made. Further, when contributions are permitted, the actual amount is left entirely up to the company. Your retirement benefits are completely unknown since no one can foretell when a contribution to the plan will be made and for how much.

Profit-sharing plans are badly out of date. They transfer all of the risks of providing a meaningful retirement benefit from the company to the worker. If you are currently covered under a profit-sharing plan, you should understand that you could very well be left empty handed when you retire.

By now you are practically becoming an "expert" in private retirement plans. Maybe you can now determine why your employer chose the type of retirement plan you have. But most of all, maybe you can now begin to understand the tremendous problems that lie waiting in the shoals to run your leaky retirement ship aground.

While we are still afloat, admittedly with leaks amidships and failing pumps, I would like to steer toward Chapter 3— How the Game Is Played.

3 How the Game Is Played

A pension rebellion is sweeping America. The tyrannical pension-plan administrators, backed up by our own employers, are under attack. They gained control over our retirement security so unobtrusively that we did not realize we were being fleeced. They did not utter a sound as inflation overpowered our expected pension benefits, heading us below the poverty line at retirement.

The pension manager, following the rules of the game, must demand the rigid observance of each section of the fine print that chips away at what retirement benefits still remain. He embraces secrecy and is made to disapprove of opposition because our pleas for a realistic pension interfere with the smooth implementation of the plan.

Pension laws have multiplied, each entangled in red tape and increasingly complex regulations, none of them halting the fleecing we face at retirement.

For most wage-earners, America's private pension plans have become a giant shell game. We are caught within the system and the shells keep coming up empty, destroying retirement dreams after decades of work and pension contributions.

The theory is that you put your money in a retirement plan and it earns money while you work so that when you retire you will get back all the money you have put in, plus all that it has earned. That has been the basic idea behind our retirement planning from the beginning. But we have to realize that this idea and the real world are not the same thing.

In actual practice small-business owners and managers have for years received most of the money going into the plan, dividing up the little that is left among those few employees with significant tenure. It is perfectly legal—small-business owners do it every day. The money going into the retirement plan is all tax-free to the company and the owner!

Since pension plans were originally designed by owners to benefit owners, this should not come as a real surprise. In fact, they were designed so that the worker had to negotiate a mine-laden obstacle course to reach the pension benefit. And when workers failed to overcome the obstacles, their lost benefits usually reverted to the owner's pocketbook.

Today learning to run the maze has become all-important if you are to avoid being cheated and are actually to grasp the long-sought pension benefit.

To help you get a better understanding of the way the game is played, we'll look at four basic principles of our pension plans.

Principle One:
Save Money During Working Years to Spend During Retirement Years

Amazingly simple, you say, yet almost impossible to accomplish by ourselves. So what happened? The government (Social Security), the unions, and the private employer plans set aside the money in our behalf. This may be the "painless way" but it has left us with virtually no control over our own retirement plans. Then came a belated realization. That the American public now realizes that each worker needs his own individual savings plan has to be regarded as the most significant accomplishment of the last few years.

Looking ahead, it could well be that saving fully half of the money will become the responsibility of each American on his or her own. This will satisfy the first principle. The failure to conform to this principle, it is important to note, has been the main impediment to the provision of an adequate retirement income. Unless Americans themselves are willing to save a major share of the money they will need for an adequate retirement income, prospects in retirement for most Americans will be sheer hell in a world of never-ending galloping inflation.

Principle Two:
The Law of Compound Interest

This principle may not sound important, but it is at the heart of every retirement plan—except Social Security. The latter, as we shall see, depends less on savings for retirement than on a "pay-as-you-go" taxing arrangement. Assume a typical plan under which you and/or your employer saved one thousand dollars each year from the time you were twenty-five to the time you retire at age sixty-five. Over this forty-year span compound interest actually will create most of the money in the plan, as we see in the following example.

	WITHOUT COMPOUND INTEREST	WITH COMPOUND INTEREST AT 9% PER YEAR
Total amount at age 65	$40,000	$368,292

In fact, the law of compound interest is so important that without understanding it one cannot understand why many retirement plans are in trouble today. A large number of pension plans have projected receiving much more (tax-free) interest income than they have actually realized. It is easy to see why this has happened. Since high rates earn more money for the retirement plan, correspondingly fewer contributions will be needed by the employer. But there is a hitch. When lower-than-projected interest rates are earned while the employer's input remains unchanged, the result is underfunding. The quite natural consequence is that the pension plan has unfunded liabilities: which means, as we have earlier explained, that there is not enough money in the pension account to pay the future benefits promised under the plan. The term *unfunded liabilities* could be used to characterize most of the pension plans in America today!

Principle Three:
The Law of Favorable Taxation

The heart and soul of a company-sponsored pension plan rests on the foundation built by the income-tax code. Without the principle of favorable taxation, the nation's employer-sponsored pension plans would come crashing down.

The solution, established from the very beginning, was to treat the employer's contribution to the tax-qualified retirement plan on a par with wages—both of which are tax deductible to the company. In a real sense the employer's contribution amounts to wages payable later in the form of a pension.

For employees the income-tax bite is delayed. This is only fair, since income tax is due only on money received during the tax year. Besides, as already indicated, much of the money set aside for the worker may never actually be received. The taxman arrives only when we retire and begin drawing retirement checks. The advantage, so often explained, is that at retirement we will usually be in a much lower tax bracket.

These favorable tax features were introduced to encourage employers to install retirement plans. In this connection it must be borne in mind that a goal of national policy was that all workers should supplement the floor of benefits offered by Social Security. That was the basic idea. However, results have not measured up. By fiscal 1977, seventy-five percent of the $6.5 billion tax savings accrued to the benefit of higher-paid individuals with incomes in excess of $15,000 (that is, $15,000 in 1977 purchasing power). As much as twenty percent of the tax break went into the pockets of really high earners with annual incomes over $50,000.

Let's look again at our example and compare only the effects on the pension fund of the employer's tax deduction. We will assume once again a compound interest rate of nine percent over forty years

	WITHOUT A CORPORATE TAX DEDUCTION	WITH A CORPORATE TAX DEDUCTION
Total Amount at Age 65	$69,726	$368,292

As a rule of thumb: Without the principle of favorable taxation, employers would have to increase their contributions over five times the current amount to maintain the same benefits scale now in effect. Only a very few private companies could afford the loss of tax deductibility and survive.

Not all retirement plans offer tax-saving incentives to the worker, however. Social Security is the big exception, and its success can be traced largely to the fact that both worker and employer contributions are mandated by law.

Principle Four:
Lifetime Income

The objective of most retirement plans is to offer a lifetime income, one you cannot outlive. Even when the amount received is less than you need to maintain a modest living standard, such plans offer security by guaranteeing that you cannot outlive your money.

The desire for a lifetime income was recognized by the insurance companies from the start and this feature has been an important part of our private retirement system ever since. By using a mortality—or life-expectancy—table, the insurance company can calculate the amount of money that will be needed at age sixty-five to assure a lifetime annuity.

The insurance company then assumes the risk, overcoming one of the nagging fears that usually accompany our mature years—running out of money before we run out of breath. In the past only the wealthy were able to overcome this fear. Today, the way the cost of living is galloping along, even those of us lucky enough to amass a small fortune in savings may run out of cash.

The unique feature of an annuity is that it guarantees a check a month for life. Annuity contracts operate under a basic principle that has been around a long time, and the concept has remained virtually unchanged over the years. The pension plan normally buys an annuity for a worker about to retire, paying the insurance company a given amount.

Assume that workers retiring at sixty-five will live about fifteen years. Then the insurance company agrees to pay the worker $1,000 a month for life, but the insurance company will have to receive about $120,000 from the pension plan. In other words, a lifetime annuity from the insurance company of $12,000 a year will cost the pension plan about $120,000 when the worker retires.

This arrangement relieves the pension plan itself of the mechanical burden of mailing a retirement check while guaranteeing the retiree a check each month for as long as he or she lives.

There are basically two types of annuities. One is called a lifetime annuity, payable only so long as the retiree lives. At death, the money is gone. The other is a refund—or "years certain"—annuity which guarantees to pay the annuity (usually for ten years) even in the event of the retiree's death before that time. In either case the annuity is always paid throughout the lifetime of the original purchaser.

There are important features of an annuity that begins at retirement. An annuity is not an investment to make money; rather it is an insurance contract to pay periodic income to the retiree. The monthly income is fixed, guaranteed, predetermined, and all that solid insurance-company jargon. It's not a chance for a windfall profit. Furthermore, the annuity contract is not like a stock-exchange security that can be traded, for once income starts being pumped out, the flow generally continues for the retiree's lifetime.

The amount of income the retired person receives is determined by actuarial tables, which are based primarily on life-expectancy tables. Since different insurance companies use various assumptions in calculating benefits (such as differences in interest rates earned on funds turned over to it by the pension plan), a little shopping around prior to retirement could pay a big bonus when you open that monthly retirement check. If you have this option to shop for an annuity, the range of differences in monthly income levels among the one thousand-plus insurance companies that offer annuities is believed to be as much as fifteen percent.

Sex also makes a big difference when you purchase an annuity. That is because most of the costs are determined by the life expectancy at the time the annuity is sold, and statistically women live longer than men. Most insurance companies figure at least three years longer. This means that the same amount of money turned over to an insurance company at retirement will buy a smaller annuity income for a woman than it will for a man.

Legal problems surfaced as soon as women began complaining about the relative size of their benefits. In the resulting litigation, the U.S. Supreme Court struck a blow for working women when it ruled in 1978 that pension plans cannot discriminate on the basis of sex just because women live longer than men.

The suit was filed by a female employee against the Los Angeles Department of Water and Power. In her suit the employee claimed that the employer had violated the job-bias provisions of the federal civil rights law by requiring women workers to make larger contributions to the pension plan than men. The court action has forced pension plans to use a new "unisex" life expectancy table, allowing the equalization of benefits between the sexes by reducing benefits for men.

The Supreme Court decision, unfortunately, was very narrow in scope. The ruling applies only to defined-benefit (pension) plans and only where employee contributions are mandated by a pension plan.

Lifetime monthly annuities, long a safe and convenient way to convert assets at retirement without having to share with the taxman, have all but passed into oblivion.

Millions of Americans already retired have belatedly found that the peace of mind they thought they had obtained through an annuity has unexpectedly been costing a great deal of money. The inflationary thief that comes in the night can take a $500 per month annuity and, at today's price escalation, reduce that check to only $250 of purchasing power in seven short years. What cost $1.00 in 1975, to put it another way, could cost $2.00 in 1982.

Unless your pension has a cost-of-living adjustment clause, and almost no private pension plans do, your guaranteed, predetermined, fixed, unwavering, set-dollar income-for-life annuity—in terms of purchasing power—could melt before your tear-filled eyes.

So much for the highlights of the basic principles of all retirement plans. It is within the framework of these principles, coupled with the original guidelines covered in the previous chapter, that the basic pension plans were developed over the first half of this century.

Now let's look at the ways private employers have designed their retirement plans for the 1980s.

Incredible as it may seem, the game is played in such a way that the legal fine print continues to allow the boss a multitude of opportunities to defraud the workers. These legal thefts, allowed employers under the protection of an indifferent Congress, continue to plague the pension system, while millions of working Americans still believe things are fair and equitable for all.

By the turn of the century some twenty million Americans currently working are expected to collect a monthly pension check from either public or private plans. The shocking truth is, however, that many of these millions will be cheated. They will take a beating either through the loss of all their expected pension benefits or through receipt of benefits which ultimately may turn out to be only a fraction of what they had been told to expect.

The next time you get all starry-eyed about chucking your job and tearing open those monthly retirement checks, just remember that the envelope could come up empty unless you know how the game is played.

Let's look at some of the ways you can be victimized by your pension plan.

One way is to "integrate" your pension plan with Social Security. This means that your private pension plan may count part of your Social Security benefits when the experts figure how much you will get from your plan.

Former Secretary of the Treasury W. Michael Blumenthal, commenting in a 1978 article in the *Atlanta Constitution* dealing with Social Security integration, said, "Millions of workers —perhaps twenty-five percent of the participants in private

49

pension plans—will receive little or nothing under their retirement plans.

"Employers who have plans for highly paid persons can now deny any benefits to those employees who earn less than $17,700. Soon there will be a dramatic increase in the number of employees subject to exclusion. By 1981, anyone earning less than $29,700—a group comprising nearly ninety-five percent of the American work force—can be excluded from one of these tax-supported plans."

Since private pension plans are allowed to piggyback Social Security, many middle- and lower-income workers are learning, in effect, that their pension plan need not provide them any retirement income beyond Social Security benefits. The boss can consider Social Security as if it were part of the company's own commitment and look at the combined benefits as the percentage of final salary the pension plan is required to replace.

The reasoning behind "integration" was to allow all workers, regardless of pay level, to have roughly the same percentage of their final pay replaced at retirement. By combining public and private benefits, it was further reasoned, integration could help correct the Social Security "bias" in favor of the lower-paid worker.

"Consequently," Mr. Blumenthal went on, "an employer's middle- and lower-income employees might get nothing from a pension plan while the tax dollars of those employees subsidize the pension benefits of the same employer's highly paid employees."

As complex as the current integration device has become, let me see if I can explain what happens in a simplified way.

Under present pension rules (which, incidentally, allow a pension plan to cover a worker for years without any mathematical way the worker could ever be paid a pension benefit) the boss can start with the pension obligation to the retiree. Second, he can subtract the retiree's benefit under Social Security. If the latter exceeds the former, clearly the boss need not make any contribution to the retiree's pension; it will all come from Social Security. So if you earn less than the Social Security wage base (which, in 1980, was $25,900 and likely to rise) you could get benefits solely from the government and nothing whatever from the company plan. As a result, most of the money going into the pension fund would end up in the pockets of the higher-paid people.

Once more, I'll provide an illustration. Suppose your pension plan sets out to provide retirement benefits equal to fifty percent of your final average salary. The first thing to check is the "offset" clause, which calls for subtracting whatever you receive from Social Security from what the private pension plan would otherwise have to pay. Take a worker retiring with a salary of $12,500, who looks forward to $6,250 in pension benefits. However, if forty-four percent of his pay is replaced by Social Security, the private pension plan needs to pay only six percent, or $750 a year, and not the full $6,250 he might first expect.

But what about the worker making $25,000, exactly twice as much as the lower-paid worker? He could receive only twenty-two percent of his retirement income from Social Security. Hence, he should receive an extra twenty-eight percent of his pay, or $7,000, from the company plan.

The facts now become clear. Higher paid workers may receive twice the salary, but they get ten times the pension benefits from the company pension plan itself.

Sounds dishonest, doesn't it? It is. So much so that in 1978 President Carter sent to Congress proposals to change the way companies should be allowed to integrate their pension plans with Social Security.

Since all contributions into the pension plan are in a sense deferred compensation and tax deductible to the employer, the Administration thinks the plans should provide at least some retirement benefits for all workers. Not necessarily a fair and equitable amount, you understand, but at least some pension benefits to millions of workers who now are expected to come up nearly empty-handed.

These proposals to make private pensions fair to all suffered the same fate that awaits most pension reform bills: the dead file. One of the bill's floor managers summed up the status of the proposed changes when he snapped, "The issue will not be considered any further this year by Congress; it will be considered again at the appropriate time." Up to this point, the "appropriate time" has failed to arise.

Let me again quote former Secretary of the Treasury Blumenthal, who made clear the failure of integration when he said, "By 1981, anyone earning less than [the Social Security wage base] $29,700—a group comprising nearly ninety-five percent of the American work force—can (under the current integration rules for pension plans) be excluded from one of these tax-supported plans."

It's not that those who earn more shouldn't have more money at retirement; it's the unfairness of allowing little or nothing in benefits for the lower-paid workers, while the same tax dollars support enormous private pensions for the higher-paid workers.

Unfortunately, in spite of the President's proposals for fair legislation from a Congress overwhelmed by special-interest groups, millions of Americans are not aware that they are now effectively excluded from their private company pension plans through the integration device.

If you are suspicious, investigate your own pension plan. You can be sure that your final retirement income will probably total much less than you expected. You might want to reread this chapter covering integration. Bear in mind that I am not talking about a possibility. The pension game is really played that way.

If the pension game is a difficult one for men to play, for women it can be nearly impossible. The average private pension received by female retirees has been a shocking $970 per year. What's more, with fifty-four percent of American women working, fewer than twenty percent of retired women are currently drawing that magnificent $80 per month private pension. That's because working women are neglected by a pension system full of loopholes. Family responsibilities frequently pull them in and out of the labor market. Further, most jobs for women offer low wages so that when and if a pension is ever payable, the amount received is relatively small. What's more, most of the requirements have little relation to real life. For example, many private pension plans deny a widow benefits if her spouse dies before retirement age.

Married women in particular are victims of this system

contrived to fleece them at every turn. Take the case during divorce proceedings. The wife argues that her childbearing and homemaking activities for twenty years were equivalent to her husband's salary on which the retirement benefits were based. She argues, with reason, that the pension earned during the marriage should be considered joint property.

But that's not the way the rules work. The private pension plans, by and large, say so. Now comes the U.S. Supreme Court, ruling that the pension benefit belongs to the husband. The wife is left at age fifty or sixty with her pail and mop—and a low-paying, nonskilled job which only an incurable optimist could believe would ever result in a pension benefit of her own.

Or consider the case where the wife, after thirty years of marriage, witnesses the death of her husband just before retirement and pension eligibility under the company plan. Her decades of work are suddenly of no economic value. Because her husband didn't actually begin drawing out pension benefits before his death, she no longer exists in the eyes of the company pension plan. Without a survivor benefit, she is faced with yet another dilemma: Who will hire a sixty-year-old woman without recent work experience?

If all this sounds dreadfully unfair, it is. Women employed outside and inside the home are effectively locked out of an individually acquired pension benefit. The people in Washington who can change the rules of the game have not made things any easier. After all, allowing reasonable pension benefits to women costs money. The bosses who offer the pensions do not like higher costs. Therefore, faced with pressure from firms that might have to shell out big bucks to widowed and divorced women, many in Congress have been unwilling to change the rules.

Until now.

The pension fraud has become so widespread that a breath of scandal has begun to engulf Capitol Hill. Last year alone three bills were introduced in Congress aimed at providing a pro-rata share of retirement and survivor benefits to former spouses of federal employees. The proposed bills would change the government's Civil Service retirement plan to include a provision that would make survivor benefits automatically part of the pension plan. In addition, in line with the recent change in Social Security, the bills would provide a pro-rata share of the plan benefits to former spouses married at least ten years.

But much more needs to be done. Private plans still remain untouched by any recent legislation dealing with the inequities that have been faced by women since the American Express Company established its first pension plan in 1875—problems that have never been admitted as real in the make-believe world of pensions. For example, a break in service (covered in the last chapter) for child-rearing as well as for military duty should be allowed without the loss of earned pension benefits. Moreover, women should be allowed to earn and vest pension benefits before they leave their jobs to raise children.

Short of any help from Congress, the most effective way to avoid being fleeced is to ask questions when you begin a new job or sign up for a pension plan. Knowing the basics of pension plans is one thing, but to cope effectively with pension inequities you need to educate yourself about the operations of *your own* plan—and do so long before you are faced with retirement.

Now let's see how the pension game works when the boss is personally affected by the outcome. About forty million people—nearly half the labor force—work for small companies and locally owned businesses, many of which do not have pension plans. The reason is simple. The boss is spending his own money, which he could otherwise take home, to pay for the company retirement plan. "Any retirement plan that doesn't heavily favor the owner doesn't have a snowball's chance in hell of ever being offered to the employees of a small company," one pension consultant told me. "For years the government has allowed owners of small businesses to rip off their employees, pocketing most of the retirement money themselves. This has not been done in the name of fairness, but in an attempt to bribe small business owners into establishing retirement plans."

A recent survey estimated that about 3.4 million small businesses (fifty or fewer employees) operate in the United States. Fully two thirds, or about 2.3 million, do not have any form of retirement plan. Of the remaining one third, about sixty percent offer Individual Retirement Accounts (IRA's) owned and primarily paid for by the employees themselves. Of all small businesses in America (as defined by this survey) only one in six has a tax-qualified, employer-sponsored retirement plan; so that five out of every six small employers, in spite of the bribe offered by our pension laws allowing the owners personally to end up with most of the money going into the plan, have yet to open a company retirement plan.

Faced with the 1974 Employee Retirement Income Security Act (ERISA), which established for the first time employee rights to at least some measure of fair treatment, many pension experts now predict that small businesses will be dropping, not opening, company-sponsored retirement plans.

Another reason for opting out might be the new federal law prohibiting mandatory retirement before age seventy. Already an uneasy realization is beginning to emerge that in trying to protect the jobs of older workers, the new law may actually make those jobs less secure.

As a result of the law, many small businesses and local enterprises may become more vulnerable to employee complaints of discrimination if they are let go before age seventy. Since most small companies do not have pension plans, many of the workers may find they cannot get along on Social Security benefits alone and they will want to continue working.

By extending the retirement age five years, we may have triggered a rash of competency tests. These are not excluded by the new law. Both large and small companies might start weeding out marginally productive people in their fifties and early sixties.

Business owners seeking to discourage older workers could, for example, increase their work load beyond their physical ability, assign them to less desirable jobs, or pass them over for raises and promotions. The worker might then feel impelled to take "voluntary" early retirement.

The sticky problems will come from the boss's desire to hire younger and possibly more productive workers at lower costs, while the older workers are faced with retirement on their meager Social Security benefits and their personal savings. Once again we see that good intentions often harvest bad legislative results.

The problem Congress should have addressed was the almost universal weakness of our private pension system. Instead they took the easy way out, by allowing workers the somewhat dubious legal right to continue to work in lieu of a realistically mandated private pension.

While we're at it, let's not forget inflation. For a number of small-business owners, inflation has put to rest the idea of a company retirement plan. They can afford to pay current income taxes—soon expected to drop even lower—and invest the after-tax money in real estate. These small businessmen have effectively shed all government controls, and more important, based on their activity in the last ten years, they themselves have a "retirement plan" that can run *with* inflation.

Small businesses are, by and large, America's last link with classic free enterprise. With their own money at risk, they are free to fail or succeed. But our whole economy has generally turned against them. Squeezed by big business, the profits earned by most have been less than might have been expected just five years ago. In fact, in these inflation times, many businesspeople could have made more money over the last five years by opting out. Taking a job with big business, they could have sold their small business and invested the cash in real estate. Their inflationary real-estate appreciation most likely would have greatly exceeded their former business after-tax profits.

It is now obvious to millions of small-business owners that company-sponsored retirement plans do not make sense. With their employees always fighting for higher paychecks, they have begun to build their own retirement plans outside the government-controlled system.

Sometimes, in fact, small-business owners have simply worked around the cumbersome federal regulations to exclude everyone but themselves. Take the case of two clever professional men who each formed a one-man corporation. Once this was accomplished, the two "corporations" formed a fifty-fifty partnership to run their businesses and actually employ the workers. The owners then set up a pension plan for each corporation, covering only themselves.

The verdict of the IRS in this case was that the professional owner's corporation actually controlled the partnership so the pension plan must cover all the partnership's employees. The tax court, however, ruled that the corporations did not control the partnership since each corporation owned only fifty percent. The court concluded that the pension plan (covering only the two owners) did not discriminate and that the contributions to the plan were deductible.

The decision, like many that have occurred over the past few years, upholds a tax device for professional businesspersons who want to cover only themselves.

But what if the boss is forced to cover all employees? What if he is forced to install a pension plan that pays, say, fifty percent of the final salary at retirement age sixty-five? Even in this case, he comes out a winner.

Take the typical small business, for example, with ten employees earning an average salary of $15,000 and with an average age of thirty. The boss might be fifty-five, earning $50,000. Assuming the pension plan can earn nine percent compound interest on the contributions it receives from the company, and ignoring inflation and future salary increases, the cost of the annuity at retirement for the boss would reach $15,100 each year. For each employee, the annual pension cost would be only $320.

Even without taking into consideration the Social Security integration device covered in this chapter, the boss will receive eighty-three percent of the company's total contribution to the pension plan. The boss may then impose a three-year waiting period before the worker is eligible to join the retirement plan. The fascinating part of this whole game is that the system continues to insure that the workers come up empty-handed at retirement.

Since the typical small business has relatively high employee turnover, even after five years of employment the worker's pension account might have received only $640. Surprised? Can you now catch the vision of the pension plan from the employee's point of view? By no stretch of the imagination can the worker believe he or she is covered under a retirement plan when the contributions over this five-year period have averaged less than one percent of salary. But that's not all. As we'll see later on, the system has now succeeded in denying the worker the basic right to open an Individual Retirement Account (IRA).

If you feel sick now, look closer. Pension plans were originally designed on the premise that the plan would continue in operation until the employee retired. In actual practice, however, this rarely will happen in the 1980s.

In fact, considering our previous example, the boss will retire in ten years, and with his retirement the pension plan will, in most cases, terminate as well.

Millions of Americans continue to remain under the illusion that the pension plans are generally fair and equitable. Congress knows otherwise. We were raised in the knowledge that there was a "right" and "wrong" in ethics and morals. But the brilliant ones in Washington have allowed the private pension mess to slip so badly that as many as seventy-five percent of the private work force can end up without a meaningful retirement plan.

For Congress, in fact, allowed a retirement system to develop in which your pension benefits depend entirely on where you work, not what you do. The nation's overall pension policy is so uneven that a minority of workers can actually retire with larger net incomes than their preretirement salary, while millions of Americans are completely dependent on Social Security.

There has to be a special place in hell for our senators and congressmen who have created their own generous, fully funded, cost-of-living-protected retirement plan while allowing millions of Americans to be effectively eliminated from any work-related private pension plan. The nation's retirement system has become both dishonest and unethical and we have become trapped within it.

4 The Patient May Die

A few months ago my wife and I went to the hospital to visit a close friend. Approaching the nurse's station, we were informed that visiting hours had been canceled; the patient had developed complications. "The patient has been running a very high temperature," the nurse explained as she returned to the stack of charts laid out before her.

Interrupting her again, I asked if she could tell me what might happen to my friend. Annoyed, she looked up from her charts and said, "Look, I'm no doctor, but around here if that high a temperature doesn't come down, the patient may die."

Today our national economy resembles my friend. If the rate of inflation, now running almost fourteen percent a year, does not come down, the patient may die.

Admittedly, inflation's origins are complex and a detailed study is not intended by the author. What to do about our recent runaway inflation is also a complex question and no one, including the author, seems to know precisely what action should be taken. It seems immune to all antibodies. If we have learned anything about inflation, we know that the days of "constant values" are long gone. The value of a dollar tomorrow is not the value of a dollar today; maybe ninety cents, but not a dollar.

To better understand the devastating effects of inflation,

let's look at how it affects your pocketbook. The first thing you might discover is that galloping inflation is a rather new phenomenon. Basically, from the time of Christ up to as late as 1939, persistent high inflation did not exist. Occasionally, mainly during periods of American involvement in wars, inflation did pop up briefly; but, taking the long view, prices moved smoothly along on a relatively even keel. They even fell for several decades late in the nineteenth century.

To put inflation in perspective, as late as the 1950s the average was only two percent. During the 1960s, inflation edged up to 2.5 percent. The last decade, however, has been a very different story. If you use the base year of 1939, where the value of your dollar equaled one hundred cents, you can not only take a look at the rapidly shrinking purchasing power of your dollar, but you can also take a horrifying look at the future.

The Purchasing Power of the Dollar
Using 1939 as the Base Year Where the Dollar Equaled
100 Cents

1949 = 58¢	to	1959 = 47¢	1/5 drop
1959 = 47¢	to	1969 = 38¢	1/4 drop
1969 = 38¢	to	1979 = 19¢*	1/2 drop

(Data: U.S. Department of Labor. *Estimate by author.)

Now for a look at the horrifying future. I have constructed my own table based on what has happened in the past and what could very well occur in the future.

The Purchasing Power of the Dollar
Using 1939 as the Base Year Where the Dollar Equaled
100 Cents

1979 = 19¢	to	1989 = 5¢	2/3 drop
1989 = 5¢	to	1999 = ?	?

In order to make it appear to the voters back home that inflation is not destroying their financial security, the masterminds in Washington keep changing the base year. In 1978 the U.S. Bureau of Labor Statistics came out with a new report declaring the dollar worth 100 cents for a new base year of 1978, with an assumed inflation rate of only eight percent. Within just a year inflation was galloping along at a thirteen percent clip. Even though there is no statistical reason to compare the 1939 base and the 1978 base tables side by side, let's do it anywav.

Value of a Dollar

	BASE YEAR 1978 100 CENTS	BASE YEAR 1939 100 CENTS
1979	93¢	19¢*
1989	43¢	5¢
1999	20¢	?

*Author's best guess of the future.

What this table points out, if in fact it makes any sense at all in the topsy-turvy world of inflated numbers, is that over a sixty-year period, from 1939 to 1999, your money will have become worthless. Or during the next twenty-one years, from 1978 to 1999, your money could drop in value a catastrophic eighty percent.

Worse yet, in basing their report on an assumed inflation rate of eight percent, the U.S. Bureau of Labor Statistics was only following the latest available forecasts.

Back in September of 1978 Henry Wallich, a member of the Federal Reserve Board, warned Americans that they may face an inflation rate of at least eight percent through the end of 1979. "Inflation has clearly accelerated from the six percent area into the eight percent area," he said, "and threatens to accelerate further next year."

The dictionary defines *accelerated* as causing faster velocity or speed. One year later, in September 1979, the velocity had spiraled inflation to an incredible annual rate of almost fourteen percent. Continuing inflation at this rate is not tolerable. You cannot make plans for your retirement, let alone care for your family, with an inflation rate of this magnitude.

It is not where we have been, it is where we are going that scares the hell out of me. Unfortunately we appear to be headed into prolonged double-digit inflation, which strikes terror into the hearts of most economists by its effect on wages alone. It has been estimated that if wages, and we assume inflation as well, increased at only six percent a year, by 2001 a plumber in California could earn $148,000 per year. But at an annual rate of twelve percent, double-digit magic over this same period would boost the plumber's salary to $581,000 per year.

When our annual inflation rate increases from six percent to somewhere around a double-digit rate of twelve percent, you now run not merely twice, but almost four times as fast just to stay in place. This is galloping inflation; only the fleetest runners survive. We even now find that, because of inflation, deceit and deception are beginning to dominate the way we live and work as individuals, in our affairs with each other, in all levels of government, and in business. The best explanation for this is the sheer terror we feel for our pocketbooks when we are faced with seemingly uncontrollable inflation. Inflation, as the economists say, does not have a straight-line effect. The inflation that grabs the headlines can only tell us what is happening today. The relentless mathematics of the Rule of Seventy can tell us what will happen in the near future. For the Rule of Seventy can paralyze with fear even the strong of heart among us.

The Rule of Seventy works like this: If the annual rate of inflation is ten percent, then divide that number into the number seventy. The answer is seven; this is the number of years it will take for the dollar in your pocket to be worth half its current purchasing power, if the inflation rate remains unchanged. A quick look at the Rule of Seventy shows how fast our country is racing toward an economic smashup. For if you can stand to visualize what the already reported fourteen percent rate of inflation is doing to the dollar, you have a very high threshold of pain indeed. At this rate the value of a dollar could drop to only fifty cents in five short years!

Clearly those of us who work, and more importantly, those who have retired on fixed incomes, cannot carry a purse full of frozen money through the Sahara Desert and long survive. We need desperately to save what value is still left in our once-proud dollar. But, as the famous line from Pogo tells us, "we have met the enemy, and they is us." All of us: government, labor, business, and each of us as individuals.

For the last year the Gallup Poll has shown that Americans regard inflation as their number one problem. What has also emerged, and this may well be a direct result of inflation, are the new results from various polls revealing that Americans, for the first time, have lost confidence in their government's ability to deal with our national problems. There was a feeling in this country that under a controlled economy, government could and would solve our economic problems. If inflation went too high, the reasoning went, the government would step in and push it back down. Today that feeling is gone. Having lost confidence in their government, Americans are spending more and buying now because whatever there is to buy will cost more tomorrow. In times of double-digit inflation there are only tomorrows.

The point I am trying to make is that inflation causes a decrease in the value of your money. This means that every succeeding dollar buys less. The Rule of Seventy simply tells you how much less your money will buy and how soon.

If you are a retiree on a fixed income, inflation will erode your buying power even more. It will take more money to live every year after the paycheck stops. According to the latest Census Bureau figures for 1977, couples sixty-five or older typically receive less than half the median income, or about $6,786 per year. Economic security for millions of retirees close to the poverty line already will crumble under the weight of the Rule of Seventy. Half of their purchasing power could disappear in the next five years.

Why has inflation taken a turn for the worse? Many Americans believe the major responsibility must lie with their own government. Even knowledgeable economists concede that government error has been a major cause of the skyrocketing rate of inflation over the last few years. Arthur F. Burns, the former Federal Reserve Board Chairman, summed up the reasons inflation got out of the bag when he said, "The main source of inflation is the tendency of modern government to expand their outlays at a rapid rate in response to incessant demands from the electorate." To fill this demand, far exceeding the government's ability to collect taxes, more money had to be printed. Printing money has always been easy for the elected officials in Washington. In fact, unwilling to take the heat from back home, they have voted a multitude of benefits directly from the public treasury. So much so that it has been almost twenty years since the government balanced a budget.

Not all of the spending is ill advised—in fact, some of it may have been necessary—but the end result has been billions of dollars of new debt each year. During the decade of the seventies, the U.S. Office of Management and Budget has estimated that the federal government accumulated red ink totaling $338 billion, with almost $40 billion of the debt occurring in the last year!

You only need to pick up your morning newspaper and turn to the financial page. Our government's finances are spelled out in detail there. The total federal public debt, through the third quarter of 1979, was listed as $820 billion.

This immense sum of money comes into perspective only when you pry out of Washington a seldom-seen document called "Statement of Liabilities and Other Financial Commitments of the United States Government as of September 30, 1979." In this report the national debt is listed as $834 billion. That is the figure that appears in the newspaper because that is the amount on which the government is paying interest. That is an easy concept to understand; most Americans today have personal debts for which they are paying interest.

But that is not the whole story. If it were, it could be covered in one page, not the thirty-four pages that make up the report. Part two of this report covers the debt for which the government has yet to go to the public trough. In a sense these are government IOU's payable to the Treasury. The list includes outstanding checks, unpaid interest, accounts payable, and other bookkeeping debts that total over $116 billion. Total liabilities—as the government likes to call debt—now amount to a prodigious $950 billion.

In this section of the report, the big numbers that leap out and grab your attention are those for public retirement (Social Security) and government retirement (civil service) plans. Federal old age and hospital trust funds (Social Security) are in debt over $50 billion, while the government's own retirement plan, covering only a fraction of the workers covered by Social Security, is in debt $68 billion!

Now come the last twenty pages of the report, telling the real story of how deeply in hock our government has become. Listed under government loan guarantees and insurance commitments, these items total an unbelievable $7 trillion plus!

Labeled "Contingency Items," they are obligations of the federal government, but somehow, through the miracle of federal paper shuffling, they do not appear as liabilities.

The loan guarantees alone total over $276 billion, covering such obscure schemes as the Federal Ship Financing Fund, the Overseas Private Investment Fund, and the National Oceanic and Atmospheric Fund. Better known programs are the Student Loan Insurance Fund, the FHA, Low Rent Public Housing, and the Small Business Administration.

The insurance commitments are another matter. On paper they total over $2 trillion. However, they are made up primarily from commitments made to the Federal Deposit Insurance Corporation and the Federal Home Loan Bank Board, and for Riot Reinsurance to help property owners obtain insurance in areas subject to riots and civil disorders. Payment for these claims would, presumably, be made only in the event of an economic collapse. Hence they are not considered a "real" debt, nor likely to be paid in the foreseeable future.

So far, by putting all the numbers together, we find that the government's "debt" and "contingencies" have now exceeded $3 trillion. The numbers now become so large that one easily loses all perspective.

Finally we reach the end of the report, which covers the debt even the government is unable to calculate, the retirement plans. Just to refresh your memory, the federal government is on the hook for, among others, the Railroad Retirement System, the Tennessee Valley Authority Retirement System, the Military and Veterans Retirement Plan, the Civil Service Retirement Fund, the Foreign Service Retirement Fund, and, of course, Social Security.

Let's look at two retirement plans to be covered in greater detail in succeeding chapters. The Civil Service Retirement Plan, for one, has now succeeded in becoming an outright disaster. In addition to the previously listed outright debt of $68 billion, the government's own report shows an additional "actuarial deficiency" of over $156 billion. In plain English this means that our government now admits that $204 billion is missing from its own retirement plan. Never in the history of the world has a retirement plan gone this deeply into debt to serve so few members. The latest figures, as of March, 1978, report that only 2.8 million active workers and 3.4 million retired workers are covered under the Civil Service Retirement Plan. This works out to a mind-boggling debt of over $32,903 for *each* worker *or* retiree covered under the system. The whole idea of the government running an individual retirement system collapses under the weight of these numbers.

The Social Security system is not much better off, as it comes perilously close to a massive financial breakdown. Page twenty-three of the 1979 issue of the Federal Statement of Liabilities estimates that, in spite of the sharply higher payroll taxes already voted by Congress, the "actuarial deficiency" of the Social Security program, from the years 1979 to 2053, will be an incredible $1.5 trillion. The "assets" to back up this mushrooming debt are the future payroll taxes of the American worker.

With the currently established payroll taxes failing to cover even the minimum costs, most members of Congress now concede that further increasing the payroll tax on the few who work to pay adequately the benefits for the many who do not has become political suicide. And well it should. The debt has now soared to such incredible levels that for all practical purposes it can no longer be supported by individual payroll taxes.

As I studied the footnotes on the Social Security section, I began to realize for the first time the extent of the sham inflicted on the American workers by their elected politicians. Millions of Americans have, in fact, been discouraged from personal savings under the belief that Social Security will take care of them. The truth is that Congress has allowed them to become hooked on a retirement system whose cupboard is bare.

Social Security will not do the job. And I say that not as an alarmist, but as a realist stating the facts. I admit that I am a bit old-fashioned. I look at the strength of a pension plan on the basis of the money already collected against the promises made to the current and retired members of the plan.

A footnote in the report states:

> If the estimates were to be prepared on the assumption
> that no workers were to be covered in the future other than
> those who were 18 and over as of September 30, 1979 [that
> is, contrary to the basis on which the Congress has provided
> for financing the program], there would be a deficiency of
> $4,225 billion for the OASDI program, computed on the dy-
> namic assumption basis.

This means that, according to the government's own calcu-
lations, which traditionally have been grossly understated, Social Security has approximately $4 trillion in unfunded obliga-
tions. That is, the system has failed to collect this mountain of
cash against the promises already made to those who expect to
receive benefits.

Four trillion dollars is equal to roughly seventy-five percent of everything that everyone owns in America today.

The Social Security system is out of control, feeding the
flames of inflation and working against the very people it was
designed to serve. I'll have more to say about Social Security
later.

The total government debt, whatever the figure may be,
represents the money we have spent without first collecting
taxes. Governments are run by politicians who, by and large,
are deathly afraid of reducing government expenditures to
save the dollar. If the expenditures are not reduced, more
money has to be printed. In order to keep the debt within some
semblance of reason, taxes have to be raised.

America may already have slipped her moorings. Every
cent earned by the average worker in the first four months of
the year is now taken in taxes. The federal budget alone has
now mushroomed to over half a trillion dollars—If you started
out at the birth of Christ spending almost $700,000 each day,
you would just now have succeeded in getting rid of half a
trillion dollars. Our government, on the other hand, in 1979,
succeeded in getting rid of that much money in a single year.
To unload this gigantic sum, the Feds had to spend over $1.37
billion dollars every day, including holidays and Sundays.

This rush to spending, and at the same time going into
debt, can best be appreciated when we observe the skill our

government has acquired in unloading the loot. It took 173 years, from the founding of our Republic up to 1962, to reach the first $100 billion budget. Only nine additional years were needed, or until 1971, to reach $200 billion. Four years later we passed $300 billion. Since our government had now fully mastered the art of spending our money, it only took two more years to reach $400 billion, then came $500 billion. Using this time frame, the unbelievable one-trillion-dollar budget is just around the corner.

The idea of government spending is hardly new. Consider this:

> Politicians have strained their ingenuity to discover new sources of public revenues. They have doubled the direct taxes such as customs due on imports and exports. They have continued the extraordinary taxes of wartime into peacetime. They have broadened perilously the field of the income tax as well as the property tax.

This was not written by William Buckley, Herbert Hoover . . . or even by Thomas Jefferson or Alexander Hamilton. Almost incredibly, it was said by Socrates in the fifth century B.C.

What's new today is the runaway cost of government, the huge, rapidly increasing public debt, and the seemingly uncontrollable urge to print money to cover the deficit. Much of the government spending today admittedly is necessary, and for the social good. But even the unthinkable can become believable when and if we allow the value of our money to disappear.

You do not have to go back to the days of the Weimar Republic's inflation of 1918–1923, when people carried their money in wheelbarrows, to see how inflation is affecting the world today. We need only look at a press release from Argentina to see that their wheelbarrow is worth more than their money. Last year commerce workers complained to the labor minister that during the previous four years (from 1975 to 1979) their wages had risen by only 3,175 percent. The workers were upset since the cost of living, during that same period, had increased by 13,850 percent! They were now demanding an emergency wage increase to meet "the abysmal drop" in their buying power.

With inflation running over 500 percent, banks were offering more than 100 percent interest without attracting any customers. Lending money was out of the question, the value of money was falling much faster than the interest rate. Saving money became absurd. Only spending money made any sense.

But Argentina is not alone. Inflation is rising in the rest of the world's industrial countries, but not nearly as fast as here at home. For the first half of 1979 the rate of inflation for the fourteen such countries was 8.3 percent against our own rate of almost 14 percent.

To be sure, the cause of inflation is more complicated than government spending alone, although that is a major factor. Another reason is the falling rate of goods and services per man hour of work. While the inflationary spiral is front-page news, the United States is also facing a growing problem in lagging productivity that threatens to stall the nation's standard of living over the coming years. If wages and costs of production go up but the amount of goods produced remains the same, price pressure goes up. Throughout much of our economy, inflation seems to have become self-perpetuating. For example, if business is uncertain whether a new factory will be able to repay its cost, it may hold back on investment in new plants and equipment. This lack of investment reduces potential production and output per man hour, and puts further strong upward pressure on prices. These higher prices can, of course, result in a demand for higher wages.

In fact, in 1979 the U.S. experienced a sharp drop in business output, with the second quarter's productivity falling more rapidly than it has since the government began keeping records in 1947.

The decline in U.S. productivity is no mere passing phenomenon. The Bureau of Labor Statistics of the U.S. Department of Labor confirms that America has been lagging badly for some time. Thus, productivity in manufacturing during the period of 1968–1978 increased only 23.6 percent. Compare this to Japan, with an increase of 89.1 percent, or France, with an increase of 61.8. West Germany increased its productivity by 63.8 percent, and Italy by 60.1 percent during this ten-year period. And it could get worse. Other countries have built a strong base for industrial expansion while we are faced with aging manufacturing facilities and dangerously inadequate capital investments.

Alden W. Clausen, president of the nation's largest bank, Bank of America, summed up the problems we face in boosting our productivity. This year, he says the direct cost of complying with "proliferating" federal controls will top $100 billion, or more than the total investment in factories, offices, and other productive facilities: "Instead of moving ahead, our economy is spinning its wheels in regulatory mud."

Economists have now concluded that changes in unit labor costs usually match inflation rates. The Labor Department appeared to confirm this in mid-1979 with a report which stated that over the past year unit labor costs went up 10.5 percent, while consumer prices during the same period rose by 10.9 percent.

The importance of the breakdown between wages and production can be illustrated by a long-held formula devised to explain why we have inflation. The formula states that when money and credit exceed the ability of the economy to produce goods, inflation will result. Therefore, if we increase wages without adding a single unit of production to the output of the economy, all we add are higher prices.

For the first time in our nation's history Americans are discovering that they can no longer invent new machines to increase production output every time wages go up.

Today the goods we must buy abroad, such as oil and raw materials, have leaped in price, not only forcing our own consumer price index up, but greatly increasing our trade deficit and lowering the value of the dollar around the world. Over the last decade our whole economy has become virtually dependent on other countries' raw materials regardless of their price. So much so that OPEC (Organization of Petroleum Exporting Countries) has become a vital supplier of oil to the U.S. If the faucet were turned a notch, our whole economy could be thrown into chaos.

Our country clearly has a tiger by the tail. We cannot let go for fear of a collapsing economy forced to run without oil, yet we cannot hang on much longer, with spiraling oil prices pushing us further into the terror of double-digit inflation. For the first time in history our choices are no longer limited to hanging onto the tail or letting go. The tiger is now threatening to devour our whole economy for lunch.

Currently OPEC is estimated to be exporting 11 billion barrels of oil each year. At an average price of about $30 per barrel, this means that an incredible $330 billion is rolling into desert oil capitals each year.

Since other countries, and primarily Swiss and German money markets, couldn't absorb this mountain of cash, and since oil sales were in dollars anyway, the Arabs, awash in money, concluded that they would invest their spare cash in the U.S. Eager for this avalanche of currency, American banks began to accept billions of dollars in time deposits. Our own government was not far behind, selling the OPEC countries huge quantities of government debt—called Treasury Bills or T-Bills. Unlike the real estate purchased by individual Arabs throughout America, the investment by the OPEC countries was short-term and could theoretically be yanked out of banks and T-Bills with little or no notice.

It has been widely speculated by many economists that should the OPEC countries decide to withdraw a major portion of their huge pile of cash at one time, America's financial market could be faced with considerable turbulence.

Lastly, we have created an inflation phenomenon over the past decade which seems to operate independently from the economic conditions that created it.

All told, some fifty-five million people are now covered by escalator clauses that automatically boost private pay or government benefits more or less at the pace at which prices rise. The negative effects of escalator clauses, I believe, far outweigh the partial shield they offer to the minority fortunate enough to receive them. Fully seventy-five percent of the population remains outside the protection of escalator clauses. A system that benefits a few at the expense of many is both dishonest and unfair. The unfortunate fact that we must accept today, as unpopular as it may be, is that it is impossible for everyone to protect himself from inflation—we can only fight inflation.

In order to fight inflation effectively, we must all pull together. As one economist put it, "People are willing to suffer, even forego personal consumption, as long as they believe everyone else is fighting inflation. When they learn that their neighbors are protected against inflation by automatic wage and benefit clauses, they give up the fight, often feeling it's better to run with the pack than be left behind."

For inflation has been called the cruelest tax of all. It hurts the poor and the middle class far more than it hurts the rich. More important, it is a hidden tax, since most people hardly realize that it is being paid. Inflation's most terrible symptom is the gradual erosion of respect for law and order. As the gap between the rich and the rest of the citizens widens, confrontation may result.

One purpose of this book is to alert you to the fact that our nation is rapidly reaching the point of economic disaster. Our country is already mortgaged to the hilt. The public debt is out of control, with no apparent restraint on future growth. Our retirement plans are being eaten alive by double-digit inflation. Our production of goods per man hour of labor is falling, driving up the price of everything we buy. And we are continuing to import billions of gallons of oil at rapidly rising prices.

Against this background of somber news, most Americans are demanding more and more money in a desperate effort to keep even. Only an incurable optimist could find evidence today that Washington is moving effectively to control inflation, or even that it has the courage to do what it takes to wind down the inflationary spiral. With the annual inflation rate the worst in our peacetime history, warning lights should be flashing all over Capitol Hill.

The unanswered question is whether the American public will recognize in time the ultimate consequences of inflation. With the 1980 national elections upcoming, the people must demand a sensible overall federal policy to control inflation. This will mean, if it is to be effective, an increase in our productivity of goods, a decrease in government spending and money printing, and a cut in the importation of foreign oil.

The bottom line is that we can no longer tolerate a spend-happy Congress, for we have now reached the point where all of us, working or retired, must give up a share to save the whole. The cure will be painful and costly; correcting past mistakes always has been.

I did not set out to be pessimistic about our country's future, but it would be wrong to be unrealistic. It is plain truth that today's double-digit inflation spiral, if unchecked, can lead to an economic smashup. We must counter the complacency of our elected lawmakers, who have been acting like ostriches. I don't know about them, but the world I live in is a world of prices that zoom and a real income that barely crawls after it. The future of our country is not in doubt, the nation is incredibly strong and viable. It will recover, as it has in the past.

I remain confident that we can conquer inflation, but first we must appreciate its devastating long-term effects on our way of life. I believe the time to start the fight in earnest is now. If you agree, write your congressional leaders and let them know how you feel. I don't know about you, but I'm not ready to believe Chicken Little and turn my hard-earned cash into bags of gold coins. At least not until I can see the sky falling.

5 Saving for Your Graying Years

As this book is being written, there is no meaningful way to help the millions of Americans who are not covered by a retirement plan where they work. Moreover, if they are covered at work and the benefits are inadequate and doubtful at best, even less can be done to provide for their retirement.

In fact, today, any attempt by an individual actually to save for retirement will be met by a barrier both of federal regulations and of powerful financial institutions who have already arranged it so that the worker ends up with precious little. The effort to save money in America today has been reduced literally to a toss-up between stuffing the money under the mattress or carrying it down to the banks or savings and loans.

What is more, the idea of saving money has almost gone out of style. So much so that when it comes to putting money aside for the future, Americans lag far behind their counterparts in England. In 1979 the Savings and Loan Foundation, Incorporated, estimated that, on the average, the British save 13 percent of their disposable income. Better yet, the West Germans save 15 percent and the Japanese a hefty 25 percent. Americans save only 5.2 percent. The major reason that people in other countries save more is that they are given, by and large, higher interest rates and important tax incentives.

In England, for example, last year the building societies were paying, on a four-year investment, the equivalent of a 14.18 percent return before taxes and a 9.5 percent return after income taxes are paid.

On the other hand, most Americans not only do not receive any incentives to save, but Congress and the taxmen have so succeeded in discouraging saving that, for many, it has begun to seem pointless. During that same period in the U.S. the savings and loans were paying, on a four-year investment, 7.5 percent interest before taxes and only 5.62 percent after taxes (assuming a 25 percent income-tax bracket).

To save, as defined by Webster's dictionary, is to "put by money rather than spend; to preserve or guard from loss; to maintain and preserve." According to Webster's definition, you have saved if you put money aside where it will be maintained and preserved and where its value will not decline. The word *savings* does not mean that your money should increase in value from year to year, only that it should be maintained and not decline in value.

Prior to inflation's becoming the dominant factor affecting the value of money, saving was generally believed to yield positive net benefits from year to year. Today the act of saving no longer improves one's wealth position; sums saved no longer hold their own in relation to the cost of living.

Long before inflation watered down the value of your dollar, Ben Franklin, in a well-remembered aphorism, expressed his view of the utility of saving for a retirement income. "A man may, if he knows not how to save as he gets, keep his nose to the grindstone."

Good old Ben set the example—for many people working and saving became an American tradition with the idea that that alone would free us from the grindstone. For most of our history as a nation these rules worked well. Government-imposed penalties, gradually increasing over the years, were not seen as important since earned interest was considered a nominal adjunct to savings. Interest rates of three percent, or even four percent, were believed to be more than satisfactory. After all, saving money meant just that, for cash was what counted, not earned interest.

Webster's definition of money saving was clearly in tune with American attitudes. Interest was of little concern and, for all practical purposes, inflation did not exist.

Today, when we look toward the future, it is as though we are looking *through* some carnival mirror. The mere act of saving money has become secondary to considerations of rates of interest and inflation.

Last year former Treasury Secretary Michael Blumenthal told Congress that current laws and regulations actually penalize those wishing to save. He cited estimates that between 1968 and 1979 federal limits on savings-account interest cost Americans a whopping $42 billion in lost earnings, with $19 billion of that burden carried by persons over age sixty-five.

But Senator Jake Garn, R-Utah, asked, as an example of the current Treasury Department's own discrimination, why it did not take its own advice and allow persons of limited means to buy high-earning Treasury Bills? (Treasury Bills are issued by our government, at public auction, to finance the public debt. They are short-term notes issued for both a thirteen-week and twenty-six-week period. Currently T-Bills, as they are called, are paying twice the passbook interest rate, but unlike a passbook account they require a minimum deposit of $10,000.)

In answering Senator Garn's question, Secretary Blumenthal stated that a sharp rise in the availability of Treasury Bills would drain money away from housing and construction and away from the private sector with a recession becoming a greater likelihood. What the Treasury did, however, was to allow banks and savings and loans the right to issue their own homemade T-Bills called money market certificates. Under the protection of the federal regulations, the minimum deposit for a money market certificate continued to be around $10,000, out of reach of most Americans, who remained chained to their low-interest passbook savings accounts.

That most depositors who could qualify wanted a better deal on their savings is made evident by the recent popularity of the money market certificates. By mid-1979, nine months after their introduction, they accounted for ten percent of all deposits in commercial banks and about fifteen percent of all deposits in savings and loans, or a total of over $130 billion.

While the savers who could qualify with a deposit of $10,000 or more were overjoyed with interest rates as high as fourteen percent on these new saving certificates, the people who pay the interest were not. Under long-standing government controls, the banking and thrift institutions' profitability has come to depend on the small investor's acceptance of the low interest rate and withdrawal restrictions now in effect.

Secretary Blumenthal did warn Congress that unless some way can be found to end penalties against small savers, "The ingenuity of the free enterprise system . . . will find new ways to accommodating investors."

During this last year the free enterprise system has not let the secretary down. What has emerged from under the current system of outright disgraceful federal regulations and equally antiquated tax penalties, basically unchanged since the Second World War, is a whole new approach to money. Saving, in the old established way, in an era of double-digit inflation, is no longer possible, since money's value can no longer be "maintained and preserved."

Passbook savings accounts are badly out of date. Inflation has passed them by. They are good for walking-around money, but amounts of over $1,000 should and can be somewhere else.

Much has been said over the years about the safety of our savings accounts. Over forty years ago, under President Roosevelt's program to restore confidence in our banks and financial system, government agencies were created to provide insurance for each depositor. The amount of insurance has now been increased to $100,000 for each account. Over the four decades that the insurance has been in force, not a single dollar has been lost to any saver. The system has worked well, protecting depositors here and there from an occasional bank failure. But the real heart of the matter is that these insurance agencies are part of the government, and, since the Depression, in the event of a national financial panic and threatened chaos, with or without insurance, any government would protect its own citizens' savings rather than allow their economic security to go down the drain. Almost no one today questions the safety of the money in a federally insured savings account. The problem now, over forty years later, is that it no longer really matters all that much. With inflation continuing to run at the annual rate of fourteen percent, the dollar will decline in purchasing power to only fifty cents in a little over five years. Regardless of the federal insurance protection, half the real spendable value of the money will have disappeared. Locking up money for future use is no longer a viable method of creating financial security. Financial advisors have been saying for some time that the very idea of saving has now become almost obsolete. In an age of high inflation, they reason, it makes sense only to spend, borrow, and invest. Millions of Americans apparently agree, for they have been spending almost twenty-four percent of their take-home pay on mortgages and other consumer debts. This is much more than normal, yet the percentage continues to increase unabated. The urge to spend seems to quicken as the rate of inflation soars.

Economists worry that the average American is illiquid— his assets cannot readily be converted into cash—and that he could be caught between high debt payments and a sharp drop in income in the event of a layoff or outright loss of work. The American workers seem to accept this risk as they continue to spend their way into prosperity. Part of the surge of spending is based on the idea that money is worth more now than later, that debt can be paid back by cheaper dollars.

Unfortunately for older Americans who still remember the hard times prior to World War II, the modern generation has so far been proved right.

To illustrate the extent to which the inmates have taken over the money asylum, suppose you want to make a purchase at the local department store for $100. If you purchase the item now on your plastic credit card, you will probably pay an annual interest rate of eighteen percent. However, if, on the other hand, you try something as old-fashioned as saving for the purchase, inflation can eat you alive. By flashing your plastic credit card, you know the price is $100. However, if inflation continues at the current annual rate of fourteen percent, a year from now that same item will cost $114. Therefore, if you elect to save over the next year, depositing $100 in the bank and paying income tax at twenty-five percent on the interest earned, you would need to realize as much as nineteen percent on your money just to pay the inflated purchase price of $114. More important, you will have given up the American dream of immediate possession.

On the other hand, the credit card purchase was made for $100 plus interest, or about $110. Since interest is tax deductible, our comparison now goes into reverse and the net cost is only $107, less than the increase in inflation alone.

Even when it can be shown that spending and borrowing (within limits, of course) are affected by the tide of inflation, the idea still runs counter to the way we live. Most people still want and need ready cash for future anticipated expenses, for a feeling of security, and for emergencies.

If you feel you must save, consider a detour around both the law controlling interest rates and the long-established reliance on savings accounts.

Millions of Americans, tired of being cheated by federal laws that tie them to paltry interest rates, have already discovered alternate methods of saving that wage a far better battle with inflation than does the traditional act of pushing money over the teller's counter.

One of the areas you might consider is a money account designed for savers known as money market funds. The fund is a pool of cash invested in short-term money market investments, such as U.S. Treasury Bills and other government-guaranteed issues, certificates of deposit from banks, and highly rated commercial paper with maturities generally not exceeding one year. These are many of the same investments millions of Americans would be glad to make on their own if it were not for the very high minimum investment amounts set by current federal regulations.

The money funds operate very simply; there is no cost to invest or withdraw your money. You can expect to have every dollar returned, plus interest. Money funds have been paying between twelve and thirteen percent interest on deposits of as little as $1,000. But best of all, you can make deposits or withdrawals at any time without interest penalties. You can even write checks against the money fund (generally in amounts of $500 or more).

Money funds are currently available at many stockbrokerage offices and money-fund headquarters. Each firm has its own special name. Some of the names include: Paine Webber's Cashfund; Merrill Lynch's Ready Assets Trust; Dean Witter Reynolds's Liquid Assets Fund; and Kemper in Chicago has named theirs Money Market Fund.

The success of money funds (Merrill Lynch's fund alone by mid-1979 contained over $6 billion) now threatens to put savings accounts as we know them out of business. From the middle of 1978 to 1979 American savers pumped upward of $45 billion into various money funds. By mid-1980, these funds could contain as much as $80 to $100 billion. The banking industry is fighting back, but unlike the sponsors of the money market funds who are deemed not to be in the regulated banking business, they must still demand a minimum $10,000 deposit and a six-month investment period for their money market certificates.

In this board game of money saving, you can now join the big investors, bypassing private enterprise, Park Place, and the Waterworks, and go directly to the government. The rules in effect for the financial institutions do not apply to the government, in this game of Monopoly. In its mad scramble to raise cash it is offering Treasury Notes to anyone. Sounds dishonest, doesn't it? And it is.

The Treasury Department has been offering two- and four-year notes with a minimum deposit of only $1,000. Paying an interest rate of over twelve percent, they offer about the same return as banks and thrift institutions requiring a minimum deposit of $10,000. They can be sold at any time through a broker or a bank, and if you are willing to make the effort to buy them, they could be a way for small investors to beat the low-interest trap our benevolent government has placed on regular savings accounts.

While the federal government is scrambling to include the small investor, cities and states are not far behind. Moving with the times, the cities and states began expanding the issuance of their own federally tax-exempt minimunicipal bonds, offering them for sale to all their residents. Once thought to be the playground of the rich, inflation has now made these federally tax-free bonds, which generally offer a degree of safety and security second only to U.S. government bonds, very attractive.

Tax-exempt bonds are issued by states, cities, counties, school districts, universities, and a host of other governmental bodies. The U.S. constitutional doctrine of reciprocal immunity makes it clear that as long as states, cities, and other local governmental units do not tax post offices, military bases, and other government property, as well as federal government bonds, the federal government must also exclude local governments as a target of taxation.

Because of the tax-exempt feature of their bonds, local governments have offered lower interest rates for years, saving the taxpayers billions of dollars in bond repayments.

Today the market for federally tax-exempt municipal bonds is huge, totaling well over $300 billion, with as much as $60 billion of new bonds issued each year. The bonds are priced at $1,000 each, and are usually sold in lots of five. Municipal bonds offer a high degree of liquidity, since they are usually traded on a daily basis on the bond market in New York and throughout the country.

Unfortunately the average working and saving American has never seen a municipal bond. Over the years, our financial system has robbed the small saver by maintaining an unusually high $5,000 or $10,000 minimum investment, coupled with a complete lack of information about municipal bonds, to the degree that middle-class America can realize little more than half the net "take home" savings income of a millionaire.

Suppose that we make a comparison between a passbook account at the bank and a tax-exempt municipal bond at the brokerage office. They both have approximately the same safety and liquidity; the only real difference might be the interest earned over the succeeding year. We will assume that the workingman is in a twenty-five percent income-tax bracket. As for the millionaire, he simply does not care about tax brackets since taxes do not apply to him at all.

**Interest Earned on Savings
in Our Topsy-Turvy World of Make-believe**

	WORKINGMAN BANK PASSBOOK ACCOUNT	MILLIONAIRE TAX-FREE MUNICIPAL BONDS
Amount invested	$1,000.00	$1,000.00
Annual interest earned	52.50	80.00
Less income taxes	13.10	-0-
Net interest earned	39.40	80.00
Balance, one year later	$1,039.40	$1,080.00

So there you are. Under our insane income-tax laws, the millionaire has actually earned, after taxes, twice as much interest as the workingman.

But today that is all changing; the workingman is fighting back, clearly illustrating how far out of date the conventional savings account has become. For years the government taxed the earned-interest income of each savings account, thereby reducing the real "take home" rate by anywhere from twenty-five to seventy percent. The higher the interest rate, the higher the tax bite. Uncle Sam simply could not lose. But the American taxpayer did, falling even further behind inflation each year.

Now the states and cities are pulling an end run on the federal income-tax collector that has sent panic rippling through the IRS, by offering what are called "minimunicipal" bonds that are free from federal income tax. But that is not all. Since the minimunicipals are bearer bonds, they can be bought and sold for cash and transferred without records, presenting a possible opportunity for tax evasion of capital gains, unreported gifts, and inheritance taxes.

Minimunicipal bonds are sold directly by the state or city issuing the bonds, bypassing the Wall Street underwriters who traditionally sell the conventional municipal bonds to large investors and institutional money funds. The minimunicipal bonds are usually sold in denominations of $100, $200 and $500, well under the $5,000 or $10,000 previously required. To favor the small saver who may purchase the minibonds, interest is paid every six months and sent directly to the bondholder.

Because of the recent success of the minibonds, an interesting comparison has come to light between the harassed taxpayer and his malevolent government. Namely, the sale of U.S. savings bonds. For over a decade U.S. savings bonds have been known to be the single worst inflation-fighting investment available to the American public, yet the geniuses in Washington, through the endorsement of famous personalities and appeals to convenience and patriotism, have built up an incredible $76 billion in sales. This is almost 8 percent of the $1 trillion in passbook accounts and savings certificates recently reported by the Federal Reserve Board.

Now the U.S. Treasury is launching yet another campaign to sell its newly issued "Energy Savings Bonds." In a magnanimous gesture, the Treasury has increased the interest rate to 7 percent, up from the old rate of 6.5 percent. But, and this is the catch, you have to hang on to the bonds for 11 years to get the full interest.

Overlooking the devastating effects of double-digit inflation, the government expects to peddle these long-term, low-interest bonds primarily to low-income working people through its payroll savings plan with such make-believe slogans as "They'll Put Your Financial Worries to Rest" and "U.S. Savings Bonds Are One Sure Way to Make Your Dreams Come True."

The real world we face today is quite different.

Apart from all the slogans, and the catchy name of "Energy Savings Bonds," the Treasury is really asking you to pay $100 for a bond that might be worth $50 in 11 years.

But if you think that is bad, consider this. The U.S. savings bonds were never designed as "one sure way to make your dreams come true." They are designed by a committee of federal bureaucrats who continue to arrange the bonds so far in favor of the government that they pay interest rates well below the market, they are not free of federal income tax, and they pay interest usually only on redemption.

The new minimunicipal tax-exempt bonds, on the other hand, are a different story. They were designed by local officials who wanted to help their own city or state raise money, while offering the local taxpayer a break at the same time.

The minimunicipal bond sales began in September of 1978 with the offering of a $500,000 issue by East Brunswick, New Jersey. The minibonds were placed on sale at the counter in the city finance department. Within hours the issue was sold out to small investors who had waited patiently in long lines outside the office door.

By January 1979 the state of Massachusetts had climbed on the bandwagon, issuing $1 million in small-denomination bonds. The first offering, Assistant State Treasurer James Hosker said, "went like hotcakes. We opened the line at nine A.M. and shut it off at eleven A.M. We could have sold five million dollars that first day." The Massachusetts offering was scheduled to yield a 5.70 percent interest return over five years, free of federal income tax, compared to a 5.25 percent return at the local bank with the interest income fully taxable. In April 1979 Ocean County, New Jersey, sold $1 million of the new minibonds. With denominations of $100 and $500 the issue quickly sold out, completing a triple play with a city, a state, and now a county successfully issuing the new minimunicipal bonds.

But the real support for the explosive growth of the mini-bond market of the future will be the computer. As it has for so many other industries, it can now dramatically reduce the paperwork and processing costs for bonds as small as $100, fifty times smaller than the previous $5,000 regular denominations.

The breakthrough, which was first used on the East Brunswick, New Jersey, bond coupons, was the use of magnetic-ink character recognition, or MICR, which, to most of us, looks like the funny numbers which appear at the bottom of personal and business checks to identify the depositor to the bank. In this case they identified the bondholder to the bank.

The bond interest coupons no longer needed to be the size of duck stamps that have to be posted by hand in a register. The admittedly inefficient system, virtually unchanged since 1840, can now be replaced with postdated checks which can automatically be mailed to the bondholder every six months as the interest falls due. The checks can be cashed anywhere, and frequently are.

The activity of the new minimunicipal-bond market has already shown that a small saver can indeed climb through the same tax loophole as a millionaire; that sales costs can be reduced since local governments can now sell the bond at retail, directly to their own taxpayers; and that the computer, through magnetic coding, has now made the sales of small-denomination bonds both possible and profitable to all concerned.

Some help for the small investor will still be required before he can move into the municipal-bond market in a big way. The resale of minibonds could present a problem because of their very low cost, but this can surely be overcome. The operation of the bond market itself has become so complex that some allowances will have to be made for the small investor. But there is no longer any question that the market in minimunici-pal tax-free bonds will balloon over the next decade as small savers realize that double-digit inflation has forced them into tax brackets where tax-free income on investments makes sense.

Yet another commonly used loophole, made possible by our crazy-quilt income-tax laws, is the tax-deferred annuity or TDA.

While the TDA is used as a savings account by millions of Americans who hate the IRS, the TDA is, in reality, an insur-ance contract known technically as a single-premium deferred annuity.

The first surprise you may have, as you explore the subject of tax-deferred annuities, is that, as their name implies, income taxes are deferred for as long as you tie up your money. This detour around the IRS is made on the basis that the annuity is offered by an insurance company, not a savings and loan or bank.

Because of this dash through the tax loophole, TDA's have become attractive to millions of Americans who now use them on the same basis as a savings account.

A quick comparison reveals a striking similarity between the TDA and the savings account: They can both return your cash on short notice, they are free to set up, although there is an interest penalty for early withdrawal, and they are backed by savings and loans and insurance companies—neither of which has a history of going sour on the investor. Where tax-deferred annuities come out in front is in the many advantages they offer you over the conventional savings account. So long as insurance companies continue to pay high interest rates— ten to thirteen percent or more—the annuity remains one of the safest and most practical ways to build a retirement in-come. This can be particularly attractive for middle-aged work-ers who otherwise have accumulated little in tax-deferred in-come.

The magic of tax deferral can be dramatic. If you invest $10,000 ($1,500 is usually the minimum amount to open a TDA account) and you are in a thirty-percent federal income-tax bracket, the example looks like this:

	SAVINGS ACCOUNT		TDA	
	10 year	20 year	10 year	20 year
Interest income after taxes	$ 9,670	28,700	15,940	57,270
Total account	19,670	38,700	25,940	67,270

Although deferral of income taxes offers the most obvious advantage of single-premium deferred annuities, there are others. If you die, the funds in your account can be paid directly to your beneficiary, avoiding probate, much like a life-insurance contract. The deferred annuity may be used as collateral for a loan or you may borrow directly on the contract.

Finally, as you reach retirement age, the funds may be converted, without incurring taxable income on the exchange, into an annuity offering lifetime income. But as if that were not enough, in recent years the tax loophole has been widened to allow the withdrawal of a truckload of tax-free money. Under the TDA contract you can withdraw up to six percent of your original investment, tax free, as a return of capital. Using the previous example, a $20,000 investment now becomes an ever-bearing money tree. Incredible as it may seem, you could withdraw $1,200 each year tax-free while the interest income, which is tax deferred, is increasing $2,000 each year.

The IRS has been chopping away at this money tree for several years, without much success, clearly indicating how inequitable even the tax system has become.

In fact, I have concluded, after years of trying to make sense of a jumbled mess of widely different savings methods, that the whole savings system has now become so unfair to the small saver that it should be scrapped. It probably will not be—special-interest groups are too powerful—and that means the burden will remain where it is, on the shoulders of those taxpayers who are not protected by special-interest groups. These will continue to slide further into the grip of inflation.

It is about time for all savers to get a tax break in this country, not just those who avoid the banks and savings and loans. While waiting for this miraculous state of affairs to come about, though, check the TDA's out at most insurance companies and securities firms. You may buy one contract and add to it as you want over the years without ever committing yourself to a lifetime annuity.

In the final analysis TDA's are a cross between an IRA account and a regular savings account. The original investment is not tax deductible, as it is with IRA's; however, the interest income, unlike that of the regular savings account, is tax deferred.

Now we get to something really scary, the longtime hero of American savers, the passbook savings account. This is the form of savings most people have become addicted to and the withdrawal symptoms will be the worst.

It was inevitable that federal controls limiting the interest rates savings accounts can earn would eventually spell the doom of the passbook savings account. It has long been a target of ridicule by knowledgeable pension experts and sophisticated savers; but awareness of its huge disadvantages is now spreading to the very heart of the system—the small saver.

Today we find rather large amounts still sitting in savings accounts yielding less than six percent. With the government limiting the passbook saver to only 5.5 percent while the savings and loans are lending the money at fifteen percent or more, the thrift institutions are faced with massive withdrawals by depositors seeking higher interest rates. The small saver is limited as to alternatives, however. But inflation itself has now spawned new plans for such savers that provide yields far above 5.5 percent, as well as attractive withdrawal arrangements.

Up until the near-runaway inflation of the winter of 1979–80, savings and loans enjoyed a handsome spread between the passbook interest rate they paid for borrowed money and loan rates earned on money lent to borrowing homebuyers. The savings and loans then were awash with profits. The price of their stock had an amazing fifty-percent runup while passbook savings flowed strongly into the industry. The out-

look for the savings and loan industry, according to a New York
security analyst, was that "over the next five years, we think
earnings can compound at a fifteen- to twenty-percent annual
rate."

Not all of the swelling profits were paid out to the
stockholders—who, incidentally, make a far better return
than the poor saver who hands his small savings over to the
teller—for much of it was used to open new branches in a
scramble to scoop up as much cash as possible. Their growth
rate far exceeds the gas-station boom of the sixties. Near
one busy intersection where I live, no fewer than seven savings and loan offices have opened in the last four years. Not
simply commercial offices, but lavish palaces catering to
your every need for comfort and convenience. And why not?
When banks are actually earning more interest than their
depositors on the deposits, nothing is too good for the small
saver.

The problem today is that the average saver is no longer
saving any money. The interest rate allowed by law does not
even preserve the capital. Everybody—except the people who
write the tax laws—now recognizes that inflation is devouring
both capital and interest at such a rate that many Americans
are losing all interest in saving money.

As I write this book, another report from the Savings and
Loan Foundation has appeared on my desk. Earlier in this
chapter I reported that Americans save only 5.2 percent of
their disposable income. Wrong. The latest figures show that
Americans are saving only 4.5 percent of their disposable income.

Worse yet, the very foundations of our society have been
shaken by seemingly runaway inflation. There is not only the
sinking rate of private savings, which portends far too little
private investment to keep the American economy ticking;
there's also the growing resistance to the high taxes that must
be paid on investment income. Indeed if such income is viewed
in incremental terms, the steepest tax rates apply to it. So
politicians are finally getting the message that politics-as-usual
won't be tolerated.

Proposals to provide relief for small savers have been

discussed for years. One suggestion would unlock federal limits on interest rates. Another would offer tax exemptions roughly on the order of the traditional tax treatment of municipal bonds. The Europeans, who have suffered from inflation over a longer period than the Americans, get generous tax breaks on savings-account interest. In Germany, for instance, the government gives a cash bonus of up to $100 a year. Or take the very interesting case of Venezuela, a South American nation which wants to make economic progress endure. Interest earned on savings accounts up to 100,000 bolivares ($23,000 U.S.) and all interest earned on mortgage certificates are totally exempt from income tax. That's very generous tax treatment indeed. Here in the U.S., however, efforts to get savers the same breaks already received by well-heeled investors have never even made it to the floor of Congress for a vote.

The average saver still is taken for a ride. He's forced to accept artificially low interest rates. And to add income tax insult to the injury of piddling interest, the small saver is required to pay high federal and state income taxes on "paper profits" recorded in his savings passbook, while the value of his money melts away. (The maximum federal tax rate on the token savings interest, let's not forget, is a crushing seventy percent.) Now we come to yet another of those "unbelievable situations" where you could actually save money at the bank and earn taxable interest income that could push you into a higher income-tax bracket. This could cost you more money in taxes than all the interest you might earn on your savings.

Let's show concretely how the small saver gets skewered six ways from Sunday. Be prepared for a shock as you check what happens to your hard-earned money once it drops inside the savings account. The illustration in the following table doesn't involve fat cats. I have assumed that you are a typical American worker with a modest income; that you are in a twenty-five percent tax bracket (nearly every family with a working wife is exposed to an even bigger tax bite); and that the current rate of inflation continues for at least a year. Note in particular how inflation literally shreds the after-tax return on savings.

$1,000 Invested in a Passbook Savings Account

	PASSBOOK @ 5.5%	BREAK EVEN	TRUE 10% RETURN
Start of year	$1,000	$1,000	$1,000
Interest earned during year	55	220	380
Less income taxes paid	14	55	95
End of year	1,041	1,165	1,285
Purchasing power lost by inflation	146	163	180
Real value of your account	895	1,002	1,105
Net loss (−) or gain (+) in purchasing power during year	−105	-0-	+105

That's it, folks. Your savings, my savings—all our savings —are disappearing like cubes of ice on a hot summer day. The arithmetic in this example makes me—like the Peter Finch character in the movie *Network*—throw open the window, stick out my head, and shout, "I'm mad as hell and I'm not going to take it anymore."

Many of us have been taught to spend our interest and never touch our capital. This is no longer possible. Our government has already spent our interest and part of our capital as well.

Let's inspect this table column by column. The passbook account, in the first column, clearly shows that you have lost 10 percent of your purchasing power even when you earned 5.5 percent interest. In other words, even though you invested $1,000 of purchasing power last year and earned a government-rigged interest, you now have only $895 of purchasing power in your account. It's sad but true. Inflation eats up more than interest can pay.

The intermediate column shows what it would take to break even, to maintain the purchasing power of your dollar. A whopping interest rate of twenty-two percent. That's what it would take, to your utter surprise. Note especially the lesson to be learned from all of this, particularly if you are saving for your graying years. This lesson concerns the break-even interest rate. When the current inflation rate is fourteen percent, the interest rate must be a staggering one and one half times the inflation rate simply for you to break even—not truly saving anything for your retirement.

The righthand column shows that to earn a true 10 percent increase in the real spendable value of your dollar, the interest rate on your savings account must now be at least thirty-eight percent!

If you want to lock up your money for a few years, you can, of course, earn more interest than the nominal 5.5 percent, even up to as much as a nominal 8 percent on some savings accounts. But the cruel fact of life today is that these numbers no longer really mean that much. Our representatives in Washington have succeeded in creating a system grossly unfair to the small saver and incredibly generous to the big lender—so much so that the methods by which we save in America seem headed for disaster.

Consider this bizarre event which occurred in late 1979 when several savings and loans went directly to the money market and came away with buckets of cash. Apparently no longer willing to wait for their regular customers to make their usual deposits, the S & L's issued their own mortgage-backed bonds, offering them to the public through investment bankers and stock-brokerage offices.

Now the unbelievable has finally occurred. If you go in the front door with $1,000 to deposit, seeking safety and quick access to your money (called a high degree of liquidity by the financial community), the best the savings and loans can offer is 5.5 percent interest. If, on the other hand, you go in the side door of your local brokerage house, you could purchase a $1,000 mortgage-backed bond—issued by that same savings and loan—paying up to 9.75 percent interest.

What is more, you not only pick up almost double the interest rate, but you have essentially the same liquidity and even better safety since the bond is a loan directly to the company and stands ahead of depositors in the event of liquidation. How long this incredible rip-off can continue is uncertain, for it seems that though under our Constitution Americans in general are to be treated equally, Americans who save money, apparently, are not.

Now I would like to dig into individual retirement accounts, where some past changes have allowed the income-tax gate to swing open a crack.

Individual Retirement Accounts

Better known as IRA's, they are one of the best-known vehicles for retirement saving on a tax-deferred basis.

An estimated two million individuals have opened their own IRA accounts since they were established in 1974 under the Employee Retirement Income Security Act. But the over ninety-five percent of the estimated forty-five million workers eligible for this effective tax-deferred way to save for individual retirement have been left out. Our bumbling lawmakers, resting comfortably on Capitol Hill with their own gigantic government-paid retirement plan, must share most of the blame for this. The laws they established for IRA's were complex and confusing, enough at the time, but what's worse yet, the rules have since kept changing. For example, the wording of the 1977 IRS publication 590 dealing with IRA's is sixty percent different from that of the 1976 edition. In fact, information presented in this book applies only to the rules which were in effect in 1979.

In general an Individual Retirement Account allows a self-employed worker, or an employee who works for a company which does not have a retirement plan, or who was not an active participant at any time during the taxable year under another tax-qualified retirement plan, to put away, on a tax-deferred basis, some of his current earnings each year. As in a company retirement plan, no taxes are paid on the amount invested each year, or on the interest earned over the years, until actual retirement. Every year an employee fails to stash some money into the plan he is giving part of it away to Uncle Sam. To further encourage us to put money into IRA's, the rules now allow a taxpayer to pump money into the account until the date he files his tax return.

If you qualify for an IRA, and admittedly that is not always easy to determine under the complex rules which have poured out of Washington since 1974, you can invest and deduct on your income-tax return fifteen percent of your compensation or $1,500, whichever is less.

Since the IRA program is partly a belated admission on the

part of the government that Social Security alone will not provide an adequate retirement, the new rules now provide for a spousal IRA. This will allow, as a similar rule does under Social Security, a retirement income for a nonworking spouse. Unfortunately, when Congress extended this coverage, they completely lost touch with the real world and the raging inflation devouring our dollar. The additional contribution for a nonworking spouse is limited to only $250 each year. If the nonworking spouse is age forty-five today, twenty years later at age sixty-five only $5,000 could have been paid into the account. At eight percent compound interest, that amount would have grown to only $12,356. Twenty years later, however, by the year 2000, on the basis of only eight percent annual inflation, that pile of cash will be reduced in purchasing power to about $5,000. Hardly a concept of meaningful retirement income for anyone, except possibly the people on Capitol Hill who made up the rules.

But if you think that is bad, consider the rules themselves: The maximum deductible is the lesser of fifteen percent of compensation of the employed spouse, or $1,750, or twice the amount contributed for the spouse for whom the smaller contribution is made. Or looking at it from the point of view of the IRS publication 590, which easily qualifies as a winner in the race for bureaucratic nonsense, you would be putting in too much if you contributed more than "twice the smaller amount paid for the individual retirement savings program for you and your spouse."

What all this means in plain English is that to obtain the maximum $1,750 tax deduction for the IRA, $875, or half, must be contributed on behalf of each spouse.

With all this confusion, it is not surprising that many Americans contribute too little or too much each year. If you make a mistake and contribute too much, the IRS can then assess a six percent penalty tax on what they call "excess contributions." This tax can apply to each succeeding year until the excess is withdrawn or used up. When you pay the tax, it is not deductible, but you can avoid the tax if the excess is pulled out of the IRA before you file your tax return.

The IRA's were designed to allow money to flow out of the plan without tax penalty when you reach age fifty-nine and a half—or if you become disabled or die. Money withdrawn before that age will be taxed as ordinary income, since taxes were not collected when the money was put into the plan. In addition, the money withdrawn can be subject to an added penalty tax of ten percent. In any event, you must begin withdrawing the money for your retirement when you become age seventy and a half.

These are the basic rules for the individual retirement account, initially authorized by Congress back in 1974. While IRA's are the only "tax sheltered" savings program available to Americans not covered by a plan where they work, those who enroll in it face a fate similar to those who buy a big car in the gas crunch. Instead of encouraging Americans to save for a meaningful retirement income, Congress has allowed their only tax-saving vehicle to run out of gas.

Over the years little has been added to the original IRA rules that would either encourage workers to open an account or, once it is opened, protect themselves from the ravishing effects of inflation.

The maximum annual contribution has been stuck at $1,-500. Today that is no longer a realistic limit, particularly for older Americans who are forced to make arrangements for their retirement income within a limited number of years.

As previously noted, the $250 limit for a nonworking wife is also inadequate. Congress is caught in a bind. If greater tax benefits were given in fairness to millions of Americans trying to provide for their own retirement, Washington would lose billions of dollars in current tax revenues. On the other hand, the same government's inflation-making policies have bad expenditure side-effects. Billions of dollars of future federal expenditures will be required to take care of millions of Americans who are forced to rely on government assistance as inflation overtakes their Social Security benefits.

Up until now Congress has not been forced to practice restraint. As a result many Americans have been left with an inadequate, overcomplex, and unfair IRA plan. To understand how unfair the plan has become, consider this: Workers who are covered where they work by a totally inadequate retirement plan are not allowed to open their own IRA account. Though their employer may be contributing only a hundred dollars to their account each year, the complex rules leave workers locked out of the benefits of an IRA. As a result millions of Americans will be prevented from saving their own money on a tax-deferred basis because Congress has continually refused to allow them to.

Employer Sponsored IRA Plans

In 1978 Congress passed the Tax Reform Act, part of which allowed employers the opportunity to establish a "simplified" retirement plan with individual retirement accounts. This was partly in response to the passage of the Employee Retirement Income Security Act (ERISA) in 1974 which directly resulted in the termination of many retirement plans by small business owners.

Rather than redesign their existing plans and then face overwhelming paperwork and reporting requirements mandated by ERISA, many employers simply dropped their retirement plans. With only about half of the private work force covered by a company pension, Congress was clearly moving in the wrong direction.

To encourage employers now to reopen retirement plans, the law allows them to contribute directly to each employee's IRA.

Under the Sponsored Individual Retirement Account (SIRA) plan the employer may contribute each calendar year to an IRA set up for each worker, including part-timers, who are twenty-five years old and who have worked for the company any three of the past five years. Once the contributions are made they immediately belong to the employee, who is then one hundred percent vested. As in a profit-sharing plan, the employer can decide each year how much money, if any, will be contributed to the plan. Once the employer decides, in theory the contribution is to be based on the same percentage of pay for each employee. Most of the other rules that apply to IRA's also apply to those IRA's covered under the employer's simplified plan.

But something got lost on Capitol Hill when the Tax Reform Act emerged from Congress. As usual, the wonders in Washington arranged it so that the average wage-earner continues to be trapped within the system. For instance, our lawmakers now allow our employers to contribute fifteen percent of our salary up to $7,500 to an IRA, while the employee in his own right can only contribute a maximum of $1,500 each year. If you think this is unfair, you are right. The amount contributed to an IRA now is determined by who makes the actual contributions, not by the individual worker's needs or pay.

But if you believe Congress went mad when they designed the employer's IRA plan, consider this: The amount each worker can receive is tilted in favor of the owner, who presumably has the highest salary.

Now the employer can choose to trim contributions by the amount paid in Social Security payroll taxes. For lower-paid workers this can mean a big cut in benefits.

Suppose your annual pay is $10,000. With a 10 percent contribution to the employer-sponsored IRA plan, you might expect a contribution of $1,000. Not so, for Congress has other ideas of fairness. By subtracting the contributions for Social Security taxes of $613, the employer now needs to contribute only $387, or 3.9 percent of pay. Now suppose the owner's pay is $60,000. Subtracting the Social Security tax of $1,404, he receives a hefty contribution of $4,596, or about 7.5 percent of pay. The contribution made for the owner by the company is well beyond the $1,500 limit available to individuals, but the contribution made for you is actually $1,113 below that allowed by law.

In spite of these rules, which are called "Social Security integration," Congress has not completely overlooked your interests. You are "allowed" to contribute, on your own, the difference between your employer's contribution and the maximum allowed by law.

Further information on IRA's is available from most banks, savings and loan associations, mutual-fund organizations, and insurance companies. A detailed study of the subject is available at a district office of the Internal Revenue Service. Ask for a copy of publication 590, "Tax Information on Individual Retirement Arrangements."*

---

*Individual Retirement Arrangement is the official designation of what is commonly known as an Individual Retirement Account.

Retirement Plans for the Self-Employed

For many years those of us who worked for a corporation were able to receive the tax benefits of a qualified pension or profit-sharing plan; the self-employed individuals were not, even though they could cover their regular employees under a retirement plan. (*Self-employed* is defined by the IRS as being either a sole proprietor or a partner who owns more than ten percent of the partnership.)

For eleven years Congress wrestled with this inequality, finally coming up with the "Self-Employed Individual Tax Retirement Act" in 1962. These plans have become popularly known as HR 10, after the act itself, or as Keogh Plans, named after the congressman most responsible for their passage.

Since Keogh Plans for the self-employed were used as a guideline for the later legislation creating IRA's, most of the rules for Keogh Plans are the same as those outlined previously for IRA's. Originally the maximum contribution for self-employed individuals was limited to the lesser of ten percent of income or $2,500 each year. Throughout the next decade, self-employed businessmen continued to apply intense pressure on Congress to raise the contribution limits. After all, they believed they were unfairly treated; for if they incorporated they could contribute over twice the amount allowed under the Keogh Plan.

Congress finally buckled under to the business community's campaign for equal treatment by increasing the limits for self-employed individuals to the lesser of fifteen percent of income or $7,500. The increased limits were contained in the Act establishing IRA's in 1974.

Once again our own elected lawmakers left the American worker, who lacked the political clout, holding the near-empty bag: Individuals who are self-employed can now contribute up to five hundred percent more than individual wage earners.

But again, that is not all, for Congress gave yet another big advantage to the business owner that heavily tilts the retirement plans in his favor. This is called a Defined Benefit Keogh Plan. These are more complicated plans in which the maximum contribution depends on several variables—age, income, and the assumed rate of return the retirement funds will earn.

97

But the hassle can be well worth it, for maximum contributions can reach as much as $10,000 or more. Many doctors, sports and entertainment stars, and other self-employed individuals in the higher tax brackets can now decide how much retirement income to aim for and put away enough tax-free cash each year to reach their goal.

The tax advantages of a defined benefit plan can also have a strong appeal for a two-income family where one income comes from self-employment and is taxed on top of the other spouse's salary. One disadvantage for the self-employed individual is that the defined-benefit plan cannot be integrated with Social Security when it covers owner-employers (subtracting Social Security payroll tax from the employer's regular contributions as covered under the section on IRA's).

Nevertheless the Keogh Plan is a classic example of the flexibility in retirement planning that Congress can offer, but seldom does. Here individuals can (within reasonable limits) make whatever contribution they deem best based on their income, age, and retirement objectives. Many believe that these basic choices should be available to all Americans regardless of "who" is actually making a contribution to an individual retirement plan. In short, the equal-opportunity law should be extended to those who want to save for their own retirement.

Unfortunately, instead of assuring equal opportunity, our government has, over the years, allowed powerful myths to develop concerning the laying aside of cash for the future. One of those myths is that each worker, as an individual, has an equal tax-favored opportunity to save his own money for retirement. If only this were true.

We need only look at the following examples to understand how far Congress has gone in making unequals of us all. Suppose at age forty-five a self-employed individual qualifies for a Keogh Plan. If the maximum amount of $7,500 were contributed each year, with eight percent compound interest, the account would total $370,672 at retirement age sixty-five. A very tidy sum indeed. All of the contributions and earned interest would have escaped federal taxation.

But suppose another individual, also age forty-five, could only qualify for an IRA. Now the tables are turned. Assuming a thirty-five percent effective tax rate, the results for the unlucky IRA saver look like this: $1,500 each year into the IRA and $6,000 saved from before-tax income. The first bite reduces the $6,000 to only $3,900 after taxes so that the actual savings each year is really $5,400, not the full $7,500 saved by the Keogh Plan participant. Another tax bite chews away at the interest earned each year on the money invested outside the IRA.

When the second individual reaches age sixty-five, the cash for retirement will total only $217,599. Even though each individual saved the same amount of money from his pay each year, the workingman, who could only qualify for an IRA, wound up with over $150,000 less at retirement. The self-employed individual was all smiles, for Congress, for him, has indeed provided numerous tax loopholes, whereas the individual worker, who ended up with a little over half as much money at retirement, found his tax situation much darker.

But what if a third individual, under the same set of circumstances, found he had no means of saving on taxes? Maybe, as a result of confusion regarding the complex and changing rules for IRA plans, or possibly because his employer had a retirement plan where contributions were so small as to be nonexistent, he was without any tax-favored retirement plan.

Now, with the individual worker investing $7,500 each year, the net amount after taxes available for saving plunges to only $4,875. At age sixty-five the retirement account will now hold $179,331 in cash, less than half the $370,672 available to the Keogh Plan participant.

Another myth about retirement planning that has persisted over the years is that qualifying for the various tax-sheltered plans established by Congress is just not worth the trouble and expense. Unfortunately without Congress legislating new tax savings the tax bite all but destroys the individual worker's retirement goals.

Continuing with our example, the amount of money lost to federal income taxes without these tax savings totaled $52,500 over the twenty-year period to age sixty-five. That is a lot of money to give away to Uncle Sam. But the point most Americans fail to realize is that the actual loss is much greater than the $52,500 paid in taxes. Had the money each year remained inside a tax-favored retirement plan, the $52,500 paid in taxes would have grown to $129,730 at age sixty-five. Under this example the individual wage earner actually lost to the taxman two and one half times the amount paid in taxes. What is clear from this brief review of individual savings plans is that Congress will continue to rip off some American workers, to the tune of fifty cents for each dollar of retirement benefits, until they are forced to provide the tax savings for all.

Tax Sheltered Annuities

The existence of Tax Sheltered Annuities (TSA's) destroys yet another myth about the equality of our nation's retirement system. In this case, members of a special-interest group literally walked away from Congress with a bag full of tax savings.

The genesis of TSA's can be traced back to the passage of the Technical Amendments Law in 1958. Under this law, employers of privately supported, nonprofit educational, charitable, and religious institutions were permitted to exclude from current income a "liberal" amount of their current salary. In fact the amount that could be excluded was huge compared to all other forms of individual tax-favored savings then available.

The tax-free plum was so tempting that the powerful schoolteachers' lobby brought enough pressure to bear on Congress to also allow educational institutions supported by public tax money to have a piece of the action. This law, passed in 1961, has permitted millions of employees of our nation's public schools to qualify for TSA's.

Today, TSA's are a way of life for teachers at universities and public schools, as well as for workers with religious or nonprofit charitable, scientific, literary, public-safety, or educational organizations, as a way to beat the tax game. Even certain nonprofit hospitals offer TSA's to their highly paid physicians and surgeons.

If you are among the select few who can grasp the gold key, the tax-saving opportunities are breathtaking. For a start you can have your employer contribute up to 16.6 percent of your salary into a TSA. If that is not enough, you can, by using something called "past-service credits," increase the contribution rate to 20 percent or more. Unlike the regular IRA's, TSA's allow a worker to go back and pick up the years of employment when no tax-sheltered contributions were made. This can be extremely attractive to older workers who after their children are grown have additional taxable income. It has also been widely used by two-income couples where one wage earner, who has a TSA, can plow a large part of his or her salary into a tax-sheltered plan. By law, investments in TSA plans must ultimately result in an annuity contract, with or without incidental life-insurance amounts.

In addition, with TSA's the limit on annual contribution is out of sight: For all qualified plans, including TSA's, a participant is limited to no more than the lesser of $30,000 or twenty-five percent of salary. What is more, the people on Capitol Hill who gave us TSA's outdid themselves when they designed the program. Unlike IRA's, you might have a TSA even if you are covered under your employer's retirement plan. In fact, some states have gone so far as to consider the employer's retirement plan outside the IRS code dealing with qualified retirement plans, and in those cases the employees can have both at the same time. In addition, again unlike IRA's, the ten percent tax penalty does not apply if you pull out the money before you reach age fifty-nine and a half.

If you are among the millions of American workers who do not qualify for a TSA, you can be sure of one thing: You are one of the Americans who pay the bills for the special tax advantages enjoyed by this special-interest group. A benefit of this size, which permits a maximum annual tax-deferred contribution of as much as six hundred percent *more* than an IRA plan, is pork-barreling in the best tradition of Congress.

Of all our government failures, the unequal tax treatment of American workers, who are desperately trying to save their own money for a retirement nest egg, has to be among the most infamous.

Instead of a simple-to-understand, fair, and realistic program whose contours can be shaped to each individual's retirement goals, the American public has been offered alphabet soup. No wonder confusion abounds throughout the land, with IRA, HR 10, TSA, and other initials representing yet more plans pouring out of Washington.

The future should include positive retirement savings programs which will encourage and assist the American public to be less, not more, dependent on Social Security benefits.

The IRA program should be liberalized in order to provide a more reasonable, independent retirement and disability fund. Any intelligent approach to retirement planning should allow an older person the opportunity to make greater tax-deductible contributions than a younger person. This should be the case if for no other reason than the fact they have fewer years to accumulate money in an IRA, at a time when their children are presumably grown and their savings are at their highest level.

For example, both the percentage of annual contributions and the total allowable amount could increase in direct proportion to age. The shameful rule that prevents a person from contributing to an IRA simply because he is already covered where he works should be discontinued. In the name of fairness, any national retirement plan should allow all workers the opportunity to make voluntary contributions to their own individual savings plan, regardless of where they work.

Another program that could lessen the dependence on Social Security would be one to allow a personal tax deduction for disability income insurance. This new Individual Disability Account (IDA) could go a long way toward relieving the suffering experienced by millions of Americans each year. Not only is their salary gone, but their savings are severely depleted, with little hope for the future. It is a cruel hoax indeed that our government plays on us by denying tax-favored incentives to protect our income in the event of disability, while at the same time spending billions of our tax dollars for disability benefits when we are unprepared for the loss.

The law should also be expanded to encourage the establishment of a plan for survivors' insurance. In order to augment the Social Security Survivor's Program, a person could deduct some of his premiums for the life insurance that benefits his family, under his Individual Life Insurance Account (ILIA).

England has for years offered a tax deduction to encourage the purchase of life insurance for the benefit of the workers' survivors. The plan has worked well, enabling a worker to provide for his family's future security and reducing his dependence on welfare.

The foregoing proposals for enlarged individual participation have been presented in summary fashion. All these concepts will require more analysis and study in order to determine a comprehensive federal retirement and security policy.

These concepts to expand and create individual retirement, disability, and survivor plans, through tax incentives, are based on the belief that most of us, given a choice, would prefer to develop our own individual financial security rather than rely upon welfare and government benefits.

Congress, however, has consistently hewed to the line that allowing Americans a tax-favored choice could only weaken compulsory government programs.

Six years and doses of inflation after the passage of the act permitting IRA's, little has changed in the way individuals plan their retirement security. Americans were led to believe that a new era had arrived when individuals could at last become active participants in their own plans. Instead, the plans have turned up empty, painfully exposing the government's continued unwillingness to help the American worker.

All Americans, to a lesser or greater degree, have become mired in financial quicksand. The way we save is scary, and the more you know about it, the more frightening the arrangement becomes. I do believe we can meet this challenge with realistic federal policies on interest rates and delayed taxation, if we act before it is too late. If there is to be any hope of winning the battle between inflation and savings, then somehow, some way, reason and fairness must be introduced into the Oval Office and into the halls of Congress.

I have not minimized the danger, and neither should you. Before the savings for our graying years can become meaningful, we must be able to earn incomes that outpace inflation and income taxes. I remain confident that we can do it.

6 ERISA: The Policeman of the Pensions

The year was 1974 and, as it has so often, the "dance of the legislators" had begun again on Capitol Hill. Amid a packed hearing room, committee members were about to hear testimony from hundreds of workers who had watched their hard-earned pensions evaporate when their employers went bankrupt.

For most congressional leaders this was real-life drama. The parade of witnesses droned on, each with a heartbreaking story—the personal loss of financial security during retirement.

Stories like that of Ed Johnston, who had worked for Perkins Machine and Gear Company of Springfield, Massachusetts, for twenty-two years. When Johnston was sixty-two, back in 1971, the gear works abruptly went out of business. Like the other 250 employees, Johnston lost his job. Not only that, but his company pension, for which he had made regular contributions for twenty-two years, had disappeared as well. He was forced into taking janitorial work at a nearby college.

Ed Johnston was one example of the many individual tragedies played out before the startled lawmakers. But the classic disaster—the one that had actually begun the drive to save lost pensions—was the Studebaker closing ten years earlier in 1964. This was the granddaddy of them all: More than two thousand workers were instantly robbed of their expected company pensions when management told its longtime workers, "Look, guys, the pension fund is not adequate to meet our promises to you. So that we won't have to come up with more money by selling assets or cutting dividends to our stockholders, we're going to turn over the entire pension plan to you. After all, inadequate as the fund may be, it's your money that's at stake, not ours."

As the testimony before the committee continued, it soon became clear to Congress that what had happened ten years earlier at Studebaker was now happening all over America. Thousands of workers like Ed Johnston already faced a bleak future. Even Congress perceived that something had to be done to save lost pensions. The problem was simple: Brakes had to be applied to pension terminations before the whole private system crashed.

Congress's answer was the Employee Retirement Income Security Act of 1974, known more commonly by its Washington acronym of ERISA. At the time of its passage it was viewed as economic legislation of landmark proportions. It was the kind of public protection rarely seen coming out of Washington, for its intent was to keep the private pension system viable and not have it become a ward of the public.

To understand ERISA and what Congress intended to accomplish, let's look briefly at the main points. I can do this only if I translate the law into plain English, for ERISA itself is a 208-page document described by many as one of the most complex and voluminous laws enacted in recent years. For each rule of ERISA there is apt to be an exception, and to some of the exceptions there are exceptions. Even government publications, which are noted for their ability to dispense double-talk, conclude "that many of the provisions of ERISA are difficult to comprehend."

What follows is based on the statute. Full details, obviously, will only emerge after ERISA has been clarified in court cases. To begin with, consider the responsibility for carrying out the law's provisions. The job falls to the U.S. Department of Labor, the Internal Revenue Service, and to a nonprofit government corporation named the Pension Benefit Guaranty Corporation.

ERISA does not require your employer to establish a retirement plan, but once he does, it requires that the plan meet certain standards. This is only elementary fairness, since a pension is nothing more than deferred compensation which would otherwise be reflected in current compensation or current fringe benefits. When all is said and done, the focal point of ERISA is protection of the interest of workers and their beneficiaries. To that end ERISA requires plan administrators —people who run plans—to tell you the most important facts you need to know about your plan, in writing and free of charge. They must also let you look at plan documents and buy copies of them at reasonable cost if you ask.

ERISA also requires your employer to disclose complete plan information to the three government agencies involved.

ERISA further requires that when an employee reaches age twenty-five, with three years of employment, he or she must be included in the company retirement plan. The law also establishes the vesting schedule—the legal right to receive your company's contributions, even if you leave your job before actual retirement. Under ERISA, an employee must be fifty percent vested after ten years if partial vesting has been available with the plan, and one hundred percent vested after fifteen years, regardless of age.

Another important feature of the law is the protection given to the worker for a "break in service." Before ERISA it was not uncommon for a worker to lose all his pension benefits through a brief interruption in work. Generally ERISA does not allow a "break in service" to occur under the pension plan when employment is interrupted for less than one year. And in most cases a break in service will not occur unless the break equals or exceeds the amount of time an employee has previously been covered under the plan.

Protecting the worker from mismanagement of the retirement-plan assets is another major provision of the law. Through its "fiduciary provisions," ERISA can now hold plan trustees personally responsible for financial losses. A fiduciary, according to the dictionary, is a person who occupies a position of trust, one who holds or controls property for the benefit of another person. A part of the law requires that individuals who have authority or responsibility for investment of plan assets follow the "prudent-man rule." In theory, if the investments are made under the so-called prudent-man rule, then those individuals making the investments will escape responsibility should losses later occur.

Understanding the prudent-man rule is difficult at best. The law defines the rule as an "act [performed] with the care, skill, prudence, and diligence under the circumstances then prevailing that a prudent man acting in like capacity and familiar with such matters would use in the conduct of an enterprise of a like character and with like aims."

ERISA also strengthens the benefits payable to a retiree's spouse. Before ERISA, many plans had no provisions for continuing on behalf of the surviving spouse any part of the retiree's pension after the retiree's death. ERISA now includes the provision for a "joint and survivor annuity"—an annuity contract that provides for income for the life of the participant with a survivor annuity for the life of the spouse. In fact, for most employees, the joint and survivor annuity must be automatic unless the employee rejects it in writing. But ERISA stopped short of requiring the approval of the worker's spouse before the joint and survivor annuity can be rejected.

The last part of ERISA, and by far the most important and controversial, is the protection offered from retirement-plan terminations. To administer ERISA's plan-termination "insurance," a nonprofit governmental agency was created, called the Pension Benefit Guaranty Corporation, or PBGC for short. This agency was to insure against the loss to workers and retirees of vested pension benefits—up to a statutorily set limit of monthly payments—in the event the pension plan terminated without enough money to pay the full benefits.

Before ERISA (going back to include Studebaker and the Perkins Machine and Gear Works), a pension-fund failure generally involved no liability on the part of the employer beyond the money already contributed to the plan. But no more. The PBGC can not only require that the employer pay insurance "premiums" into the reserve fund for each covered worker, but can also claim up to thirty percent of the employer's net worth to help pay for the unfunded benefits.

These are only the main points of one of the most comprehensive pieces of financial, tax, and retirement legislation ever passed by Congress. Unfortunately, as so often happens to a major bill as it winds its way through the congressional maze, ERISA left many of its teeth on the committee-room floor.

The part of the law requiring full disclosure to the worker contained so many loopholes that much of the plan disclosure-material now looks like Swiss cheese. A typical case occurred recently where a worker, who died unexpectedly at age fifty-four after eighteen years on the job, had believed that his widow would then receive his pension benefits. He had read his pension booklet, but his great mistake was in believing what he read about his plan. After his death, when his widow filed a claim, she received nothing from the pension plan.

The law requires that you receive something called a "Summary Plan Description." The problem is that the law also allows a disclaimer clause. This clause, found in virtually all SPD's, states that only the plan's formal documents, usually held by the company, shall contain the fine print. Several grass-root organizations are now starting to spring up, challenging the use of disclaimer clauses by private pension plans.

Exempt from the protection of much of the act, including the insurance provided by the PBGC, are workers covered under retirement plans set up by the federal and local governments (who else?), certain church plans, and multiple-employer plans, which usually include many union plans.

The PBGC currently insures pension benefits for about one third of the labor force—thirty-three million workers covered under more than eighty-eight thousand private plans. The governmental and multiple-employer plans, most in need of the protection against unfunded liabilities (not enough cash in the pension plan to pay for currently earned benefits) still rest outside the PBGC's protection six years after the passage of ERISA. This includes about two thousand multiple-employer plans covering eight million workers with total assets of $25 to $30 billion.

A significant number of these plans are currently on very shaky financial ground. As many as eight million workers continue to be covered by troubled pension plans without any protection against either a reduction in long-promised key benefits or outright collapse of the retirement plan itself.

Multiple-employer plans were last scheduled to be covered under the PBGC in 1978, but Congress has repeatedly postponed extending this coverage. As of now PBGC coverage is tentatively set for May 1980.

Congress fully intended to cover multiple-employer pension plans at the outset, believing that workers covered under those plans should enjoy the same benefit guarantees as workers with other private employer plans. The unions and employers involved in big plans, however, thought otherwise. They argued that big plans were much less likely to shut down since they were supported by so many different employers. Furthermore, they pointed out that not one single multiple-employer plan had failed prior to the then-proposed ERISA legislation.

Congress was impressed enough to delay coverage for multiple-employer plans, but in delaying coverage they set up two separate insurance funds. Annual premiums for the private plans were set at one dollar for each worker and only fifty cents for workers covered under the multiple-employer plans.

Looking back over the past six years, ERISA has indeed become a vital protector of America's pension system. It has restored workers' rights by forcing their employers to dust off their existing plans to question the adequacy of investments, to take a hard look at possible discrimination, and to reexamine eligibility requirements and vesting schedules. ERISA has also made workers aware of some details of their plans that previously they were unaware of, and, equally important, has given them certain rights to know what changes occur during their employment with their company. (ERISA also gives us the IRA program, adopted in Canada years ago and long overdue in this country.)

ERISA has worked well to restore workers' confidence in our private retirement plans. A large measure of this confidence comes from the belief that ERISA, as the "policeman of the pensions," will force employers not only to make adequate contributions in the future, but also to pay up on the massive unfunded debt now on the pension books.

But the most important benefit from the passage of ERISA may have been the forced reexamination of the financial condition of America's private pension system. For obvious reasons this is the heart of the matter. A worker's "bill of rights" to equitable contributions and benefits is meaningless if the pension plan itself is on the verge of collapse.

Few Americans realize that private pension plans were in deep trouble even before the passage of ERISA. A Department of Labor study showed that about 13,000 pension plans folded before the law became effective. Worse yet, there were 83,500 workers who qualified for benefits under their old plans, who face losses of $208 million without the protection of PBGC

It is bitter irony indeed that most of the workers who testified before Congress to insure the passage of ERISA will not reap its benefits, since the law does not cover individuals whose plans failed before July 1974. The Labor Department, which might pay benefits to workers who lost their pensions prior to the passage of ERISA, has been "looking" into the question of equal treatment for some time. A Labor Department official admitted last year that the cost of a program to pay for benefits wiped out between 1969 and 1974 would not be significant. The official concluded that it's now a benefit issue. This analysis illustrates how government works. For six years the benefit issue was studied before a final conclusion was reached that a strong case exists for guaranteeing lost benefits, before and after July 1974.

Both the Labor Department and Congress now appear willing to help the workers recover their lost pension rights. A bill should be introduced in Congress shortly.

For Ed Johnston, who has been waiting nine years for Congress to act, it may come too late. Last year, then age seventy, he was handicapped by cataracts and a paralyzed left arm and reduced to living on Social Security and veterans' benefits. More to the point, it now becomes apparent that Congress also has finally learned that a pension delayed is a pension lost.

In creating the PBGC, Congress devised a very unusual kind of insurance. In addition to collecting an annual "premium" for each covered worker, the insurance plan requires that any guaranteed benefits left over after the insurance fund runs dry must be picked up by all other companies under a scheme called Plan Termination Insurance. The fact that all companies are now liable tends to warp the way businessmen make decisions. Companies with weak pension plans pay the same "premium" as those with strong plans whose risk of default is minimal. A weak company with a shaky pension plan now has little to lose by making substantial pension promises: if it goes broke, thirty percent of its assets could amount to very little, leaving the PBGC and other companies to pay the "premiums" to make good on the fancy pension benefits.

It is now becoming clear that the designers of ERISA overlooked the basic fact that pension plans really aren't insurable. Insurance is based on the law of large numbers (this law applies to statistically similar but independent events; for example, everyone will die sometime, but everyone will not die at the same time). Under the plan devised by Congress, as the massive unfunded debt begins to come to the surface—largely through the effects of inflation—the domino effect will tumble the PBGC.

The defaulting pension claims against the PBGC could force its "premiums" so high that many companies would be compelled to abandon their pension plans, creating even further debts. The PBGC, now inundated with claims, would be forced to cut off benefits to avoid bringing down the entire pension system and, would itself, in turn, have to seek a bailout from Congress.

No one expects all pension plans to go belly-up at once, but there is deep concern that the PBGC is heading for dangerous territory with most of the debt it is guaranteeing exposed.

During the first six years the PBGC has avoided a head-on collision. The agency has been able to spread an effective safety net under the nation's private employer plans, rescuing about sixty thousand workers whose plans went under without sufficient assets to pay the benefits promised. But everything is not what it seems, for over eighty percent of the small plans terminated so far have involved still solvent employers.

The birth of the PBGC has clearly created an Achilles' heel, because now employers can abandon their debt-ridden pension plans, leaving other companies in the system to guarantee the benefits. While the PBGC has been able to pay off the occasional failure, the number of troubled pension plans now looms so large that many companies are planning to pull out in fear of the additional burden they might face in the future.

Nervous workers think about taking early retirement to avoid being caught short among the collapsing plans. "Nobody wants to be the last person in the plan," PBGC executive director Matthew Lind stated. "It's like the *Titanic* atmosphere. Everybody wants to leave the ship first."

In establishing ERISA, Congress again mandated financial responsibility without providing the cash. From its inception PBGC's funding has been woefully inadequate. At the end of fiscal year 1976, the insurance fund was carrying a $41 million deficit. That is, payment for the debts already assumed exceeded assets on hand by $41 million. By 1977 the deficit had risen to over $60 million. Though the annual "premium" had been hiked in the interim from $1.00 to $2.60 per worker, the new yearly charges put hardly a dent on the burgeoning debt.

In the latest report, dated September 30, 1979, the government now acknowledges that the debt is "somewhere" over $142 million. With the debt soaring each year, paying the "premiums" at all has become a Sisyphean feat. Howard E. Winklevoss, a University of Pennsylvania professor and pension consultant, was quoted recently as observing that "if there were a [serious] recession, there's no way in the world that the PBGC could pay benefits for all the funds that would fail." And for good reason. Experts today estimate that total obligations of all private pension plans are about $350 billion. Assets are estimated to be around $250 billion. This means that if all private pension plans went broke, the PBGC could be saddled with as much as $100 billion of debt.

That's the rest of the story. The amount is so huge that it represents about forty percent of all the assets so far contributed to our private pension system.

Another stumbling block to the successful operation of the PBGC's insurance fund is the terrifying fact that only about five percent of the U.S. companies account for about seventy-five percent of the nation's private unfunded pension debt. And that debt is growing rapidly. Inflation is pushing final retirement benefits sky high. For many major companies, estimates run from a fifteen to a twenty percent jump in unfunded pension benefits each year!

The pension insurance program established by Congress to cover only single employer plans clearly cannot pay the debts now faced even by these big plans. If even a few collapsed over the next ten years, the PBGC—yet again—would itself go bankrupt.

On top of this the multiple-employer plans, yet to be covered under the PBGC, have become so shaky that many are already on the verge of going broke. ERISA defines a multiple-employer plan as one to which more than one employer is required to contribute; which is maintained pursuant to collective-bargaining agreements; to which no one employer makes more than fifty percent of the aggregate contributions; and under which benefits are payable with respect to each participant without regard to the cessation of contributions by the employer who had employed the participant, except to the extent that such benefits accrued as a result of service with the employer before such employer was required to contribute to such plan.

In actual practice, multiple-employer plans involve many competing companies which contribute to one large pension plan covering thousands of workers who themselves belong to a common union or industry. Contributions into the plan are usually established through collective bargaining.

As we have already seen, to finance the pension insurance fund for multiple-employer plans, when and if they are actually covered by the PBGC, the "premiums" were set at fifty cents per worker. When "premiums" were increased with respect to private plans, however, the PBGC didn't even ask for an increase in "premiums" for multiple-employer plans because they didn't know how large they should be. Again we see that the "premium" income originally expected to finance the insurance fund simply isn't adequate for the job.

The Pension Benefit Guaranty Corporation's own report, released in 1979, predicts that at least 160 of the approximately 2,000 multiple-employer plans may go broke during the next ten years. Probably much sooner. The unfunded debt alone of these plans could leave the PBGC holding the bag for about $8.5 billion. This would force the so-called annual "premium" to leap upwards, leaving the PBGC with a debt of over $1,000 per worker for those participants still covered under a multiple-employer pension plan.

Faced with this arithmetic, Congress has effectively defaulted—allowing eight million workers, almost *one in four* covered by private plans, to remain unprotected. "The workers are sitting on a time bomb," exclaimed one Washington insider, "and Congress is scared to death to offer insurance for fear it would open the floodgates."

The unfortunate truth is that Congress has delayed the implementation of adequate coverage of multiple-employer plans so as to protect the PBGC from itself. Today the widely held belief in Washington is that many of the shaky multiple-employer plans would simply take the opportunity to fold as soon as they got PBGC coverage. With fewer and fewer employers left to pay ever-increasing premiums, PBGC's multiple-employer insurance fund would then quickly go broke.

Make no mistake about it, Congress has been aware of the private pension situation for some time. How do I know? Let's look at *The Wall Street Journal* for October 10, 1977. The headlines screamed: Multiple-Employer Pension Plans May Fail Without New Legislation, Officials Warn.

> WASHINGTON—Federal pension officials are warning Congress that about 40 multi-employer plans are on the verge of collapse and that legislation may be needed to stave off a wave of failures.
>
> The Pension Benefit Guaranty Corporation, an agency set up by Congress in 1974 to insure workers' pensions against their plans' failure, told key congressional committees it fears a rash of failures by multi-employer plans early next year unless the current law is changed.
>
> The law currently requires the agency to guarantee the pensions of beneficiaries in all multi-employer plans beginning next January 1. But the agency is asking Congress to postpone that deadline for a year or two, because it says time is needed to change the law to head off a possible string of pension plan failures it fears could occur once the guarantees become mandatory.

Unable to find the courage to face the pension mess head-on, Congress sat on its collective hands. Ten days later *The Wall Street Journal* of October 20, 1977, reported: Senate Panel Votes to Delay Insuring Some Pension Plans.

> WASHINGTON—The Senate Finance Committee voted to give the government's pension guaranty agency another 18 months before it's required to insure retirement benefits of workers covered by multi-employer pension plans.
>
> The Pension Benefit Guaranty Corporation says the

extra time is needed to change the law to head off a series of pension-plan failures that might occur once its guarantees become mandatory.

The corporation is afraid that guaranteeing a number of shaky multiple-employer plans will put it deeply into the red, and that many other funds will go broke if the corporation raises premiums enough to cover the resulting deficit.

The last extension has come and gone. Another date has been set for May 1980. Congress appears to be frozen into inaction not only by the fear of provoking an avalanche of pension-plan bankruptcies through insurance, but also of the shock waves that would reverberate across America when the actual pension mess should be fully exposed.

The jam many multiple-employer plans now face reflects the same kinds of forces that are plaguing Social Security: shifting economic and social trends. Because many of the plans cover declining industries such as shoe manufacturing, coal mining, milk delivery, and leather workers, financial problems have sprung up for the declining number of workers who are left. They must now pay the pension costs for an expanding number of retirees. The multiple-employer pension plans have developed into so many time bombs, bound to explode exactly when everything appears safe. The opportunity for such an explosion already exists in a billion-dollar loophole big enough to accommodate a milk delivery truck.

Consider the case of the Milk Industry-Teamster Local 680 pension fund in New Jersey. Even when such plans are not yet covered by the PBGC, the law actually makes it possible for a multiple-employer pension plan to bail out when the unfunded pension debt is more than thirty percent of the business's assets.

The milk industry pension plan had a $20 million unfunded debt. Under the law the employers paid $4 million to the government and walked away from the troubled plan. The retirees will continue to receive their pensions, but the checks will now come from the PBGC. With the books now wiped clean, the employers are free to start up another plan, again offering attractive benefits that could result in yet another massive unfunded debt.

Matthew M. Lind, then head of the PBGC, commenting on the employers' freedom to unload prior pension debt onto the government's books, said, "It's not illegal, but I think it's wrong. It makes termination a very attractive deal for them."

Another loophole in the law allows still more employers to bail out of shaky pension plans. In this case, employers contributing to multiple-employer plans need put up money only if they contribute more than ten percent of the total contributions. Many employers can now leave their unpaid liabilities behind for free. They can avoid even a cash payment of other liabilities by posting a bond, since they are actually liable only if the multiple-employer plan goes broke within five years of the time they pull out. Labor Secretary Ray Marshall summed up these employer dodges by stating, "These rules could have the effect of encouraging employers to leave a plan at the first sign of financial trouble, penalizing employers who remain with a plan until its termination."

Again, this is only what can be seen. Although the PBGC is not required to take over multiple-employer plans until possibly May 1980 or later, it has already rescued three plans on a voluntary basis, including the New Jersey milk-fund case cited above.

Six years after coming into being, the PBGC is facing a dilemma of credibility. If it is, in fact, the pension of last resort, how can it allow some debt-riddled plans to collapse without protection while continuing to insure others?

So far, by voluntarily saving highly visible plans like that in the milk industry, the PBGC has kept only the surface of the problem visible. The hitch is that more and more people are now beginning to look under the water line, and becoming frightened at what they see. One of the reasons is that the agency itself doesn't know how many employers are dropping out of multiple-employer plans, shifting their burden of debt to the currently insured private plans.

Moreover, estimates of the crushing debt underlying the pension plans are only now coming in. Former director Lind has predicted that the agency might have to assume an incredible $5 billion over the next decade just in multiple-employer plans alone. Even supporters of the PBGC now concede that the agency will have to sop up an enormous amount of private pension debt over the next few years—probably as much as $15 billion.

It is a scary truth that no one really knows the extent to which the debt has built up over the years in the nation's private pension plans. Offering insurance on this type of risk is like selling fire insurance to a man with a lighted torch in his hand. Worse yet, the PBGC has already insured many of the larger pension plans currently ablaze.

To meet the pending crisis of multiple-employer plans, both the Administration and the Pension Benefit Guaranty Corporation have donned their fire hats and rushed to the scene of the blaze. Their idea of fire control, which is a parallel to the case of Social Security, is simply to reduce benefits. The idea is not to run away from all workers, just the estimated eight million of you who are covered under multiple-employer pension plans.

Proposals in the works are intended to make it less attractive to terminate multiple-employer plans by preventing companies which abandon plans from escaping their financial obligations. These proposals would also give financially shaky plans more flexibility to withstand bad times, besides reducing or postponing the PBGC's rescue attempts so that the premiums employers pay can be kept to a manageable level.

Under the deceptive proposals, companies and unions could continue to promise the worker steadily increasing benefits—until the time the plan runs into deep trouble. Then all promises would take a nosedive, for benefits would then be reduced to levels no higher than those in effect up to five years earlier.

If a pension plan continued to remain on the verge of collapse, additional benefit cuts could be made before the PBGC would be required to come to the rescue. President Carter wants the PBGC to cut back the benefit protection even further as one of the new proposals made to save the idea of "insuring" pension benefits. Under this proposal the PBGC would only guarantee modest-sized monthly retirement checks, with the higher benefits only partly insured. Thus, as the worker's monthly retirement benefit increased, less and less of the expected pension would be insured by the PBGC. Worse yet, once the PBGC was forced to step in, the benefit

117

levels would be fixed, without any adjustments made for inflation.

It remains to be seen whether these new proposals will make it any less attractive for employers to dump their debt-ridden pension plans on the government's insurance program. Many observers doubt that it will. Considering the temptation to unload pension plans that are already deeply in debt and headed, during the next few years, into sharply higher levels of red ink, such dumping may easily grow excessive when it becomes clear that pension insurance is available.

The Administration's proposals appear, to many of the eight million affected workers, to abandon them at a time when they have no one else to protect their interests. If ERISA was established as an umbrella over our private pension plans, then it is a very leaky one in an increasingly savage storm. In order to cover the multiple-employer plans, the rain is now to leak on one in four workers when, in fact, all parties deserve equal shelter under the same umbrella.

The prospect of getting soaked is not a happy one for anyone. Inflation is already eating away at their meager pension benefits to such an extent that their only hope may lie in grasping the full benefits they have already been promised. They may well ask whether too high a price is being paid to save the government's pension-insurance program.

Band-Aid amendments applied by Congress will not save the program. The loss of pension benefits by millions of workers will not save the program. What we have is a textbook case of interminable congressional delay that can only lead to an eventual collapse of the PBGC—and with it, the end of the American workers' confidence that his pension benefit will actually be paid.

In a sense, ERISA is becoming nothing more than a limited aspect of the broader issue of the requirements of a total federal retirement policy. Clearly such policy should include the continued payment of already-promised and paid-for benefits to each worker covered under a private retirement plan. That was the original goal when ERISA was hammered out by the lawmakers back in 1974, reflecting the fact that, fundamentally, the pension is deferred compensation.

Now, six years into the program, it is becoming clear to

many observers that the legislation has not achieved its goal. This is largely because the authors of ERISA failed to understand the financial reality of pension funding. The speedy shuffling of paper by the Department of Labor, the IRS, and PBGC, as well as congressional staffs, has only resulted in regulations and legislation with little relation to reality. The question most overlooked in congressional cloakrooms was, "Whose money is at stake?"

Prior to ERISA, it was not the employer's money. He had the option of making payment in full on the pension promises he had made, or simply turning over the retirement fund to the employees and walking away. Recall the Studebaker fiasco, where the workers were surprised with an empty bag of pensions and the company was off the hook. ERISA attempted to place the risk where it belongs, back on the company making the pension promises (a commitment in the form of deferred compensation).

Instead, the legislation that finally emerged from Congress shifted most of the risk to the Pension Benefit Guaranty Corporation. The employer is now back to square one: the choice between fulfilling the promised pension benefits or turning over the entire fund to the PBGC. One amazed Washington insider concluded, "What this means is that the PBGC now bears the risk for unsuccessful plans whereas the employer benefits from unsuccessful ones."

We have now reached another "unbelievable situation": The company can advantageously trade current wages for future pension promises, since the risk associated with the promises is now shared with the PBGC.

But that is only half the story. For the PBGC has proposed to Congress that what little risk is left to the employer—the possible loss of up to thirty percent of his net assets in the event of pension-plan failure—be covered via yet another insurance program. This is called Contingent Employer Liability Insurance, or CELI.

Only our wonders in Washington could design government theft insurance after the theft had already occurred. But selling the insurance may be another matter. If the CELI is voluntary, only the bad risks will buy it. If the insurance is mandatory, it is most unfair to those who are adequately funded.

Let's look at how this nightmare could shift the pension liability from a company's back to the government's own PBGC insurance fund.

Over the years Lockheed Corporation, as it bounced from prosperity to near-bankruptcy, simply did not ante up enough cash to pay for the pension benefits promised its workers. The unfunded pension debt at the end of 1976 totaled $276 million. In contrast the total net worth of the corporation was only $167 million.

The drama could now easily be staged. PBGC's white horse would be waiting in the wings. Galloping onstage, the mighty stallion would now scoop up the defaulting pension plan—if default should occur—and ride off into the sunset.

Lockheed would only be liable for thirty percent of its net worth, or $50 million. The PBGC's mighty stallion would be saddled with the huge pension debt of $226 million, and Lockheed would be off the hook.

Now comes the proposed Contingent Employer Liability Insurance. If this insurance scheme is adopted, nearly all of the $50 million could be saved. As absurd as this seems, Lockheed could now transfer most of its huge debt of $270 million to the government's insurance fund, which could then look to the other companies contributing to the PBGC to actually come up with the cash.

The unrealism of the PBGC is that it transfers the pension debt from the employer who allowed it to come into existence in the first place to the government's own insurance fund. In this tortuous way, it is the nation's taxpayers, only half of whom are covered by private pension plans, who must in the final analysis pay the bills. If the concept of insurance is to work at all, then payment for it must clearly be changed from a flat rate for all to a risk-rated premium that reflects the degree of danger that a given pension plan could slide toward bankruptcy. At least some sense of equity might then return. The old-fashioned notion would be revived, that those employers who ran up massive pension debt in the first place should be held responsible for their fair share of the insurance premiums.

But the reverse is revealed as disclosures concerning the PBGC come to light. Congress has discovered once again that it is easy to pass laws but far from easy to see that they work equitably, especially in the financial sense. In the case of the PBGC, Congress may have ended up only writing a blank check.

For all pension debt is but a promise to pay in the future. When that promise is guaranteed, it constitutes an ongoing burden for all pension plans—weak or strong. It raises the tough question whether the government really should guarantee future income to that half of the work force covered under employer-sponsored retirement plans.

If it is our belief that all private pension benefits should be guaranteed for half the workers, who are fortunate enough to be covered, then we must be prepared to face the implication of the following fact: If the employer does not pay, the government will. The passage of ERISA, which has come close to making the government the pension-payer of last resort, only hastens the day when *the* one and only pension will be that provided by the government in its own monopolistic fashion.

7 The Crumbling Benefits Where We Work

The time: 1986. The place: the boardroom of one of America's larger corporations. The subject: the company's retirement plan.

A hush falls over the room as the president rises to speak.

"Gentlemen, I have an important announcement to make. After careful consideration, and a look at the potential future costs, your company has decided to terminate its pension plan. As of today, those employees already retired should continue to receive their pension checks. Those currently at work may keep whatever is in their pension account. This was not an easy decision to make, but we all felt it was necessary in order to ensure the financial solvency of the corporation."

The president then turns to his vice-president in charge of employee benefits. A man of considerable girth, the latter picks up a wad of papers from the table and begins to speak on behalf of the pension-plan committee.

"Gentlemen, let me say this. We have come to the point where we cannot afford to provide adequate retirement incomes for workers who haven't reached retirement age. Unless something is done very soon—and our track record is not encouraging—about seven thousand retirees and widows will find their checks drying up at some future date. And those who leave the department, the agency, or the organization before qualifying for a pension will find it all but impossible to recover all the money they have paid into the plan over the years."

That is all there is to say. The president has finally acknowledged that inflation has overtaken the company's ability to pay ever-higher pension benefits from an already nearly empty purse.

For years a "secure" pension plan meant that the employer was willing and able to provide a fixed level of benefits, based on a final salary at retirement, and that the plan was adequately funded to provide the benefits promised under the plan. But no more. The unworkable structure in which current workers support benefits for more and more retired workers is near outright collapse. The state of pensions prompted Ian Lanoff, Administrator of Pension and Welfare Benefits for the U.S. Labor Department, to comment last year, "This is a crisis that touches us all now, or will touch us in the near future. It is not as dramatic as the energy crisis or as obvious as skies dark with smog, but it is a deeply moving crisis reflecting lost hopes and quiet despairs."

The Graying of America

Every pension plan—including Social Security—is threatened when the number of active workers fails to grow as fast as the number of pensioners. This disparity has been caused by a lower birthrate and the reduced savings rate, which, in turn, has caused investments in business to suffer. This can then result in a lower productivity rate and higher inflationary costs.

The problem of paying for promised pension benefits has been building for some time as more and more private companies have found it all but impossible, based on these conditions, to put aside the staggering amount of money required to fund the plans adequately.

Worse yet, pension-fund managers aren't coming clean.

They are greatly understating the costs of future retirement benefits.

Various estimates, based partly on the corporations' own reports, place the unfunded private debt somewhere between $40 and $50 billion. Since much of this information must come from the companies already awash in pension red ink, the reported figures may be grossly understated. The unfunded pension debt may actually exceed $100 billion. When employers are finally forced to pay the bills, stockholders may find that very little money remains in the company till.

The most obvious test of a pension plan's strength is the extent to which assets have been set aside to cover the expected pension benefits. When not enough assets have been set aside, the pension plan, as we have before noted, is said to have "unfunded liabilities." Ballooned by double-digit inflation, and thus by burgeoning wages, costs that constitute the base for reckoning pensions, today's pension obligations are soaring.

A study contained in a 1978 issue of *Business Week* reported that unfunded vested pension debt for one hundred major U.S. companies increased by nineteen percent from 1976 to 1977, or $18.5 billion, while total corporate profits grew only ten percent. (Vested benefits are only those a company would have to pay workers if its pension plan were terminated now. These are to be contrasted with the full cost of allowing for the impact of the inflationary spiral on future salaries—the base for establishing benefits which someday must be paid.)

The pension crunch is pinching the very hand that feeds the benefit flow. As the figures just cited suggest, these one hundred major U.S. companies have pension obligations that are growing almost twice as fast as the corporations' ability to make money. This fact portends very serious trouble for America.

Two things must be said. First, company obligations to retirees are zooming so fast that corporations don't have time to catch their breath. Lots of companies could get clobbered before they've had time to carry out adjustments. Chalk this up as yet another of inflation's many hidden costs.

Second, pension obligations are a cost of doing business. Over the long haul, companies have got to cover all their costs, pension included, with something to spare that shows up as the bottom line. But what happens between today's raging inflation and the "long run"? Firms will go out of business—and many retirees will take a bath with them. How many companies will sink can't be determined in advance, but we can be sure that far more won't make it than the number that would in a noninflationary environment.

More than a few U.S. firms face competition from foreign rivals, and the overseas competitors may not have the same obligation to pay pensions. Some foreign companies may not have to pay pensions at all. Other U.S. firms have only domestic rivals, but pension problems may result nonetheless. Suppose Brand X's domestic rivals have a small wage bill in relation to all costs of doing business. When that happens, our old friend Brand X takes a drubbing by losing out to the company with the small wage bill; with higher labor and pension costs pushing up their prices, their sales will fall.

Some striking cases have come to light recently, illustrating the way inflation undermines a company's ability to pay pensions. The undermining occurs even though the company remains in business and reports what appear to be good financial results to stockholders.

Once more, let's take the years 1976 and 1977 to illustrate how the uncontrolled cancer eats away the financial life of some of America's greatest corporations.

Lockheed, as the professionals realize, is at the head of the pack. In just one year its unfunded vested pension debt increased from 166 percent to 195 percent of the company's total net worth. The stockholders haven't really owned the company for years. Nor does the pension plan own Lockheed, since the total net worth of the company is little more than half the pension debt. Ownership, if it can be called that, rests with the empty sacks of money that have yet to be paid into the company pension plan.

Or consider the case of LTV, the fifty-seventh largest company in sales in 1978. With sales of over $5 billion—*billion* that is—the company's unfunded vested pension debt, compared to its total net worth, increased from 103 percent to 125 percent from 1976 to 1977. These are admittedly scary figures, but a host of giant companies are not far behind in a losing battle to keep the pension debt under control.

For another case, look at Bethlehem Steel's fight to save its pension plan from disaster. Trying desperately to stay the flow of red ink, Bethlehem saw its unfunded pension debt rise from only forty-eight percent of its total net worth in 1976 to fifty-six percent in 1977. Now the pension plan owns a controlling interest in the company, and unless the debt is checked soon, the stockholders of yet another company will be left empty-handed.

America's pension crisis has pervaded the entire world of big business. For companies like National Steel, Trans World Airlines, struggling Chrysler, Pan American, Uniroyal, American Motors, and Republic Steel, just to name a few, the pension debt figure is more than forty percent of their total net worth and rising rapidly.

Who are the next candidates to fall into the pension morass? (We define this morass as being unfunded vested benefits that amount to between twenty and forty percent of a company's total net worth.) Well-known firms like Bendix, Westinghouse, Alcoa, Goodyear, Allegheny Ludlum Industries, are rapidly sliding toward the danger point.

Even the really big giants, companies you have come to know—and maybe love—are in deep trouble. General Motors increased its unfunded vested pension debt between 1976 and 1977 by an estimated $500 million, creating a towering pile of empty pension cash bags totaling as much as $3.5 billion, or over twenty percent of its total net worth. Ford Motor did even "better," relative to its size, increasing its pension debt by thirty-three percent, from $970 million to $1.3 billion! Joining the billionaire club of big-time pension debtors, Ford acknowledged that this one factor in the price of building a car, for instance, has risen faster than the cost of steel, or even the cost of labor. We are witnessing an explosion in pension costs. And you can bet your sweet life that the pension figures are understated. Even with only the admitted costs considered, pensions add far more to the showroom price of a GM car today than any other cost item, not only because their cost is rapidly rising in line with our spiraling inflation, but also because there are so many more retirement-pension checks to mail each month.

The graying of America has taken over General Motors. In the early 1960s GM counted twelve employees for each pensioner. Today the number has slipped to only four. To make things worse, it is estimated that by the year 2000 there will be just two. In fact, we are rapidly approaching the day when, clobbered as they are by inflation and overwhelmed by sheer numbers of retirees, the cost of pensions could push the price of a car beyond the pocketbook of most Americans.

As usual, the public has been kept in darkness. To be sure, not all large companies are haunted by pension debt; in fact, probably as many as half of our firms have yet to incur one of any size. Once again, as with the Social Security disaster, it is the major, well-known companies that account for most of the pension debt. Representing only five percent of all U.S. companies, these firms account for as much as seventy-five percent of the aggregate unfunded pension liability. If you remember the chapter on ERISA, a huge part of this debt is not even protected by the PBGC's federal pension insurance.

With red beginning to cover corporate books, many companies are already pumping *more than twice* the rate of profits into pension plans, with no apparent effect on the rising debt. By any measure of dollar counting, the pension debt has become so great—and is rising so rapidly—that it may put a severe drag on profits. Such companies are very like anvil salesmen with their own merchandise in the trunk.

As if that weren't enough bad news, the really appalling aspect of the problem is that apparently no one really knows to what extent the pension monster is overtaking America's larger companies. Even in this time of never-ending regulations and meticulous disclosure requirements, there apparently is no way to state in advance a realistic estimate of the pension drag on companies' profits. The accounting and actuarial (estimated future costs for pensions) treatment of the pension debt on company books is often a classic case of confusion. In fact the companies have so much latitude in the way they calculate pensions that they can practically come up with any level of payments and debts they like.

To a great extent the reported status of a pension plan depends on the company's assumptions as to the growth of wages and the return on the pension plan's investments. As unbelievable as it may seem, some companies are still estimating a four or five percent growth of wage costs in an economy that is roaring along with a fourteen percent or better inflation rate. The reason future wage costs are important is that most pension plans scale retirement benefits to the employee's salary near the time he starts to draw benefits. If companies underestimate the extent of wage increases, then their contribution to the pension plan will fall short of what will actually be needed to pay the sharply higher benefits.

As the years roll by, this shortfall keeps ticking away like a timb bomb under the President's chair.

But the real clinker in the pension reports could be the assumed rate of return that many plans use in calculating their debt. If the interest assumption is optimistically set high, the pension plan will appear to be in better financial health and the company can put up less money to cover the promised benefits. In fact, the interest assumption has a potent effect on the company's obligation to fund the pension plan. Pension experts have estimated that an increase of one percent in the expected interest return could mean a twenty-five percent reduction in pension costs and liabilities.

What all this means is that retirees and the public must continue to rely on the figures received from company pension plans—even though the reporting companies have shown a marked tendency to report a bank robbery as just a misappropriation of funds.

From what little we can learn, however, we know that the pension debt has been exploding over the last five years—largely because of inflation.

Winston Churchill once observed that "there are people who regard private enterprise as a predatory tiger to be shot. Others look upon it as a cow to be milked. Not enough people see private enterprise as a healthy horse—pulling a sturdy wagon." Today most people fail to see that there are limits to the load even the healthiest horse can pull. The added burdens of bloated pension plans and runaway inflation may prove too much for private enterprise.

The money crunch triggered by soaring inflation and reflected in skyrocketing interest rates now threatens financial panic among managers of pension funds. In October of 1979 IBM sold $1 billion in bonds and notes. With one of the best credit risks after the U. S. government itself, a yield of 9 3/8 percent seemed like an answer to a pension plan's prayers. Six months later, U.S. Treasury bills were yielding sixteen percent on a three-month investment and no one wanted to touch a long-term debt instrument. IBM's bonds now were selling for only seventy-five cents on the dollar—a paper loss of one quarter during a short interval of time.

With the higher interest rates offered on new bonds and notes today, America's pension plans have experienced sharp paper loss on the mass of older securities in their bond portfolios. Remember, this isn't speculative money. It represents the traditionally most respected assets that stand behind pension plans all over America.

With their engineer's slide rules slipping along in offices across the land, the people who run pensions have been unable to come up with a logical plan to trim back the rising deficit. The pension debt might now be described as coming under a new sort of "domino theory."

First of all, most pensions are based on wages earned near retirement so inflation in wages creeps up on a pension like a relentless morning tide. Next, companies also frequently increase pension benefits retroactively, creating new debt. Further, in addition to paper losses on bonds, major pension investments—like those in the stock market—have, frankly, "gone to hell in a hand basket." Already in the stock market to the tune of some $300 billion, private pension plans have become the largest institutional investors on Wall Street. Unfortunately, there is little choice when they are forced to invest a wad of money this large. Bonds have been discredited, at least for the time being, and real estate takes a lot of know-how besides being not all that much of a sure thing anyway. Short-term investments of high quality—until very recently—yielded paltry interest returns. Most pension plans have very little confidence about investing for the future, usually splitting the difference by putting long-term investments half in bonds and half in the stock market.

A thought attributed to Mark Twain allows that October is one of the peculiarly dangerous months in which to speculate in the stock market. The others are July, January, September, April, November, May, March, June, December, August and February. Mark Twain may have been right; the once popular inflation hedges, like common stocks, have lost much of their old luster. Over the last twenty years stock prices, as measured by the Dow Jones Industrial Averages, have increased 80 percent while the cost of living has soared almost 140 percent over this same period. In fact the stock market has been deadly to investors since 1966. That was when it finally broke over the Dow Jones 1,000 mark for the first time. Struggling like a racehorse with heavily loaded saddlebags, the market has maintained an uneven pace, never permanently breaking over the 1,000 mark. In all of 1979, for example, it was comfortably resting in the 800–900 range.

The true condition of the stock market, however, can only be discovered if we wind back to Chapter 4 and the topic of inflation. That's where we talked about funny money. Or, putting it another way, after adjusting for inflation, the 1,000 Dow Jones mark is worth less than 500 in 1966 terms.

Now if you think you can beat the market by trading, you should reconsider. The odds have been stacked against you for some time.

One of my stockbroker friends told me recently that his clients have been making money shorting the market (selling stock they don't own in the hope that they can buy it back later at a lower price).

"Hell," he said, "the stock market has gone so sour only the pessimists make money anymore."

"What do you mean?" I asked.

"The real money is being made in antiques, art, and jewelry. Even the bankers have entered a new world of investing, offering their clients a fully managed portfolio of art and antiques."

"But what about the stock market?" I asked again.

"I don't know," he replied. "Money as an investment seems to have gone out of style."

In spite of my friend's advice, the pension plans for the present will, in their investments, remain "out of style." They must deal with plain old, dirty money. The trouble is that plain old, dirty money has not been good to pension-plan managers; they have been losing the battle with inflation in a spectacular way.

A. G. Becker, a Chicago investment firm, published a study in 1979 indicating just how spectacularly bad retirement funds have been in fighting inflation over the last fifteen years. Between 1964 and 1978 about 3,500 retirement funds managed an average return of just four percent a year, when inflation was running along at 5.4 percent—and in a steeply rising curve at that. More recently, over the last five years, the annual return on stocks has been an incredibly poor 2.2 percent. (And, according to the best current estimates, pension assets are made up of fifty-one percent stocks, thirty-nine percent debt, and ten percent demand and time deposits!) The return on bonds was better, reaching 6.1 percent, and for cash invested for short terms, 7.4 percent. During this period the study points out that inflation was marching along at an eight percent average pace, but becoming more poisonous with each passing year.

What all this means is that over the last five years, according to the Becker study, the return on pension plans has skidded to a crawl, averaging less than four percent. And that, my friend, is only half the reported average rate of inflation during this same period. The value of the pension funds has been shrinking badly in real terms.

Most workers continue to believe that their pension money is being invested and managed in a competent way. After all, the nation's largest and most prestigious banks and investment firms handle the money. Well, perhaps, but the A. G. Becker study reveals that the results have been less than might otherwise be expected from such a talented group of money handlers. Merrill-Lynch may be bullish on America, but their confidence has not spilled over to the pension funds.

Something more sinister, however, emerges from the question of control of this $300 billion chunk of money. If the workers look closely, they will see that their pension money now permits a handful of people to determine the future of our economy.

These money managers have the power to acquire something like effective control of major corporations in this country. In other words, the pension funds are already close to taking over the hand that feeds them.

The Securities and Exchange Commission, for example, considers ownership of over five percent of a company's stock equivalent to control—given the fact that the common stock of most companies is scattered among many thousands of separate stockholders. By this measure, the pension funds—individually or as a group—now control many of America's largest corporations. With this control comes the ability to influence key sectors of our economy.

A major conclusion emerges from all this. It would seem to me that the workers who contribute to the pension plans—after all, it's their deferred compensation—should have a greater say in how and where their own money is invested.

Short of a miracle the system is unlikely to change. If you are among the millions covered under private pension plans, you will continue to remain in the dark as to where your money is. Furthermore, you can only hope that the downright embarrassing return on pension assets will improve, and improve substantially!

In a sense the stock market, no longer a hedge against inflation, has turned its back not only on the pension-fund managers, but on all of us who expect eventually to receive a retirement check. The tragedy of the widely fluctuating stock market can be brought home in a personal way when you sit down with a new retiree and review his expected retirement benefit.

During the recent stock-market plunges, the effects have been devastating. From my retirement-counseling experiences, I remember particularly the painful story of a person who, unaware of the recent stock-market nosedive, decided to retire. His account had held over $70,000 in assorted stocks. Unfortunately, when he retired a few years ago, taking out his money, the value of his account had shrunk to only $48,000. Not only were his retirement assets unexpectedly cut by over thirty percent, but like most workers covered under private plans, he had been left without a hedge against the inflation that is sure to devour his modest pension check in the years to come.

As for the future, the costs of private pension plans will keep rising. The "domino theory" of soaring pension-benefit levels unmatched by at least equivalent returns on investments means that more and more pension plans will begin to fall in true domino fashion.

Meanwhile it seems certain that in the coming years many will press for the inclusion of cost-of-living clauses in private pension plans. If management is to provide all of the required funding, pension costs will have to increase far beyond twelve to sixteen percent of payroll. They may easily have to be hiked to as much as twenty-five percent. This would be a more than significant change when you consider that only five years ago many pension plans were funded on the basis of only ten percent of payroll.

One of the most depressing aspects of our nation's private pension system is that, despite the situation resulting from the gargantuan size of the unfunded debt, pensions in the private sector are typically too few and too small. How things change when you shift to government workers! These people not only are universally covered, but their pension benefits are generally the best to be found anywhere.

There's a reason for the generosity offered federal employees. Unlike everybody else, the feds can promise the moon in money terms. They can do it because they alone can print the money to assure payment. Who else regularly runs up gallons of red ink in the budget? In recent inflationary years, with full employment and with modest unemployment, the federal budget is in the red to the tune of tens of billions. The federal deficit, despite the ballooning of prices, hasn't been kept below $30 billion in years. And this is the reported deficit. In addition Congress gets away with "off-budget" expenditures—items running into billions that aren't counted in the regular budget. Some of the red ink is covered by borrowings from the general public, which are not inflationary per se. But a lot of the deficit—a disgustingly large part of it—is covered by newly printed money that only brings more inflation.

With this instructive digression behind us, let's return to the private pension problem. Recall Chapter 2, where it was shown that the underlying problem boils down to vesting and benefit schedules that have been deliberately set low to protect the employer's own plans. Not all employers are vulnerable on this score, because some provide quite handsome benefits indeed. But most of the plans place recipients below the poverty level.

In fact, in 1976 only seven million retirees received a private pension income, and the amount averaged only $2,204 per year. Many workers in private industry who have worked hard to live the American dream are now waking up to discover a nightmare: poverty at retirement. With only half the private work force covered, the vesting rules effectively reduce that half to little more than half again. Let's look at the arithmetic. The average American man has been estimated to change jobs every 4.6 years; the average woman, every 2.8. But the average private pension plan usually pays full benefits only if a worker stays with the employer for ten years or more. Moreover, because many people hop from job to job in an effort to raise their income relative to the rising cost of living, pension experts believe that no more than forty percent of the workers will actually get a pension. Many experts believe the figure will actually turn out to be lower, maybe twenty-five to thirty percent.

The true condition of the private pension system is apparent from these figures. With only half the workers covered, and roughly half of those covered expected to collect a retirement check, the plain truth is that less than one in four who work in the private sector can expect to augment their Social Security benefits with a realistic company pension.

In spite of this poor showing—with private pension benefits sliding lower each year in terms of real dollars adjusted for inflation, while the unfunded debt slated to cover the benefits roars out of control—there's a yet more sinister side-effect to the pension debate that, little noticed by the public, is threatening to restrict even further our ability to compete for business.

Take the United States steel industry, for example, which is fighting for its financial life against the influx of lower-cost imported steel. Mr. Wayne Atwell, an analyst at San Francisco's Davis, Skaggs and Company, commented in a 1978 *Wall Street Journal* article that "pension obligations represent a serious problem for the U.S. steel industry due to a large unfunded liability and rapid growth in benefits." One of Mr. Atwell's main conclusions is that hopes for greater efficiency in U.S. steelmaking by the closing down of old, inefficient plants, may not be realized because the current overhanging burden of pension obligations will compete with capital for modernization.

A specific case in point. In 1977 Bethlehem Steel wanted to close a marginal plant. But to do this they had to take a $375 million charge to set up a special fund for the unpaid pension debt involving twelve thousand laid-off employees. As Mr. Atwell points out, "This works out to $31,250 per employee versus a reported unfunded vesting liability of $10,993." What this means is that before the plant closing, the company books showed a pension liability of only one third the amount that was needed when the plant was actually closed and the company had to come up at last with the hard cash. Mr. Atwell states the industry was considering a twenty-five-million-ton reduction in capacity in order to improve its cost efficiency for both the domestic and export markets. However, he estimates that "if those write-off costs are representative, it would cost the domestic industry $5.7 billion to close down twenty-five million tons of capacity. We don't believe the industry could stand such a drastic alteration of its capital structure and, for this reason, we believe large-scale close-downs are highly unlikely. To an extent, the industry is held captive by its unfunded pension liabilities."

Unfortunately our steel industry is not alone in its fight to improve manufacturing efficiency by lowering its labor costs. Our economy is plagued by older plants that, in themselves, reduce the overall efficiency of the American economy.

In 1979 Johnson and Higgins, an employee-benefit firm headquartered in New York City, asked Louis Harris to conduct a study of American attitudes toward pensions and retirement. The study was based on interviews with a national cross-section of 1,330 full-time employees, 369 retirees, and 212 companies. The attitudes toward private pensions reflected the lack of public awareness of the major problems covered in this chapter. In fact, most employees (seventy-eight percent) claimed to be basically satisfied with the way their plans are designed and administered. Only one in three (thirty-one percent) expressed less than full confidence, while a sixty-eight percent majority had a great deal of confidence that their plans would pay the promised benefits. A significant segment—eighty percent—felt that "every employer should be required by law to provide a reasonable pension plan for his employees." But a striking ninety-three percent want a provision not found in most private plans—a provision for benefits which will increase with the cost of living. Business leaders, however, were found to consider cost-of-living benefits to be much less important than did current or retired employees.

The practice of integrating private pensions with the amount a person receives from Social Security (refer back to Chapter 3) when determining the size of pension benefits was rejected by a clear-cut majority of current and retired workers. The owners, who save a bundle of money through this offset method, felt by a margin of seventy-seven to twenty-two percent that Social Security benefits should be taken into account when determining the size of a pension benefit.

Louis Harris found that business leaders and current and retired workers are most negative about union retirement plans and Social Security. What do they like most? It was inevitable that a plurality of current and retired workers—at least those that knew the score—felt that plans for government employees offered the highest benefits for the money contributed. In fact, they would prefer this type of plan over all others if they had to rely on only one plan for all their retirement income.

But the most significant finding of the study regarding private pension plans may have been the fact that nearly half (forty-nine percent) of the working and retired public would favor a change in the pension law which would permit employees to contribute to pension plans at work and deduct their contributions from federal taxes until they retire. This proposal received strong support from the business community, where eighty-nine percent said they would approve of the change.

Just to refresh your memory, in Chapter 5 we covered individual retirement plans. For reasons most people have been unable to accept, the current IRA law does not allow a worker to make his own tax-favored contributions into an IRA if he is covered by a retirement plan where he works.

The Louis Harris survey on private pension plans concludes with a very optimistic and welcome note. Since the graying of America will substantially increase the number of workers reaching retirement age beginning in the 1980s, the survey expects today's employees to exert considerable pressure for higher benefits from business and government as they approach retirement.

At the same time, and I believe this is very important in

light of the depressing pension situation described in this chapter, the survey concludes that part of the solution to future increases in pension costs may lie with the employees themselves. The survey found that they are willing to make contributions to their company pension plan if their contributions can be made in exchange for larger benefits or earlier benefit eligibility. But probably most significantly, more than two thirds of the workers interviewed said they would be willing to contribute to a plan, or to contribute more than they do now, if it would increase their retirement benefits.

Many companies have long recognized the need for individual savings as part of the overall company retirement plan. Such a savings program, known as the *Thrift Plan,* was begun by International Harvester back in 1965. Participation in the program is entirely voluntary; a worker may discontinue his or her saving plan at any time. Thrift plans usually work much like that established by International Harvester: for every two dollars the employee saves, the company contributes one dollar. All company contributions are invested in company common stock. The employees have several options: government bonds, savings accounts, company stock, or a combination of all.

But Washington authors of the shameful federal tax laws prohibiting you from deferring, along with your employers, income-tax money on your contributions to a pension, will probably remain unmoved by the pension dilemma. In this case Congress has failed again to understand the classic phrase "Government is not the solution, it's the problem." For in a sense this restrictive tax law regarding your own contributions into your employer plans is a thief. It robs you of the taxes you must pay on money you will probably not see until retirement. Then it robs you again by the loss of interest income on the money you paid in taxes simply to make a contribution toward your eventual retirement. In fact, the United States is one of very few industrial nations whose tax policy discourages employee contributions.

It seems to me incredible that the lawmakers on Capitol Hill could be frozen into inaction by the fear of the looming pension disaster, the threat that the private retirement system will collapse around our feet, and yet turn a deaf ear to the workers who are seeking to shore up that very system with their own money.

With our own private pension system in disarray, let's look at recent developments in European pension planning.

The wave of the future seems to be coming in the form of national compulsory employer-sponsored pension plans. This is an approach to the problem of providing retirement income security through a combination of Social Security and legally mandated employer-sponsored pension plans.

Not only our own country, but the developed countries of Western Europe are finding it difficult to pay Social Security benefits that are always on the climb.

With Social Security taxes rising, the concept of a federally mandated private-pension system has gained wide acceptance in the Netherlands and Switzerland. It has been pushed for various reasons. For one, many believe that keeping a place for private plans provides a better overall balance between the government and the individual, and, equally important, provides an important source of capital for national economic development.

Others contend that the straining Social Security system is hardly the place to provide adequate retirement benefits for all workers. Still others would like to see a state-controlled retirement and welfare system, and they believe this is the most realistic way to achieve their goals.

Let's look more closely at the Swiss approach to private compulsory pension plans. Their major desire was to ensure that the Second Pillar of retirement income be made available to all employed persons. (The Swiss Three Pillar income replacement program consists of: (1) Social Security, (2) private plans, and (3) personal savings.)

Faced with the same archaic vesting schedules and the possible loss of accrued future retirement credits at each job change, the Swiss invented a system in which pension credits would be fully transferable.

The plan that actually emerged in Switzerland incorporated many of the same pension improvements long sought in America. The Swiss compulsory pension plan includes:

— A Social Security and private pension equal to sixty percent of average final earnings for a single person with forty years of coverage. I should point out that these are "integrated" plans designed to provide the desired total income from both government and private plans.

— All employees over age twenty-five with minimum earnings must be covered. Full and immediate vesting will apply to each worker during his or her employment.

— The company plan will be required to provide a pension equal to at least forty percent of the worker's last three years' average covered salary, prior to retirement.

— Each company will be responsible for funding the basic retirement benefit (as outlined above) but—and this is an interesting idea—a national pool will be responsible for providing future cost-of-living adjustments.

— The socially oriented benefits will also apply; death and disability coverage will be required as early as age eighteen for full-time employees. Both a pre- and a post-retirement widow's pension will be available at 60 percent of the normal benefit.

To ensure this national compulsory pension system, the Swiss voters approved an amendment to their federal constitution in December 1972.

The Swiss experiment with a compulsory private-employer-sponsored pension system is expected to become law in 1980. The Netherlands appears to be ready with a very similar plan in the near future.

What about America? Are we headed in the same direction? Proposals to mandate private pensions in the United States have been introduced in Congress several times. The prime reason for mandating private pensions in place of ever-higher Social Security benefits has been the pressure to avoid higher payroll taxes. I think it makes sense. After all, I believe it offers a far more equitable and attractive approach to our national retirement problems than greatly expanding the already overburdened and deeply in debt Social Security system. Moreover, I believe, the huge amount of money that would be required to pump up the Social Security program would go nowhere. It could cause a loss of $300 billion from the private pension system that is a vital factor in providing the necessary capital for our expanding economy.

When I began to write this book, an old sage in the investment business warned me that much of what he knew never came from books. "Seat-of-the-pants experiences were all that mattered," he told me. As our conversation turned away from stocks and bonds, I asked him what he thought of Social Security's effect on our economy.

"Damn funny program," he said.

Curious, I wanted to know what made it so funny.

"Why, it takes money away from the worker and sends it straight back to the government. Then the government sends it straight back to the retired worker. Never does anybody any good 'cept the guy who's retired."

"But that's what it's for," I explained, "to provide retirement benefits."

"No," he said, "you're wrong. It's also supposed to provide part of the investment capital to provide that job in the first place."

"That doesn't happen with Social Security," I agreed. "I guess you're right."

"Damn right I am," he said as he tugged his beard. "Social Security is like an old car. You can keep it running while it nickels and dimes you to death. But after spending all that money, you still got only one car. With a private pension plan you can use that same money and buy a dozen cars. Now at least," he sighed, "you can get some use out of the money before you retire."

In any event, if the day does arrive when serious consideration is given in this country to a compulsory private-pension system, Switzerland could serve as an example worth studying. After all, Switzerland, with virtually no unemployment and a government committed to fiscal policies that have maintained a stable Swiss franc and almost zero inflation, appears to have more than one lesson worth learning.

Another European approach to retirement planning is also worth noting. It is called "gliding out." For many workers, the day the job stops becomes one of the shocks of a lifetime. They must retire literally overnight from decades of work with little or no advance planning.

Gliding out of the day-to-day work schedule is already practiced in France, England, Sweden, and the Netherlands. Basically, gliding out enables a worker to move gradually into retirement through a scheme that allows a combination of part-time work and part payment of his pension. The usual plan takes effect between the ages of sixty and seventy. Older workers can work part-time or full-time every other week, so that regular hours are maintained during the gliding-out period. Under the Dutch Extra Leisure Scheme, the number of days off work each week increases from one half at age sixty to two and one half at age sixty-four.

Considering our present retirement mess, phased retirement plans should be worth considering. Where they have been used extensively they have nearly eliminated absenteeism among workers aged sixty to sixty-five. There has also been a considerable improvement in the older employees' standard of health. More important, the old Otto von Bismarck concept of age sixty-five and out has been changed to a more personal approach, allowing workers to glide more comfortably out of their working life.

Now for some good news. Sometimes it takes the scent of scandal or a pension system drowning in debt to make pensions into headline news. But it finally happened. In Executive Order 12071, issued July 12, 1978, President Carter established the President's Commission on Pension Policy. Although the commission was more than three years in coming, it is now in operation. The two-year study, financed by a $2 million grant from Congress, went into operation in 1979.

The commission's goal is to make an across-the-board assessment of the existing systems. The commission members will look at much that was covered in this chapter, including disability and survivor programs, noncoverage, ownership of pension funds, and will make an attempt to determine what the appropriate level of retirement income ought to be in this country.

The commission was reportedly established to represent the interests of the average person and to educate the public about retirement-income issues. The commission is made up of ten members and a chairman, C. Peter McColough, who is chairman of the board of Xerox Corporation. The other current members are:

Henry L. Bowden, a lawyer and former city attorney for Atlanta, Georgia;

John Bragg, a state representative from Tennessee;

Lisle C. Carter, Jr., president of the University of the District of Columbia;

James Clark, Jr., a state senator from Maryland;

Paul R. Dean, law professor and trustee of the United Mineworkers Health and Retirement Funds;

William Greenough, chairman and chief executive officer of the Teachers Insurance Annuity Association College Retirement Equities Fund;

Martha Griffiths, lawyer and former congresswoman;

Harvey Kapnick, chairman and chief executive officer of the accounting firm Arthur Anderson and Company;

John H. Lyons, president of the International Association of Bridge, Structural and Ornamental Iron Workers;

Dorothy W. Nelson, dean of the University of Southern California Law Center.

Almost from its inception the commission has had to come face to face with the graying of America. The members were told that by the year 2035 the number of people age sixty-five may increase by more than 120 percent. The commission's job is a tough one. The graying of America and the superthief—inflation—are at the heart of the problem we all face in developing a realistic federal policy on retirement income.

If you are interested, the commission meetings, most of which are held in Washington, D.C., are open to the public. For information write: C. Peter McColough, Chairman, President's Commission on Pension Policy, 736 Jackson Place, N.W., Washington, D.C. 20006, or call (202) 395-5132.

8 End of the Rainbow

America has often been promised good things that were never delivered. But the American public may have been promised a pot of gold that *cannot* be delivered. The bills for unpaid debt facing private pension plans pale before those that taxpayers will eventually have to pay to provide the incredibly generous retirement benefits for public employees. In fact, Social Security looks absolutely solvent compared to the public retirement plans.

In short, the pot at the end of the rainbow has never been full. The gold has been missing for years. Congressmen, governors, mayors, in fact every politician worthy of his name, has run up a colossal tab for public pensions that are frequently more generous than anyone in private business could imagine in his wildest dreams. It's the immense size of the unpaid public pension debt that is striking fear into the hearts and minds of elected politicians across the land.

Up to now the convenience of underfunding public retirement plans has allowed public officials to avoid making difficult and frequently unpopular increases in the budget. They have simply borrowed effortlessly from future taxes to ultimately finance the growing debt. After all, there's an almost irresistible temptation to avoid coming up with the hard cash on a prudently scheduled basis. Aren't the effects of the bloated debt likely to become apparent only after the present group of elected officials have left office?

In fact, many people are now aware of the ease with which pension debt can be prevented from ballooning most public operation budgets. A case in point: Oakland, California. In 1970, with a population of 360,000, it ranked thirty-ninth in size among all U.S. cities. By 1975 its population had shrunk to 330,000, falling to the forty-fifth largest city. Today the city has shrunk again, reducing even further its tax revenues. Normally this would be a problem for a city burdened with a debt-riddled public pension plan. Not for Oakland. The city faced a more pressing problem in the need to coordinate changing ethnic groups with state and local programs designed to emphasize the livability of the city. As a result, much of the cost of future pension obligations was simply ignored. Today the city would probably have to set aside five dollars for its pension debt for every four dollars of current payroll. A new employee with a salary of $20,000 would, in effect, cost the overburdened taxpayers $45,000 simply to catch up.

Now some more bad news. These figures are based on an outmoded assumption: an eight-percent inflation rate. If we assume that the current inflation rate of fourteen percent is here to stay, all bets are off. The new employee with the annual salary of $20,000 could now cost the city $75,000. In a classic example of miscalculation cities across America are making financial commitments faster than they are saving for the future. As a result, the aggregate of unfunded public-pension debt dwarfs the private plans—even though public pensions cover only thirty percent as many workers. The imbalance is so great, in fact, that out of every dollar of property taxes collected from Los Angeles homeowners, fifty cents goes to support the massive pension drain of the city's pension and retirement fund. Many of these same taxpayers are retired themselves and they are fighting soaring taxes and runaway inflation in a furious attempt to save their own homes.

The horrifying thing is that half the taxes simply will not do. The city of Los Angeles has already run up a scandalous $2.6 billion unfunded pension debt. Each man, woman, and child living in Los Angeles is already in debt almost $1,000—and they don't even know it.

e city's policemen and firemen provide a classic example
pensions gone mad. Such personnel can retire after
ty years of employment, regardless of age, with ulti-
ts as high as seventy percent of their last year's
nakes working almost a crime, punishable by stay-
Also, pension benefits are "indexed"—that is,
creased annually to match the full rise in the
c   result is that the future debt is already so
hi   n Los Angeles now admit it will take sixty
ye   hey start today.
ve Officer C. Erwin Piper, who has been
on t   an fifteen years, recently had his staff
prepa   s generous pension plan for police and
fireme   City Council.

"I'   ever gets out of committee," Piper
was quo   izing the difficulty of ever reducing
a public

"I hav o respect for politicians," he went on. "I think the
politician is a first-class prostitute because he has more interest
in getting reelected than he has respect for the institution he
serves."

But if you think the pension giveaway for police and firemen is outrageous, consider the plight of the California State
Teachers' Retirement System. They are struggling to avoid as
much red ink as possible. Covering more than 344,000 members, the system is the second largest public pension in the
state. The pension fund already faces an enormous $9 billion
debt, yet it is estimated that, on the basis of the state's existing
funding formula, the debt will reach $52 billion in only the next
twenty years.

"Like the Social Security fiasco, those teachers retiring
today will be pushing up daisies before the system collapses,"
a pension consultant, who asked that his name not be used,
explained. "It's the teachers who have just come into the system over the last few years who are going to be in trouble."

"How do you know?" I asked, pushing for a further explanation.

"Look at the school system yourself," he said. "They're
closing schools all over the state. Not just grammar schools
anymore, but now junior high schools and high schools them-

selves. The number of teachers is shrinking fast. Hell, at the rate they're going, by the end of the century most of the people in the plan will be drawing retirement checks, not working."

But the topper of them all has to be the trend still followed by governments in dealing with the pension crisis. In the case of the State Teachers' Retirement Plan, the California state legislature recently approved "benefit enrichments," which in some cases were substantial, for a pension plan that no one has yet found a way to make pay for the benefits already promised. Most public officials, not willing to recognize the mountain of past pension debt as *their* responsibility, have behaved like ostriches in a sandstorm. With their heads stuck in the sand, they have found it easy to give away something they don't have to pay for right now. Again—the case is similar to that of private plans—not all public pension plans are in trouble. Many are well managed—maybe as many as half the plans— but so little is known about the financial condition of public pension plans that no one really knows.

What is known is that the pot of gold has already disappeared on several occasions. The Pension Task Force report revealed that in 1972 the Hudson County, New Jersey, Employee Pension Fund was temporarily placed in receivership awaiting a bankruptcy ruling by the courts. Retirement benefits were also temporarily suspended in some of the local police and fire plans in Michigan, Arkansas, Mississippi, and Oklahoma. Some public pension plans in Colorado and Connecticut have reduced benefits to active workers in an effort to prevent their plans from going deeper into debt.

The crisis pervading public retirement plans is not new— it is just now becoming news.

What might come as a surprise to most of us is that federal, state, and local government pension plans are as diverse among themselves as they are different from private plans.

Back in 1975 there were 6,630 different state and local government plans and 67 different federal plans. The state and local plans covered 10.4 million members and the federal plans —excluding the military—covered another 2.8 million. Civil service, the federal government's primary retirement plan, covered all but about 183,000 active workers, who were covered under the remaining 66 plans.

The first local pension plan was established for the police force by the city of New York in 1857. Well before the first private plan was founded in 1875, the state and local retirement plans were off and running.

In 1911 Massachusetts developed the first state plans, but the real growth occurred, paradoxically, during the Second World War. Between 1941 and 1947, twenty-two states adopted pension plans. The federal civil service retirement plan dates from 1920.

The passage in 1974 of the Employee Retirement Income Security Act (ERISA—covered in Chapter 6) required that private plans meet tough federal standards. As usual, government plans were exempt from this landmark coverage, which was designed to protect and defend the average worker against the dangers of too little cash and too much fine print found in most retirement plans today.

With the passage of ERISA, information about private plans began to pour into Washington. But Congress was also becoming aware of massive problems that existed among public pension plans covering state and local government workers.

It is surprising that since 1857 very little information has ever been available concerning the operations or financial condition of most public pension plans. In 1978 the Committee of Education and Labor of the U.S. House of Representatives published the findings of a two-year study of public pension plans by the Pension Task Force of the committee. For the first time solid information was emerging. The report, which covered all federal plans and ninety-six percent of all state and local plans, contains a parade of shocking facts that reveal the far-ranging dimensions of the public pension disaster. On inadequate funding, the task force report concluded that plans "are not operated in accordance with the generally accepted financial and accounting procedures applicable to private plans."

In fact, thirty-three percent of all the public plans have not even had an actuarial valuation in over five years, with seventeen percent already operating on a pay-as-you-go basis. The remaining two-thirds, which base contribution rates partly on actuarial funding methods, are also in deep trouble. Nearly three-fourths may be seriously understating current and future costs of pay increases by ignoring the full effects of inflation.

Last year the General Accounting Office studied seventy-two state and local pension plans. The new study found that seventeen retirement plans haven't any reserves at all; only nineteen were putting aside as much as the 1974 federal law requires for private plans. With local and state pension liabilities continuing to balloon, the GAO warns that "Prospects for significant improvement in the foreseeable future aren't bright." Because, as the GAO points out, to start adequately funding the public retirement plans would mean big tax increases at a time when the voters have clearly indicated an unwillness to pay ever-higher tax bills.

This means, of course, that you and I, as taxpayers, are headed for big trouble. The public pension debt, quietly ascending behind a smokescreen of deceptive budgets, represents obligations of such enormous size that it will remain a burden for taxpayers well into the next century.

The details present a disquieting picture. Take the Federal Civil Service Retirement Plan. It has incurred staggering debt despite the fact that Washington has far greater ability to meet pension costs by virtue of the Fed's power to print money to meet obligations in nominal terms.

Between fiscal 1970 and 1976 the unfunded liabilities of the federal plan were reported to have more than doubled. During the same short period, payments of benefits to retirees more than tripled. State and local governments are not far behind. In 1977 the unpaid pension debt of Massachusetts was estimated at $7.6 billion, or $1,306 for each resident. In California, the figures are $13.6 billion, or $660 respectively; and for Illinois, $5.7 billion, or $507 for each resident.

With federal, state, and local public retirement plans having to deal with tremendous debt, the inescapable conclusion is that someone has been coasting along for a free ride. Sure enough, the Pension Task Force confirmed the shocking fact that those of us who work for private industry have allowed both the public worker and his government employer to enjoy a free ride at the expense of the taxpayers. How much of a free ride? The Pension Task Force study concludes that federal workers pay less than nineteen percent of the amount contributed by their employers and less than sixteen percent of the total revenue received by federal employee retirement plans. State and local workers perform a bit better, paying about half of what their employers pay, but contribute only thirty-five percent of the income received by the various state and local retirement systems. Read the table and weep.

Finances of Public Employee Retirement Systems
(In billions of dollars based on 1975 figures)

	EMPLOYER PAYS	EMPLOYEE PAYS
Federal	$13.2	$2.5
State/local	10.1	5.4

In defense of the civilian employees, the table lumps the 2.8 million members of the civil service retirement system with the 2.1 million active members of the military retirement system to reach 97.5 percent of all federal retirement plan members covered under these two plans. Since active members of the military do not make employee contributions to their "pay-as-you-go" plan, employee payments listed under federal plans are actually lower than might otherwise be expected. In fact, if we exclude the military from the figures, the picture for 1975 might look like this:

Finances of Public Employee Retirement Systems
(In billions of dollars based on 1975 figures)

	EMPLOYER PAYS	EMPLOYEE PAYS
Civil Service	$ 6.7	$2.5
State/local	10.1	5.4

Civil service workers as a whole now pay about thirty-seven percent of the amount contributed by their employers, but they account for only about twenty-seven percent of all the receipts of the federal employee retirement plans.

The free-ride approach to retirement, disability, and survivor benefits is so disturbing because public plans, by and large, were originally designed so that half the cost would be paid by the worker and half by his government employer. The principle of fifty-fifty, after all, guided the way Social Security was to operate for those workers covered in the private sector.

The actual situation as of 1980 falls far short of the original goal. On the basis of 1975 data, as previously indicated, federal civil service employees pay only twenty-seven percent, and state and local government employees pay a mere thirty-five percent of the total contributions into their respective plans.

As bad as that story may appear, you haven't heard the worst of it. That account is just about the contributions into the public retirement plans. Excluded is the full cost of the prospective vast benefit program already promised well into the next century. The best estimates—and these were made in 1977, long before the latest surge of inflation into the double-digit range—are that current contributions at best cover only two thirds of the ultimate retirement-benefit costs.

On the basis of this information, I have prepared the following table which I believe more accurately reflects the actual financial situation of public retirement plans. Again, let me say that the data falls short of being current by three to four years, which, with today's supercharged inflation, makes the numbers look even better than they actually are.

Finances of Public Employee Retirement Systems
(In billions of dollars based on 1975 figures)

	EMPLOYER PAYS	%	WORKER PAYS	%	ESTIMATED UNPAID DEBT	%	TOTAL ESTIMATED COST
Civil Service	$ 6.7	49	$ 2.5	18	$ 4.6	33	$13.8
State/local	10.1	44	5.4	23	7.7	33	23.2

So there you are. Federal workers, according to my figures, contribute only eighteen percent of the cost of their benefits. The federal government—that is, you and me as taxpayers—is expected to pay fully eighty-two percent of the future bills of the Civil Service Retirement System. Once again, the already overburdened federal taxpayer is left with nothing.

State and local workers do "better," covering less than a fourth—twenty-three percent—of the expected retirement bills, while taxpayers at state and local levels are expected to come up with seventy-seven percent of the money.

We can now compare and contrast public and private workers. Suppose you are about to retire from private industry —maybe you were covered under a private pension plan, or perhaps your own IRA or Keogh Plan provided the retirement coverage. You are faced with the task of putting together the various pieces that make up your total retirement-income picture. For instance, consider the most recent thoroughgoing studies, those conducted in 1974. Recall from the previous chapter on private plans that only one in four workers is likely to receive a private pension. The "lucky" workers covered by a private plan and Social Security might expect to receive as much as sixty percent of final pay if they are in the low-income wage category and as much as fifty percent if they are high-income wage earners then making over $25,000. Clearly these figures, based on 1974 data, are badly out of date. The recent soaring inflation has swollen one's final 1980 salary. Moreover, Social Security—under the 1977 amendments which will be covered in the next chapter—actually reduces benefits in relation to final pay as compared with 1974.

Therefore, my estimate—perhaps I should call it a guess— is that the average worker in private industry covered by a pension and Social Security at retirement age of sixty-five now receives about forty-five percent of his final preretirement pay. This is probably optimistic.

But, as you might have expected, public workers enjoy peaches and cream by comparison. Federal, state, and local governments are run, first and foremost, by politicians. By and large they do not want to face the political consequences of explicitly raising the cost of doing the public's business. So, as a rule, they do not. They give away a comprehensive retirement package today; but conveniently they gloss over the situation of those who are going to pay for it—your children.

Here's the story from the Pension Task Force study expressed in simple-to-understand terms. Using the average for all earning levels, including Social Security benefits where applicable, the Task Force estimated a very attractive outcome for almost a quarter (twenty-three percent) of state and local government workers retiring on January 1, 1976, at age sixty-five with thirty years of service. These lucky people could retire with a hefty seventy-five to ninety-nine percent of their preretirement net income replaced by a pension. That was the estimate in the *average* situation.

But there is a special place in retirement paradise for fully fifty percent of state and local government workers. The Pension Task Force found that, on average, this group could actually expect to receive *more* net income than they got from their former preretirement salary! Up to an incredible 124 percent, by all accounts. Twelve percent of these lucky state and local government workers could have received a "pay increase" at retirement of as much as twenty-five percent or more! It is a strange world indeed, where seemingly no one is paying the bills.

Even more worrisome than the flow of red ink in which our public pension plans are steeped is the news that many large public plans are now providing political slush funds to bail out the very people who help to create the debt in the first place.

"Political slush funds for the use of mayors and governors" who have access to "millions of dollars in ready cash just sitting around to be spent," tells the current story of many of the public pension plans, according to Representative John Erlenborn, R-Illinois, who addressed a national conference of pension-plan trustees and administrators in 1978.

Representative Erlenborn, referring to the Pension Task Force report, concluded that many such plans are "running afoul of not only federal regulations, but common sense."

Take the case of New York City. John Lindsay, while enjoying his glamorous passage as mayor, exchanged style for performance while transferring the bills to tomorrow. He fled to television—always his best environment in dealing with the public—just before the wormholes in the city's finances caused the roof to collapse. The city's financial picture had grown so bleak that only the federal government (for political reasons) or the city's pension plan (for political reasons) might buy the city's new issue of bailout bonds.

When Congress insisted that New York City must help itself if it was to receive additional bailout money from Washington, the local officials went directly to the largest pile of cash they could find—the five city pension funds. But this was not a new idea. City pension funds had already played a major role in keeping the city financially alive. By mid-1978 the pension funds were saddled with an estimated $2.65 billion in New York City securities and another almost $1 billion in Municipal Assistance Corporation (MAC) bonds.

The people who ran the city's retirement plans (the trustees) already knew what an appalling investment they were being "asked" to make in order to keep the city alive. Referring back to the point made in Chapter 6 on ERISA, the trustees were deeply concerned about their fiduciary responsibility. As it turned out, the congressional bail-out plan also conveniently excluded the trustees from their fiduciary responsibility when they bought the New York City bonds. And buy the bonds they did.

In their single-minded attempt to save the city from financial collapse, the public officials simply ignored the retirement security of city workers. With one third to one half of the five pension funds' assets invested in city bonds and securities, New York City's bankruptcy, if it should occur, could end the hopes and dreams of retirement security for thousands of city workers.

Representative Erlenborn contended that New York's "use of public pension funds to buy bonds which were virtually unmarketable anywhere else was a 'prime example' of how pension funds could be used for political purposes." Further, the Task Force Report found that "in many cases" the public officials who run public plans are "free to use pension funds as bargaining chips during contract negotiations with labor organizations." The irony in this is that the city's pension plans had already reached their limit in debt—debts yet to be paid by a near-bankrupt city—with no one left to protect the future retirement benefits of those covered by the city's pension plans.

To return to our congressman from Illinois. Along with other members of the Labor Standards Committee, he was going to introduce a bill in Congress to require public pension plans to meet the same tough federal standards required of private plans under ERISA. The bill was to be known as PERISA—Public Employee Retirement Income Security Act.

The fate of this legislation is still very much in doubt. Consider the behind-the-scenes political drama. It's something to behold as politicians permit a "policeman of the pension" to emerge in their own bureaucracy. "That's like asking the mayor to appoint a new police chief to investigate the mayor for mismanagement of public funds," I was told recently by a pension consultant. "Hell," he said, "everyone already knows the money is missing—or has been played around with—and creating PERISA would blow open the whole can of worms.

"What's causing the panic among politicians is that PERISA would probably force them to clean up their vesting and then begin to pay up the debt at a time when the taxpayers have already said no to higher taxes."

"What do you think will happen?" I asked.

"My guess is that eventually we'll get PERISA; the public will demand it. Already, from what I've seen, maybe only twenty to twenty-five percent of all public plans could technically meet ERISA's funding requirements."

Worse yet, the politicians may have trapped us into keeping the failing public-pension system we already have. Specifically, the passage of PERISA could force state and local governments to jump yet another hurdle in order to fund their pension plans. As the Pension Task Force reported, some state constitutions do not permit making changes in past or future accruals for currently covered workers. The report also warned that even though federal courts have not ruled yet, the Due Process Clause of the Fourteenth Amendment may protect future accruals for all public workers. (Accruals, in this case, means money set aside to pay the expected retirement benefits.)

Let's move on to the financing of public plans. A good focus is the operation of the Civil Service Retirement System, which provides federal employees with retirement, disability, and survivor benefits. Since federal employees are not covered by

Social Security, they contribute seven percent of their base salary and their employer—the federal government—matches the contribution to the plan. This seems to work the same as Social Security, where combined employer-employee contributions average about fourteen percent of salary.

But be careful! It is quite unlike Social Security in that the Treasury Department in 1971 began to make special additional payments to help meet the terrible costs of the program. These payments are in addition to the Treasury's annual level contributions to amortize new congressional enactments enlarging benefits. Such new benefits are to be amortized over a thirty-year period.

Interestingly, by fiscal 1975 these payments from the Treasury had already totaled twelve percent of the federal payroll. The expectation was that if the employee and employer continued to contribute seven percent of base salary, Treasury payments would soar to nineteen percent of payroll. That would be more than the amount originally designed to operate the system on employer-employee contributions alone.

So general tax revenues are actually already being used to bail out the civil service system. Washington has been tapping the general fund for the past nine years. All the while the public continues to debate whether public tax revenues should be used to finance parts of the Social Security program. This inconsistency is downright appalling. Aren't both benefit programs government mandated and controlled? The only conclusion I can reach is that when benefits become so incredibly generous that they threaten financial collapse of the program, general government tax revenues will almost inevitably be used to save the system from itself. If so, Social Security can't be far away from government handouts as well.

After several years of Alice-in-Wonderland reporting, the true condition of the federal government's own retirement system is finally coming to light. By the Feds' own figures as of September 30, 1979, the unfunded debt had reached the astronomical sum of $204 billion. (The debt is made up of $68 billion of outstanding public debt securities and $136 billion of assumed actuarial deficiency.) For the roughly 95 million Americans employed in the civilian labor force in 1978, the debt already represents an individual future liability of over $2,000.

But if you work the pension debt back against the 2.8 million civil-service employees yet to pay the bills, you find an amazing political blunder the likes of which the world has rarely seen. According to figures supplied by our own government, by 1979 the unpaid future pension and retirement-system debt amounted to the elephantine sum of $72,860 for each covered active civilian federal employee!

A 1977 civil service report, which circulated inside the agency but has only recently became public, discloses even more depressing news. The figures the government publishes, which you and I are supposed to accept, in fact greatly understate the actual long-range costs. This insiders' report states that federal employees currently pay less than one sixth of the projected costs of their pension benefits!

However, the visible payments are only a fraction of the true long-range costs of pension benefits. Each year workers earn pension benefits that will eventually be paid at retirement. The government, however, is ignoring the effects of inflation. As the kettle of inflation continues to boil, retirement benefits are sure to be pushed sky-high by the time many of the workers actually retire. Inflation also will give a hefty boost to the cost of pensions already granted. It will do so through the automatic cost-of-living adjustments that Congress first authorized in 1962.

These details convey quite a message. The "official" reports pouring out of Washington which continue to insist that projected costs of pensions are only fourteen percent of payroll should not be believed. If you can stand the pain, try this arithmetic: The civil service's own report projects these costs on several assumptions. One assumption is that if inflation averaged only four percent a year, the costs to pay for both the expected pension benefits and the gradual amortization of the debt would zoom to between forty-six and forty-eight cents of each dollar of salary. If the inflation rate were eight percent, the costs could easily equal $1.60 for every dollar of payroll. With the current rate of inflation almost fourteen percent, the numbers become too discouraging to print.

If the runaway costs for the Civil Service Retirement System were honestly charged against the agency, many critics contend that the already obvious would then become glaring:

it is often wasteful to use federal employees—at possibly higher pay levels than those provided by private enterprise—to do jobs that could be performed more cheaply by private taxpaying contractors.

Full retirement benefits for federal employees are payable under several options, each a combination of age and service. One option is age fifty-five with thirty years of service. Another is age sixty with twenty years of service—only ten years for a member of Congress. The benefit is figured on years of service and the average salary during the highest three consecutive years. Contrast this with the case of Social Security, which is based on years of coverage, but averages the maximum earnings base from 1951 to actual retirement. Once the retirement or survivor benefits are established, they are increased automatically twice a year to reflect accumulated changes in the consumer price index. For most civil service personnel, the transition from work to retirement is smooth and financially almost painless.

The transition from work to disability is also virtually painless for many federal workers. For starters, the definition of disability is considerably more liberal even than Social Security's. In fact, the civil service system pays benefits whenever an individual is unable to perform the duties of his or her usual occupation. Social Security's tighter definition requires that the individual must have a disability so severe that he is "unable to engage in any substantial employment which exists in the national economy, regardless of whether such work exists in the immediate area in which he lives, or whether a specific job vacancy exists for him, or whether he would be hired if he applied for work."

The extremely liberal eligibility requirements for disability benefits in the case of federal workers have caused a torrent of checks to pour out of Washington into over 323,000 pocketbooks. That's right—323,000—or an incredible one out of every eight active federal workers covered under the Civil Service Retirement System.

To be more specific, a federal worker can now claim full disability retirement if he has completed at least five years of service and meets the previously referred-to test of disability— namely, that he is unable for medical reasons to perform any part of his job. With a guaranteed monthly check for at least forty percent of the average of his highest salary for three years, the disabled worker is free to take a job in private industry and continue to collect federal benefits, unless for two consecutive years he earns eighty percent of what his old job now pays. Again, as is not the case with Social Security, which limits outside income on an annual basis, this rule can easily be manipulated by arranging a high salary one year and a low one the next.

Thomas Tinsley, deputy associate director for benefit policy in the Office of Personnel Management (formerly the U.S. Civil Service Commission) has taken quite a stand. He was quoted in a 1979 *Forbes* magazine article to the effect that "this [disability] system is no more milked than any any other system." In fact, according to Mr. Tinsley, the long-term disability program for civil service employees has often been used to clean out the ranks. By getting rid of unwanted employees through the disability program, the federal government can avoid the often messy and protracted battle that usually results when an employee is dismissed.

"If you're trying to reduce federal employment, you want to make it easier for more people to leave. Disability gives you room for turnover in the ranks. Every organization needs change, particularly when you get changes in national policy," Tinsley stated.

Using the disability program as a personnel management tool may be fine for the federal government since it has never learned how to terminate an unneeded worker. But it is incredibly costly for the taxpayers who ultimately must pay the benefits to a worker who is, in fact, not disabled. As if these shortcomings were not enough, the Civil Service Disability Program, like all government programs—including Social Security— suffers from a bad case of abuse. The malingerers are running wild, with little danger of being caught. "The only way I know," says Tinsley, "is when some neighbor gets mad at the guy and writes me a letter."

Because the government-created money used to pay for unnecessary disability benefits rolls in on an endless sea of red ink, the civil service system admits it often is not worth the time and effort to locate those who abuse the program. In fact, the people who operate the runaway disability program do not as yet cross-check their records with those of the Internal Revenue Service to see what disabled beneficiaries are actually earning.

The whole system has evolved into a nightmare where workers are encouraged to play games instead of work. Since the retirees are fully protected twice yearly by cost-of-living adjustments, their annual disability payments have zoomed to over $2 billion. And they keep rising fast. Civil service's *total* cash benefits came to only $1.7 billion back in 1966. Ten years later they rose to $8.6 billion. By 1978 the total outlays roared over $11 billion, with about twenty percent of that staggering amount going to support the overly generous disability benefit program.

Who is to blame? Not the workers who abuse the system —they are just taking advantage of a lenient situation. It's so lenient that the Office of Personnel Management (Civil Service) concedes that, shocking as it may be, only about half of the 323,000 ex-federal workers receiving disability checks are truly disabled. The blame for the civil service disability mess, which unfortunately is typical of many public retirement systems, clearly rests with Congress.

Out of touch with reality, Congress continues to spend colossal amounts of taxpayers' money to support an incredibly generous federal employee retirement system.

This point can be clearly understood by comparing the price tags for retirement systems. We need only match up the total benefits paid with the number of active workers who are supporting the program in each of the several worker categories. The results of this comparison, based on what information I could piece together, strikingly reveal the generosity of the federal government.

Again, let me state that this is only one of many approaches that can be used to determine the relative cost of retirement-benefit programs. What makes this comparison important is that both the graying of America and the future effects of inflation can best be illustrated using this arrangement. These are the factors that will greatly increase the cash benefits to an ever-expanding number of retirees at ever-higher levels of retirement income.

**Amount of Annual Cash Benefits Paid Compared by
Category
of Covered Worker Using 1978–79 Data Compiled by
Author**

	WORKERS COVERED	BENEFITS PAID	AVERAGE PER ACTIVE WORKER
Civil Service	2.8 million	$ 11 billion	$4,000
Social Security	85.0 million	103 billion	1,210
State/local	10.4 million	10 billion	960
Private	41.0 million	19 billion	460

Getting back to the civil service long-term disability program, let's look at what Congress has done to control the last word in bureaucratic horror stories. Nothing, that's what. Thomas Tinsley, the watchdog of federal pensions, concedes, "I haven't seen a bill even introduced into Congress to stop the games which are being played." The distressing fact is that the games will go on being played. Why? Because you and I, as taxpayers, will continue to support an overgenerous public retirement system even while private retirement benefits are likely to decline in terms of both actual dollars and then purchasing power. The reason for this dual effect is simple. The federal government—and it alone—can print money on top of its stiff taxes. State and local agencies, for their part, can effortlessly tax us and borrow their way into tomorrow. Put differently, you would have a better chance of buying gas at thirty-five cents a gallon than tightening the public pension spigot. Try this on for size—I quote directly from the National Planning Association's book on Pensions for Public Employees: "The bulk of public pension costs are ultimately paid by taxpayers. Although public employees contribute to their pensions, public plans are financed primarily by appropriations to the employing governmental unit. These appropriated funds come from tax revenues. Therefore, if increased funds are required to support pension expenditures, these funds will be collected from the entire taxpaying population."

That means you and me. For starters, we use the more conservative estimates. If *no* changes are made, the cost for the federal employment retirement plans will leap to thirty-one percent of payroll during the 1980s. (Again, that assumes the rate of inflation takes an unrealistic nosedive down to something like an annual rate of six percent for the decade!) However, even at thirty-one percent of payroll, the taxpayers will still pay *more* than the employee and his employing agency, who will contribute a total of only fourteen percent.

If you are a masochist, and I suppose you need to be to read this chapter, you will not be disheartened to learn that many of our state and local programs during this last decade have, like the federal plans, operated on this very principle, sinking into hopeless debt.

Even though state and local plans are not required to meet federal minimum funding requirements—they are virtually perpetual entities—there comes a time when the gigantic unfunded debt can no longer be ignored. Moreover, the debt represents a substantial claim on future tax revenues and it raises the very real possibility that future taxpayers might search for ways to avoid paying the already promised benefits.

In addition the massive unfunded pension debt can weaken investors' confidence in state and local bonds, forcing the payment of a higher interest rate. Even the unthinkable could occur—the unfunded debt could become so large that bond issues would be all but unmarketable.

But throwing the speeding debt into reverse creates major problems of its own. Assume we set out to develop a program for amortizing these unfunded pension debts over a forty-year period. We can be sure that major tax hikes and perhaps roaring inflation would all but eat us alive. If the $300 billion (the author's very conservative estimate of the total state and local public-pension debt) were amortized over forty years, the first year's payment would amount to about $2 billion.

Secondly, the annual repayments would automatically increase each year to reflect inflation's ballooning impact on future promised benefits. You guessed it: At the rate of inflation we would now have reached, the required benefit payments could increase to such an extent that funds would be unavailable for amortizing the original debt.

If we are going to be realistic about cutting back on the immense public pension debt, all state and local taxes—taken on average—will have to *increase* substantially over the foreseeable future.

But consider this: Even if you and I were willing to tolerate a tax hike of this magnitude, it is unlikely that the additional money would ever be paid into the pension fund because, like starving people, the governors and mayors would be drawn to this banquet of accumulated pile of cash to beef up nonpension programs. Such action could permanently halt any attempt to actually repay the long-accumulated pension debt.

Paying up on the unfunded pension debt of federal employee programs is another matter. Unless federal taxes are increased or nonpension expenditures are reduced by an amount equal to the funding payment, we would wind up with nothing more than paper-shuffling between the Treasury and the Civil Service Retirement Fund.

In effect, federal bookkeeping can, over the years, allow the debt to increase without its ever becoming a part of the unified federal budget. Only when the time has come to pay off the accrued benefits will the pension debt finally appear in the budget. The debt would then at last be recognized as more than a paper transaction; it would either have to be financed by more government borrowing or by increased taxes. In other words, in big government it is not enough to have a surplus in the Civil Service Retirement account; adequate funding necessitates a larger surplus or a smaller deficit in the total federal budget.

What can be done to save us, cried the three little pigs as the wolf banged on the door! If we ask the three little pigs, who have failed to put aside the cash to shore up the house, we can expect a report that will recommend future changes in benefits to future workers effective at a future date. Just such a conference was held last year in San Diego. The International Foundation of Employee Benefit Plans' annual public-employee conference surveyed over two hundred of its registrants and found that seven out of ten agreed that there is a "crisis" in public retirement plans.

Possible solutions from the people inside the house were:

— About fifty percent voted to delay normal retirement age, regardless of years of service.
— About fifty percent supported the merger of municipal and county pension plans with their state retirement systems in order to increase efficiency and economy.
— And finally, those attending the conference, by a majority that you wouldn't believe, said that they support pension reform for

"new (as yet unhired) employees" if that would build a heavy door and keep the wolf out.

Unhappily, the wolf has already broken the hinge; it is too late for patch-up reforms suggested by those currently expecting to receive the overly generous cash payments. Three major developments have triggered an avalanche of cash payouts: early retirement; irresponsible financial planning in some state and local governments; and poor coordination among Social Security and the over six thousand public plans.

Let's assume that there is no way we can keep the wolf from breaking down the door short of runaway taxes at the federal, state, and local levels. Certain steps should be taken now to get the monumental public disgrace out in the open, at least, and under control.

First, we should seek universal coverage of public employees under Social Security so that all workers can retire on a combination of both employer-sponsored retirement plans *and* Social Security.

Secondly, all public retirement plans should be required to meet the tough federal standards contained in the proposed Public Employee Retirement Income Security Act—PERISA. Until this law is effective, the plans should be required to meet the ERISA-like actuarial, accounting, reporting, disclosure, and fiduciary standards. (Estimates today are that perhaps only twenty to twenty-five percent of all public plans could technically meet ERISA's funding requirements, while a majority of the plans would fail to meet ERISA's overall standards.)

Finally, once the extent of the vast unfunded pension debt is known, each state and local government must chop back the overly generous cash benefits, reduce the retirement benefit as a percentage of preretirement income, and report honestly to their constituents the full cost of the public retirement systems now in place.

For, in the final analysis, it is the long-suffering taxpayers who must decide how much of their future income they want to mortgage solely for the benefit of the public-employee retirement system.

9 Social Insecurity

The Ponzi scheme is based on the real life adventures of the Boston swindler Charles (Carlo) Ponzi. He entered America through the Port of New York in 1903 at the age of twenty, an Italian immigrant, penniless and unable to speak English. By 1920 he had moved to Boston, and, without business associates or money, had established a business with the imposing name of Securities Exchange Company.

He had discovered that International Reply Coupons could be purchased from post offices and redeemed in America for a profit of as much as two hundred percent, depending on the then international exchange rate. The reply coupons were originally established as a way to prepay postage for relatives or friends, many living just above the poverty level and often hard pressed to come up with the extra few cents needed to reply to the letters from overseas.

The fact that reply coupons were seldom used by the public and could only be redeemed for postage stamps did not deter Ponzi; he was set to make millions from an idea that appeared to make sense on paper.

At a time when the Boston banks were paying four percent annual interest, Ponzi's idea was to accept "investments" from the public redeemable in only ninety days at fifty percent interest. Soon the money literally poured into the small office of the

Securities Exchange Company. By some estimates as much as $15 million flowed into the scheme from thousands of small investors before the collapse of Ponzi's company within the first year of its operation.

The idea would work, Ponzi knew, only so long as the "interest earned" was paid out of new money from subsequent investors. Like a giant chain letter, the plan succeeded beyond his wildest dreams as more and more money came in to cover the maturing ninety-day notes.

As the pyramid grew, the pile of cash became so large that the bottom of the pyramid began to crumble. When Ponzi was finally forced to turn away the first investors empty-handed, the whole scheme toppled. The lesson that the unhappy investors learned was that to profit from a Ponzi scheme, it is not enough to be the first one in; you have to be the first one out as well.

The similarity between Ponzi's Securities Exchange Company and America's Social Security system is both alarming and real. To profit most from the Ponzi scheme, as well as from Social Security, it is not enough to be the first one in. You need to be the first one out as well. Those workers who retired into the system in the 1940s received virtually all of their retirement benefits from active workers paying into the system. They had redeemed their retirement benefits with one or two small deposits. During the 1940s and 1950s, retirees qualified for future retirement benefits not on the basis of what they had paid into the system, but only on the basis of the benefit schedules set by Congress.

Almost from Social Security's inception, Congress realized the electoral wisdom of offering immediate benefits regardless of individual contributions, and of frequently raising benefits or including coverage for new segments of our population while omitting to raise taxes. Since the individual benefits paid out were no longer directly related to each worker's payroll taxes, the system quickly became a pay-as-you-go plan. Therefore, over the years, each age group has come to depend for its retirement benefits on the forced contributions of those Americans still at work.

Getting the system back to solid ground requires that Congress go into reverse: cut back benefits and substantially raise taxes to pay for the future expenses. Proposals to save the system by cutting back benefits and raising taxes have, however, brought angry outcries from all across America, from spokesmen for the aged, employers, unions, and even from lawmakers who are feeling the heat from their constituents.

So, for the last forty years, things have remained pretty much the same.

To better understand the Social Security system today, let's go back and follow its developments over the last four decades.

As early as 1920 the National Civil Service Retirement System for federal employees was established to provide "income maintenance." The plan to provide benefits to retiring workers where none had existed before became so successful that by the 1930s income maintenance for both the unemployed and the aged became a pressing national issue.

In November 1934 President Roosevelt stated, "What I am seeking is the abolition of relief altogether. I cannot say so out loud yet, but I hope to be able to substitute work for relief." The Social Security Act of 1935 was a positive step in that direction, since the benefits would be prepaid from workers' earnings.

Social Security was conceived and established in a time of American innocence and unbounded faith in the future. The Great Depression was finally coming under control and Congress wanted to begin rebuilding government support for what was then known as old-age assistance. The original purpose of Social Security was to prevent "old-age dependency." The program started out simply to provide retirement benefits to all Americans so that, as now, the Social Security payments could provide a basic level of support during retirement. What many Americans may not know is that Social Security payments began on an "individual equity" account system. The idea, old-fashioned as it may seem, was that every worker should get back at least as much as he put into the plan from a trust account which was established in his name.

The idea of "individual equity" was often stressed and actually felt to be crucial to obtaining public acceptance of a compulsory program. By the time the system went into operation on January 1, 1937, the plain, simple truth was finally told —that there really was no individual account, no guarantee that any money paid into the system would ever be returned to the worker, and that Congress could change the benefits at any time.

Even though Social Security has evolved into a broad-based welfare plan, the four basic principles of the original 1935 act have survived nearly intact over the intervening years.

— Benefits are to be financed by a special tax on wages, paid in equal parts by the employee and the employer.
— The payroll tax is set at a flat rate, up to a maximum amount of earnings.
— Benefits are only to be viewed as a partial replacement of wages.
— To qualify for benefits, a covered worker has to reach a certain age and pass an earnings test. Unlike those of welfare, the Social Security benefits are not based on assets or unearned income, but the earnings test does limit the amount of "earnings" allowable for a retiree.

The Social Security Act established three programs: Old Age Assistance, Unemployment Insurance, and Public Assistance programs. The first of these programs has become dominant and today Social Security is commonly referred to as the Old Age and Survivors Plan.

Since its inception the system has reached out to include a host of new benefits, moving farther away from the public's conception of the original plan created to prevent "old-age dependency."

As a result the entire program known as Social Security has been surrounded by powerful myths and by an almost complete lack of understanding as to how the system operates.

Try this true/false quiz:

T ☐ F☐ Payroll deductions go directly into the Social Security fund.
T ☐ F☐ The deductions from your paycheck will be used to pay your retirement benefits.
T ☐ F☐ It is an insurance scheme whereby individual contributions are tied to future benefits according to the payments into the system.
T ☐ F☐ Actual benefits paid are not related to need.
T ☐ F☐ Most recipients are poor and in need of additional assistance.

If you answered false to each question, you receive a perfect score. For most Americans, however, the answers may be as interesting as the questions, since almost all of our basic assumptions about Social Security are untrue.

The first question is false since Social Security taxes from your paycheck, and your employer's tax as well, go into the general fund. The trust funds are not a pile of cash or real wealth of any kind. They are simply an item on the balance sheet of the government books. Only pieces of paper, simply an IOU from the Treasury to the Social Security system. The government takes your Social Security tax payments and spends them partly on Social Security, but also on other things.

The trust fund "assets" originally designed to protect our future retirement benefits will have been reduced to less than thirty percent of the annual cash outlay for 1979. The real "assets" of the trust fund are Social Security's authority to collect taxes in the future. The future then is secured by a promise to pay.

The second question is false because we no longer have an individual account. In fact, the money received from your paycheck deductions is used to pay benefits for current Social Security recipients.

The third question is false since there is no insurance element in the Social Security system, despite the fact that many still cling to this idea. The system, in all its glory, has been reduced to a simple pay-as-you-go benefit plan. Future benefits are also unknown since they may, and usually are, changed by each succeeding Congress.

The fourth question is also false since, to a large extent, Social Security payments are based on need, with a greater percentage of preretirement pay replaced for low wage-earners than for others. Congress based many of its decisions on the belief that many elderly simply need more money to maintain a basic standard of living. Minimum benefit levels have for years been based on individual need, whether the recipient is single or married, or disabled and unable to work.

The last question is false since Social Security is paid to every covered worker regardless of financial circumstances.

One reason we know so little about Social Security today is that the original system was presented to the American public as a means of providing for their own retirement through individual monthly contributions. The actual benefits would then be paid out of the trust fund which had collected the money during their working lives. What we have today is exactly the opposite of President Roosevelt's original conception.

We have moved from the old to the young the burden not only of old-age retirement, but a host of other socially desirable welfare benefits for everyone. This means that once we run into a depression or a crisis, whether caused by the falling birthrate or by inflation, there will be no way out. For today, at any rate, we are caught in a never-ending cycle of using one generation to pay for the benefits of another. It simply is not possible even to borrow the amount of money that would be required to balance the system, estimated to be over $4 trillion. The debt has become too great to even imagine.

Almost everyone now agrees that the current system is out of control; in fact it is so large and so incredibly complex that it is not certain if anyone really knows what is happening today, let alone what will transpire over the next few years. One thing that does seem certain is that Social Security will continue to be the largest single tax many Americans will pay in their lifetime.

Some people believe that the future can be told from the past. If that is so, a look at the past can easily portend a shrinking purse and an unremitting need.

Since we are talking about money, yours and mine, let's take a look at what has been taken from our paychecks to support the Social Security system.

When the plan was put into effect in 1937, the original payroll tax imposed on the worker was only one percent up to a maximum of $30 per year, slowly moving up to a maximum payroll tax of $95 per year by 1957.

Thus, even though Social Security's income from payroll taxes remained almost level over the first twenty years (the maximum $30 tax remained in effect until 1950), averaging only $42 per year, the benefits were expanded almost as fast as Congress could seek out and find new voters. They included payments to workers' spouses, children, children disabled before age eighteen, disabled workers age fifty to age sixty-four, and survivors' benefits to spouses, divorced and/or dependent, and many others too numerous to list here.

For it was in 1950 that politics began to overpower Social Security's entire operation. Congress had become alarmed that the "insurance system"—even the lawmakers asked us to believe there was insurance when in fact there was none—was not taking over the country's welfare burden fast enough.

Congress remedied that situation by deliberately shifting needy people from welfare to Social Security. They wanted to help the few who had retired and at the same time make it easier for more workers to qualify for benefits. After all, during the first fifteen years of its life the system paid out very little in benefits since most Americans paying into the system had yet to retire.

Therefore, in addition to transforming Social Security into a welfare/retirement program, Congress more than doubled the size of the minimum pension for retired workers and cut back substantially the number of years of covered work required for eligibility.

The Senate Finance Committee reported that the bill was designed "to decrease the number of people who will have to depend on the assistance program." The net effect of the bill, however, was to plunder the system, since it became necessary to tap the Social Security trust fund for millions of people who were covered but who had made, at best, only token contributions to the system.

The burden on the trust fund of paying these unearned benefits, at a time when Congress was unable or unwilling to raise payroll taxes, has proved a major reason why the Social Security program presently is near collapse.

During the next ten years—1957 to 1967—expanded benefits again began to pour out of Washington, eating into the system's finances at such a rate that Congress finally had no choice but to resort to the steep upward climb of payroll taxes.

The new benefits during this period included disability payments for workers, who are covered at any age; dependent coverage for full-time college students from eighteen to twenty-one; disability benefits for a wife, divorced or not; and the right of a female worker to retirement benefits at age sixty-two. Unfortunately, though Congress recognized many of these legitimate needs, it was still unwilling to raise Social Security taxes enough to pay for many of the new benefits.

By 1967, thirty years into the program, the maximum tax was only $290 on the first $6,600 of annual salary, known as the "taxable wage base." Over this ten-year span the total maximum tax an employee could have paid was $1,541, or an average yearly payroll tax of only $154.

Only during the last ten years—1967 to 1977—has the giant Ponzi plan appeared to stumble and falter under the weight of paying out a multitude of benefits with fewer and fewer workers pumping the life-saving money back into the system. Old Charlie Ponzi was right, of course. Only so much cash can be shoved out the front door without more and more money coming in the back door.

By 1977, a full forty years into the program, everyone, it seems, was collecting so many different benefits, in addition to a simple retirement income check, that the cash was pouring out the front door into the pockets of over thirty-four million Americans at the incredible rate of over $100 billion a year.

The ghost of Charlie Ponzi had finally come back to haunt the system. Congress simply had to face the reality that the bill for decades of incredible mismanagement was coming due. And so with outright bankruptcy staring them in the face, our lawmakers created their latest masterpiece, the Social Security Amendments of 1977 (PL 95-216).

Ignoring their past mistakes in long-range pension planning, the legislators proudly announced that they had put the system on solid ground for the rest of this century.

In 1950 the Senate and House committees predicted that "fifty years hence, estimated benefit payments will be almost $12 billion per year." In actual practice the annual cost of cash benefits topped $100 billion in only twenty-seven years. The new long-range forecasts are more realistic. In spite of the sharp payroll-tax hikes scheduled in the future and the slash in already promised benefits, the Department of the Treasury's forecast is that Social Security will run a deficit of $1.5 trillion between 1979 and 2053. Hardly a system on solid ground for the rest of this century.

As usual, deception was foremost in the minds of Congress when it came time to explain their actions to the folks back home. After all, the legislators must have reasoned, they had saved the monster they had created from devouring itself, and

171

that was all the voters really needed to know. As a result the American public has never fully understood the extent to which Congress raised the payroll taxes over the next decade and reduced the future benefits.

The revolt against soaring payroll taxes has been triggered by the incredible future increases now mandated by Congress. The period from 1977 to 1981 is a good example. Back in 1977, the maximum annual employee tax was only $926. By 1981, under present law, the tax will leap to $1,975, an increase of over $1,000 or 113 percent in only four years.

Over the last decade alone, Social Security taxes have increased a whopping 425 percent, jumping from $374 in 1970 to $1,588 in 1980. By 1987 Social Security will represent nearly fourteen percent of payroll compared to less than two percent in 1940. Today, only the federal income tax is higher than Social Security, but the day is fast approaching when, for many of us, Social Security will indeed be the highest tax we will pay each year.

But let's assume that we can make a stab at what might happen over the next ten years, from 1977 to 1987.

By 1987, now fifty years into the program, the worker's maximum tax would be an incredible $3,046 on a salary of $42,600, moving up from $1,071 on a salary of $17,700 at the start of the decade.

To better focus in on the past forty years, as well as to peek into the future, let's look at a simple money graph. This is the same money you would see if you sat at Social Security's front door over the years and counted the cash.

The graph on the following page is compiled from published Social Security tax rates, with the author's best estimate beyond 1987 where the actual Social Security tax rates are yet to be determined.

In spite of the fact that Social Security taxes have already risen much faster than inflation, the cost of living, or government spending in general, it has now become clear to almost everyone that the sheer magnitude of the tax increases planned over the next twenty years could bring the entire system, as we know it today, crumbling down.

Worse yet is the fact that you must use what is left of your paycheck to cover Social Security taxes after you pay your

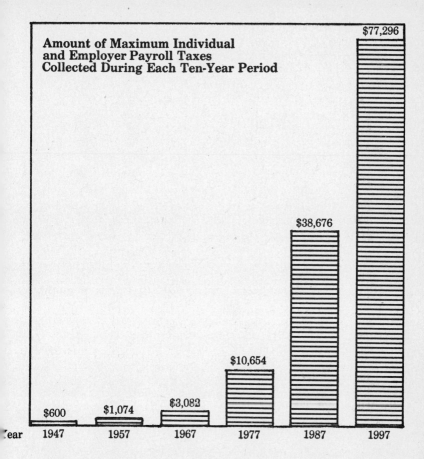

**Amount of Maximum Individual
and Employer Payroll Taxes
Collected During Each Ten-Year Period**

$600	$1,074	$3,082	$10,654	$38,676	$77,296
1947	1957	1967	1977	1987	1997

Year

income tax. Unlike any private or company retirement plan,
Social Security tax comes after Uncle Sam and your state government take their big bite out of your gross pay.

This calls for a brief reference to the perverse operation of
income tax in an inflationary environment. When the federal
income tax was legalized back in 1913, it was thought of only
as a one or two percent affair, and then only with respect to the
true fat cats in the country. The workingman was never expected to pay such a tax. In any case, tax rates graduated with
respect to income—they call it a "progressive" tax because that

YEAR	YEARLY WAGE SUBJECT TO TAX	MAXIMUM TAX (BOTH EMPLOYER AND EMPLOYEE MUST PAY THIS AMOUNT)
1937–49	$3,000	$30.00
1950	3,000	45.00
1951–53	3,600	54.00
1954	3,600	72.00
1955–56	4,200	84.00
1957–58	4,200	94.50
1959	4,800	120.00
1960–61	4,800	144.00
1962	4,800	150.00
1963–65	4,800	174.00
1966	6,600	277.20
1967	6,600	290.40
1968	7,800	343.20
1969–70	7,800	374.40
1971	7,800	405.60
1972	9,000	468.00
1973	10,800	631.80
1974	13,200	772.20
1975	14,100	824.85
1976	15,300	895.05
1977	16,500	926.25
1978	17,700	1,070.85
1979	22,900	1,403.77
1980	25,900	1,587.67
1981	29,700	1,975.05
1982	31,800	2,130.60
1983	33,900	2,271.30
1984	36,000	2,412.00
1985	38,100	2,686.05
1986	40,200	2,874.30
1987	42,600	3,045.90

Source: Research Institute of America

makes it look better—were supposed to operate in a special way. If your income was twice mine, you were supposed to pay more tax—not necessarily twice as much. A higher or graduated tax rate was supposed to apply to differences in real income, or the purchasing power of money income.

Until recently hardly any attention was paid to the income-tax aspect of funny-money income. Whole textbooks on taxation were written with no more than one footnote on the matter of what should happen under inflation. Differences in income were supposed to represent differences in the power to buy—differences in real income.

Then came the inflationists in Washington. The year 1965 is as good a starting point as any. Huge budget deficits and enormous printings of new money became the rule. Ballooning prices started hitting us where it hurts. Incomes doubled in devalued dollars. But they stayed almost unchanged in purchasing-power terms. Graduated income-tax rates were not supposed to be applied to funny-money income. But do you think the politicians were guided by the basic philosophy of income tax? No way! They couldn't resist making a fast buck. At first their excuse was that inflation would soon go away. This or that new federal program was supposed to prick the inflation balloon. Then, when the loot came rolling in thick and fast, the politicians' pitch was that the government had all these programs, and it couldn't afford any drop in tax revenues.

Few Americans got wise to how they were being taken by the majority of politicians. But north of the border people were more alert. They raised a big fuss, threatening incumbents with the sack. So in 1973 Canadians stopped government cheating behind the skirts of inflation. The Canadian income tax was "indexed." Each year the money you report to the government on your tax return is reduced by that year's inflation rate. So Canadians either aren't bumped into higher tax brackets at all, or are hit gradually as their real income rises slowly.

Why did the Canadians move in the right direction back in 1973? It wasn't because their inflation rate was much worse than ours. The fair thing was done because a vocal minority raised a big fuss, played up the cheating that occurs when government fails to adjust nominal income for inflation that the government itself causes.

175

In our own country, all we get is an occasional token change to keep people quiet. For most of the American middle class, and above all in nearly every case where there's a working wife, the cheating of the taxpayer under income tax is shamefully high. The term for it is "bracket creep." Inflation unjustly shoves him into higher tax brackets.

The facts speak for themselves. Consider what happened in the decade ending in 1976. The average wage rose by some seventy-seven percent and the consumer price index moved upward by about seventy-five percent. (Note that typical wages barely kept pace with zooming prices.) That is, American workers experienced no measurable rise in their real or purchasing-power income. Yet, because of the graduated tax tables quietly used by the grabbing feds, the total income-tax burden at the federal level could have increased by a gigantic 144 percent, while the maximum Social Security tax rose by a colossal 310 percent.

And don't forget that graduated income tax also hits you in many states—the big state-income-taxers being California, New York, Massachusetts, and Wisconsin.

During the next ten years the government income-tax men and the Social Security tax collectors are set to reap an unjust reward, since most of us will receive actually worthless salary increases that will automatically push us into the higher tax brackets.

Consider, as we review our future tax planning, how from the government's angle everything seems to fit neatly together, as our annual taxable salary for Social Security increases from the current maximum of $25,900 to the top figure in 1987 of $42,600. First we will be caught in the income-tax spiral. The federal income-tax levy will leap upwards for a husband and wife using a joint return, from about twenty-eight percent (the income tax on the last few dollars of income) to a whopping forty-two percent on their latest last few dollars of income.

Unless we have all gone mad or someone has figured out a new way to add and subtract, from 1980 to 1987 personal income taxs rates could then go up (under this example) about fifty-five percent. Social Security taxes could concurrently zoom by ninety-five percent. In real dollars, then, both the personal income tax and the Social Security tax could be going up much faster than our real dollar salary.

But if we are dismayed as typical employees, consider this: If we are self-employed—say we are one of the millions of Americans who operate small businesses throughout the land —we could be faced in 1987 with a Social Security tax of $4,000 for which we might have to earn a salary of $5,700 just to have enough left over after income taxes to pay the Social Security tax. The self-employed taxpayer will now clearly see that he is spending a fantastic 13.5 percent of his total income just to pay for Social Security.

Clearly something must be done about this variation of Catch-22. If we don't do something, the income-tax collector and Social Security people will force us onto the graduated tax tables as our inflated salaries continue to increase over the years.

In defense of Social Security it must be said that the benefits we eventually receive are tax-free. For most other retirement plans, whose annual contributions are tax-deductible, the benefits are not taxable until the worker draws retirement pay. The advantages of these private or employer-sponsored retirement plans are twofold: The money saved for retirement grows much faster when the contributions and reinvested interest on the contributions are tax-deferred, and when benefits are actually received, it is expected that the retiree will also gain in that he will be in a much lower income-tax bracket than he was during his working years.

The advantages of private plans are unlikely to be offered to those of us who pay Social Security taxes. The cost to the government is simply too high. It has been estimated that in fiscal year 1978, approved private retirement plans that delay income taxes until retirement cost the government about $10 billion in lost tax revenue.

There's an interesting sidelight to Social Security, the benefits from which are now received tax free: In the early days of the program, the Treasury Department ruled that funds received in retirement were a "gratuity."

There is now, however, a growing belief that at least half of the benefit we receive from Social Security should be treated as taxable income. In late 1979 the Social Security Advisory

Council voted ten to one to recommend to Congress that they adopt this change. The taxation of benefits can prove complicated, but the general theory is that the portion of the Social Security benefit that would become taxable is the part paid for, in effect, by your employer. The Council estimates that change will reflect the way inflation pushes ordinary people into higher tax brackets so that about forty-four percent of the people who receive benefits will have enough taxable income to be affected. If, on the other hand, you are among the four in ten who have adequately saved for your retirement despite unfair income taxes under inflation, the Council estimates that the additional tax revenue pouring into the Treasury will amount to as much as $1.5 billion to $2 billion each year. In the years to come this opportunity to dip into your wallet on so massive a scale may be hard for Congress to resist.

Before you throw up your hands, stick your head out the window, and scream, "I won't take it anymore," one final note is in order regarding the money collected by our friends at Social Security. It seems that one of the major reasons our retirement benefits are in deep trouble today is that the payroll taxes received by Social Security are not used exclusively for old-age benefits. In 1978 the payroll tax was 6.05 percent, *but* just under one third of the total money collected went to support the disability and hospital insurance programs. In 1987 it is projected by Social Security that of the total tax of 7.15 percent, only 4.90 percent will go to the old-age retirement account and 2.25 percent to the disability and hospital insurance fund.

These two programs are in no way related to the old-age assistance and retirement program, but they continue to be paid for inside a program that was originally sold, and is still known, as a means of providing financial assistance to retired workers.

Now comes the question most Americans are asking today as they cut and scrape to set aside the huge payroll taxes each month: With all this money flowing into Social Security, why is the system coming apart at the seams? Simply put, the system has been asked by Congress over the years to pay out an increasing variety of benefits, paid for by a decreasing number of workers, on a scale that not even a Ponzi plan could support.

If you can visualize Social Security as a giant balance scale, you might be able to see workers putting money on the left side and recipients taking money off the right side. As long as the scale remains in balance, on a pay-as-you-go basis, the system can survive. But now the scale is rapidly tilting to the right side as more and more workers stop putting money on the scales and instead move to the right to receive benefit checks. To get a better idea of how many people are on each side of the balance scale, we need to know how many workers are paying money into the system for each recipient receiving a benefit. Based on the information available today, there are about thirty-one pensioners for every one hundred active workers. By 2025 the Social Security Administration believes there will be fifty-one pensioners for every one hundred active workers. As with most statistics surrounding Social Security in the past, these are probably overly optimistic and the actual two-to-one ratio will most likely occur well before the year 2025.

A simple chart can quickly show the speed with which the balance scale is tilting toward the incomprehensible vision of each active worker supporting his or her own parents.

The basic reason so many Americans are crowding over to the right side of the balance scales is the fundamental changes occurring in the country's demographics. In all fairness to Social Security, anticipating the graying of America which has occurred over the last forty years would have been impossible. Now, almost before the system's disbelieving eyes, America is emerging as a country whose population is rapidly graying toward Social Security retirement checks at the same time the baby boom is turning into a definite baby bust.

The decreasing birthrate is not good news for Social Security. It has already had a major impact on the number of workers paying into the system.

For example, in 1950 the number of births per 1,000 women fifteen to forty-four years old was 106. By 1970 this had dropped to only eighty-eight, and by 1980 it is projected to be less than sixty-seven per 1,000 women. From these limited and admittedly sketchy details, it becomes clear that over the last thirty years the birthrate may have fallen by as much as sixty-three percent. The practical results for Social Security are that a great many of the workers who were expected to climb on the

Estimated Number of Workers Paying into Social Security for Every Pensioner Receiving Benefits under Old-age, Survivors, and Disability Programs

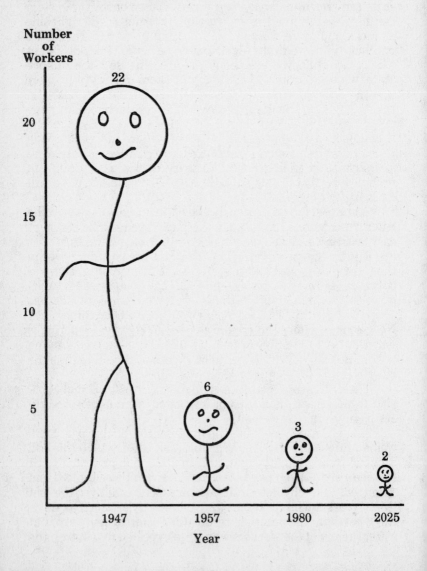

left-hand side of the scales and start paying billions of dollars into the system simply do not exist.

On the other hand, the number of workers waiting to collect their monthly checks is rapidly rising because significant improvements have been made in such areas as health care, childhood-disease control, childbirth, and nutrition. The longer life span has spawned a new generation of active retired Americans, creating vast new markets for the travel, recreation, and craft industries.

The graying of America has now reached almost epidemic proportions. According to the Department of Commerce, when Social Security essentially began paying benefits in 1940 only 6.8 percent of the population was age sixty-five or over, a mere nine million people. By 1980 it is projected that 11.2 percent of the population will be sixty-five or over, increasing to twenty-five million. And by 1990 it is projected to be 12.2 percent, with over thirty million people age sixty-five and older.

To make matters worse from Social Security's standpoint, Americans are retiring in greater numbers at age sixty-five with many electing to receive their monthly checks as early as age sixty-two.

From a cash standpoint, the system will now be forced to pay out billions of dollars in benefits to an increasing number of retirees, who are both retiring earlier and living longer.

On top of all this, inflation has hit the system with the same force with which it has hit your own paycheck. To compensate for inflation, Congress intended to maintain the real value of retirement benefits by having monthly retirement checks increase automatically as the cost-of-living index went up. As it turned out, the final 1972 amendment was so complicated that it compensated for inflation by gearing benefits to a formula that paid retired workers beyond what Congress had intended.

For example, if the system set out to replace fifty percent of preretirement pay, and if the final salary was $800 per month, the worker should receive a monthly benefit check of $400. Now if the cost of living increased ten percent, the retiree's benefit might rise to fifty-five percent of his preretirement salary. What actually happened was that the new benefit went up fifty-five percent on his new wage base of $880 per month. The retirement check would then be fifty-five percent of that figure, or $484 per month, a twenty-one percent increase in retirement benefits against a rise of only ten percent in the cost of living.

In the mystical language of the Social Security system, this was called "overindexing." Whatever it is called, this one flaw in the way the system calculated retirement benefits, because of the sheer size of the system, resulted in "overpayments" and billions of dollars of "losses" that were not anticipated. This "error" in the law has been widely publicized as a major reason the system is sliding toward bankruptcy.

Symptomatic of the illness affecting Social Security is the way Congress, over a period of several years, simply sat on its hands while massive amounts of money leaked out of the system. An important feature of the 1977 legislation, we are now told, was the amazing feat of "decoupling" which will allow benefits for retired workers to continue to rise by the increase in the cost of living—but no higher—and still eliminate much of the previously estimated future deficit.

Now let's look at the benefits which have been paid out and those we can still expect to receive from the system. Benefits are a "sometime thing," rapidly expanding to cover new beneficiaries and, paradoxically, both increasing and decreasing for retirees. In the original law, benefits were never intended to remain constant, and amendments to the system since the original Act was passed in 1935 have occurred in 1939, 1946, 1950, 1952, 1954, 1956, 1958, 1960, 1961, 1965, 1967, 1969, 1972, and 1974, and the latest—and one of the most comprehensive—amendments was passed in 1977.

According to Social Security, as of June 1977 about 62.8 percent of the beneficiaries who receive monthly benefits were retired workers and their dependents, 14.2 percent were disabled workers and their dependents, and twenty-three percent were survivors and others.

But, as is often the case, it is what the Social Security report does not say that illustrates the way the system has really changed over the years—into a social-welfare benefit program wherein over fifty percent of all recipients are children and young adults under the age of thirty.

At this point a good question might be: Has Social Security, in spite of its massive welfare-oriented objectives, provided an equitable retirement plan?

The answer is yes and no.

Many critics of the system have often said, "Give me the tax money so I can invest it in my own retirement plan. I know I can do better." If we remember old Charlie Ponzi's law—first in, first out—most Americans retiring by 1987 could not.

For example, assume a worker entered the system at the inception of Social Security in 1937 and after forty years retired at age sixty-five in 1977. If he and his employer paid the maximum payroll taxes each year, he could retire into a pot of gold. The maximum taxes paid over this forty-year period would have been about $15,500. The maximum annual retirement income for the worker and dependent spouse, age sixty-five, would have been about $8,400. In other words, in less than two years, ignoring inflation, he could have recovered all the taxes he and his employer had paid over the previous forty years!

However, suppose the worker in 1937 put the same tax money each year into a private retirement account where interest was compounded tax free. By 1977 the savings could have amounted to $31,865. He might then have purchased a lifetime annuity (ten years certain) for about $277 per month versus his family Social Security benefit of $700 per month.

From this simple example you can see that over the last forty years the Social Security taxes should have been increased by more than five hundred percent just to purchase a lifetime income of $700 per month.

Now let's look at the next example: a worker entering the system in 1947 and retiring at age sixty-five in 1987. Again we assume that the worker and his employer paid the maximum payroll taxes each year, and, as a result, the worker is entitled to receive the maximum retirement benefit.

The payroll taxes paid over this forty-year period would total about $53,500, or three and one half times more than those of the worker who retired only ten years earlier. The maximum yearly benefit for the couple would also be up from $8,400 to $14,400, reflecting the increase in the cost of living and, presumably, the higher payroll tax bill. For the couple retiring in 1987, it will now take them almost four years to recover the taxes paid over the previous forty years.

Again, if we assume the worker in 1947 put the same tax money each year into a private retirement account where the interest was compounded tax free, by 1987 the account could have accumulated to about $111,824. If an annuity were then purchased (at today's rate), the couple could have a monthly income of about $972 versus the maximum Social Security benefit of $1,200.

The Social Security benefits are still out in front for a couple, although for a single worker they are about the same under either Social Security or a retirement annuity. Payroll taxes during this period increased substantially, more accurately reflecting the benefits paid, but not enough to fully fund the program.

Now for our last example: the worker retiring at age sixty-five in 1997, after working forty years.

The payroll taxes over this forty-year period have now zoomed to an estimated $130,000, almost two and one half times the amount paid by the worker who retired ten years earlier. The maximum yearly benefit for the couple has also increased from $14,400 up to an estimated $25,000. It will now take the couple over five years to recover their taxes paid over the previous forty years.

By now the equity scales at Social Security are tilting in the other direction and, in fact, the worker, because of the constantly rising payroll tax rates, might do better on his own. Had he started investing the payroll taxes in 1957 as outlined in the previous examples, by 1997 he could have accumulated about $353,309. This could have purchased for the couple an attractive monthly annuity (at today's rate) of $3,072 versus the maximum estimated Social Security benefit for the couple of only $2,085.

Under our examples the worker retiring twenty years later in 1997 paid 8.5 times more taxes than the worker retiring in 1977, yet the benefits at age sixty-five for a couple increased only three times during that twenty-year period.

From these examples it is apparent that, over the first forty years of the system, payroll taxes were substantially less than were needed for the entire benefit package under Social

Security. As a result the tilt in the balance scales will require for correction a spiraling tax rate beyond the end of this century.

A Look at the New Social Security Law

Social Security is aware, as each of us should be, that one way to save the system—and its generous promised benefits—is simply to reduce the spigot's flow: cut future benefits.

So let's look at the new law which finally has cut benefits on a broad scale. This is the Social Security Amendments of 1977 (PL 95-216), passed by Congress on December 15, 1977. These amendments are generally considered to represent the most significant Social Security legislation since 1972, and possibly since 1950. No matter how you view the changes, many of the new amendments were desperately needed in order to protect the system from itself and help it survive. As a result of it the rules are now changed and it's a whole new ballgame.

Somehow it doesn't seem fair to change the rules of the game when many of the players are now in the clubhouse. But that is required to happen after 1977.

The first change in the rule book was the revised (or decoupled) benefit formula for adjustments in retirement payments tied to the cost-of-living index, which we alluded to earlier in this chapter. This was a major change to reduce retirement checks in the future.

Impact: Save billions of dollars in future years.

Another change was a substantial increase in the payroll tax rate. The net effect of this increase will be, as has frequently been publicized, a tripling of the payroll taxes during the next ten years, excluding further increases in taxes that are sure to come because of inflation.

Impact: Gain an additional $227 billion—or more—over the next ten years.

Another change was a reduction of the percentage of final preretirement pay you can receive when you retire. If you retired in 1978 under the old law with a final salary of $20,000, Social Security would have "replaced," or sent a retirement check, for about thirty-two percent or $6,400 per year. Under the new law, ten years later (or 1988), Social Security can only

185

replace thirty-one percent of that $20,000 salary, or $6,200 per year of relatively low-purchasing-power dollars. Of course, in ten years you will probably be earning $30,000, but then Social Security can only replace twenty-one percent of that salary. The real value of a Social Security retirement check should be based on the percentage of the final salary it will replace.

In effect, what the new law has done is to further protect the retirement system, but at a cost of substantially reducing the percentage of your final salary you can receive in monthly retirement checks.

If all workers received the same return on their taxes, the replacement rates of their preretirement pay would be almost identical. Social adequacy, or what the average retiree requires in income, as conceived by Social Security, will now allow a replacement rate of fifty-two percent for low earners, but only a twenty-seven percent replacement rate for maximum earners. Thus, even tripling the amount of taxes over the next decade will not produce a fat increase in benefits for average or higher-paid workers.

What Social Security has publicly stated is that it would like to contrive a situation where an "average" worker could receive a replacement rate of about forty-five percent. Under the 1977 amendment, Social Security's idea of an "average" worker was someone who makes $10,000 per year. This does not appear very realistic, given our sad inflation when the basic payroll tax base for year 1980 includes workers earning as much as $25,900.

But consider this: If both a husband and wife have earnings levels that qualify for maximum benefits, they will receive only one third higher benefits than if the wife had no covered earnings; yet they will pay twice as much in payroll taxes.

If Social Security is going to continue to be perceived as a program fairly serving those it covers, it may be necessary to put more emphasis on individual equity rather than on social adequacy. This could result in substantially higher tax rates than are already scheduled, but it might avoid the massive discontent in the years to come when many Americans will begin to realize that the payment of abruptly higher taxes has resulted in only modest increases in retirement benefits.

Impact: Save substantial amounts of money, amount unknown.

Another change as a result of the 1977 amendments is the amount of money we can earn after we retire and begin cashing those retirement checks. In Social Security bureaucratic language, this is called the retirement (or earnings) test. This part of Social Security goes back to 1935 when the original program was conceived by Congress.

At that time the labor movement, concerned with the "inadequacy" of jobs in America, was particularly concerned that the average wage level might be depressed if an appreciable number of older employees drew benefits and continued to work at the same time. By 1942, when benefits were first paid, the law allowed the retired worker monthly exempt earnings (the amount a retiree can still earn and not lose Social Security benefits) of $14.99. Not bad, considering the federal minimum wage was forty cents an hour, or sixteen dollars per week, only four times the exempt amount.

The exempt-amount-of-earnings clause has now become more commonly known as the "Eddie Cantor Clause." When the actor Eddie Cantor appeared on a TV show in 1957, he never dreamed that he would be giving his name to a part of the law that determines how much a retiree can earn and still collect monthly benefit checks. Since Eddie Cantor was sixty-five, and the exempt amount in 1957 was $1,200, he only "lost" one month's check from the earnings he received from the broadcast and was eligible to collect his benefit for the remaining months of that year.

That was how things went for many years. No matter how much you might earn on a TV show or other big windfall during the month, the most you could lose was just *that month's check*. Believe it or not, the Social Security Administration worked with Eddie Cantor to promote this great money-saving idea and, not surprisingly, the publicity resulted in millions of Americans concentrating their work and earnings in one or two months of the year so they could collect the full benefits for the balance of the year.

Back in 1957 Social Security sought to remind Americans that retirement benefits were an earned right, subject to the limit of exempt earnings, and were not welfare. The good news is that the exempt amount—the amount of annual earnings permitted for full benefits—has been increasing over the years. The general rule is that every two dollars of earnings over the exempt amount will result in the loss of one dollar of benefits. The exempt amount for 1980 is $5,000 for beneficiaries age sixty-five to seventy-two, less if you are under age sixty-five. After age seventy-two, the earnings test will no longer apply; this age will be lowered to seventy effective after 1982.

From 1981 to 1982, the new law will increase the exempt amount for those age sixty-five or over $500 each year. After 1982 the limit is scheduled to increase automatically as wages go up.

It is difficult for most Americans to understand why they should lose retirement benefits that have been paid for throughout their working lives simply to save the system some money. If a worker retires on Social Security only, and many Americans do, the need for money will become more pressing with every passing year. Throughout their working lives Americans strive to increase their salaries, to reach for a better life for themselves and their families. It does seem unfair, then, that any attempt to earn additional wages during retirement should be met with a possible loss of paid-for benefits.

But that is what will happen under the new law. The old "Eddie Cantor" clause is out the window. In the future a Social Security beneficiary can only get the advantage of the one-twelfth rule in the initial year of retirement. This means that anyone now receiving retirement checks will lose that right to lump income on a monthly basis. This may come as a real surprise to many current retirees who have for years staggered their earned income into as few months as possible.

Impact: This change to reduce benefits will save the trust fund an estimated $159 million in fiscal year 1978, an estimated $224 million in fiscal 1979, and billions of dollars over the next decade.

Another major difficulty which the 1977 amendment covered was the disability-insurance provisions of the Social Security program. Faced with runaway expenditures for disability insurance during the last few years, and with the future looking like a cash-hungry monster ready to devour the entire system itself, Americans who believe in the Social Security system are now justly concerned about disability benefits.

More and more Americans are claiming that they are so disabled that they must not only collect disability checks, but retire early as well. At a time when medical science is making great strides in treating heart disease and other various medical problems that disable workers, the number of claims for disability is skyrocketing, including a wave of younger people opting out for disability benefits.

Over the last few years a combination of factors has been at work driving up the number of claims. For one, a change in the law now makes it easier for people to claim that they are disabled. Consequently more people have become aware of the disability coverage contained in the Social Security program. Equally important, over the last few years there has been less reluctance to accept federal and state assistance of all kinds. Further, Social Security's requirement that a worker be at least fifty years old has been changed so that there is now no minimum age for disability payments.

The task of determining who is qualified for disability benefits has also become so complex that the bureaucratic machine for handling applications includes some 680 administrative law judges. By contrast, there are only 495 judges in the whole federal court system. There are also more than 10,000 state-level disability examiners backed up by thousands more Social Security employees involved in processing the claims. Yet, with all this help, the maze of paper has created a backlog of almost 100,000 cases with something like 20,000 more cases on appeal.

Social Security Commissioner Stanford G. Ross, in reviewing the appeal process, said, "The administrative process for determining disability is obviously cumbersome and erratic, and badly in need of overhaul. The appeals process results in a complete redevelopment of individual cases at several levels, and the federal courts are being burdened with over 8,000 new disability cases every year. And the program inflicts severe economic penalties on those who try to return to work. The program has, in fact, become a trap for many, with significant economic incentives for people to get on the rolls and others to stay there rather than to try to work and return to the mainstream of American life."

Ironically, one of the reasons that disability payments

under Social Security were delayed so long before acceptance into the system in 1956 was that the experience of private insurers against wage losses due to disability had been so financially disastrous. The insurers could not enforce the eligibility rules under the policies sold, against the pressures put on them by the courts and physicians trying to help workers whose unemployment usually was more the result of the labor market than their health.

At a House subcommittee hearing on Social Security in 1978, Representative Richard T. Schulze, R-Pennsylvania, observed that "a man who won the annual race up the Empire State Building apparently was on full disability this year. He did it in maybe twelve minutes."

"His wife said he could run," observed Representative James A. Burke, D-Massachusetts, "but he couldn't sit down."

The Social Security Disability Insurance (SSDI in bureaucratese) has now become anything but a laughing matter. In a 1978 speech, then Secretary Joseph A. Califano, Jr., of the Department of Health, Education and Welfare (which includes Social Security), admitted that the program is "a caricature of bureaucratic complexity" that has "drifted into crisis" and is "in need of fundamental reassessment and overhaul."

During that same subcommittee hearing held by the House, Representative Abner J. Mikva, D-Illinois, stated that benefit levels now create "too great a temptation" for "cheaters and malingerers." "Marginally" disabled people are "overloading the rolls and giving the [disability] program a bad name." Many people feel that Mikva's point is not far wrong. Consider this example: The maximum family benefit for a young disabled worker with dependents last year was somewhere around $1,000 a month (based on average previous earnings of only $15,900 a year). When a young person learns that the benefits are all tax-free, the annual income of $12,000 begins to look too good to pass up. Further, the disabled worker should not have any work-related expenses and his or her spouse can now make up to $5,000 a year on the side without any loss of benefits.

In fact, the overall Social Security program has changed so dramatically over the years that today's average payment to a retired worker is actually less than the average payment to a disabled worker, even though the disabled worker may have paid next to nothing in Social Security taxes.

With the system coming apart at the seams over the soaring cost of disability benefits, the final straw may well be the marginal cases who could work but whose real disability is more psychological than physical—they simply do not like their job, their boss, or the idea of walking away from all that tax-free cash.

The long-range effects on a system beset with marginal cases can be devastating. It has been estimated that every erroneous award of a disability claim means an average waste of about $60,000 over the life of the benefit. The main reason, unbelievable as it may seem, is that once a person's disability claim is accepted, it is rarely reversed. As long as the disabled worker does not go back to work in a job covered by Social Security, there is no real way of even checking up.

Social Security regulations state that "to qualify for disability benefits, a working individual must have a medically determinable physical or mental impairment so severe that it prevents the performance of any substantial gainful activity for at least twelve months or is expected to result in death."

In spite of these tough regulations, the courts have helped so effectively to liberalize the stated eligibility requirements that, during the last ten years alone, the number of disabled workers receiving benefits has more than doubled. Adding their families, the total is close to five million Americans who are now supported in a major way by the disability provisions of the system.

It was back in 1956 that Social Security was expanded to allow cash payments to workers who became disabled and unable to work. By 1967 about twenty out of every thousand workers covered under the plan were receiving a disability check. Ten years later, in 1977, the number had shot up to thirty workers out of every thousand. By 1981 the Social Security Administration itself estimates that at least sixty-eight workers out of every thousand—more than double the number today and 340 percent more than just fourteen years before—will be cashing disability checks.

The soaring costs have drained the disability trust fund. In fact, the fund has been operating at a loss since way back in

1975. Without the 1977 changes in the law, it would have run out of money in late 1978.

The people graph on the following page shows the startling jump in the number of recipients and the huge amounts of money the program is expected to require in the future. (The numbers are an estimate by the author, based on his own research; they are not official Social Security reports.)

Congress was told last year that unless the government overhauls its Social Security disability program, financial disaster is inevitable by the year 2000.

Gerald S. Parker, vice president of Guardian Life Insurance Company of New York, appearing before a subcommittee on Social Security of the Committee on Ways and Means, warned that "if the disability benefits program is not controlled, it will come far sooner than that, and there will ultimately be far fewer than two workers for every beneficiary. We think it goes without saying that those few workers are not going to be willing to support the nonworkers at an excessive level." Mr. Parker concluded his remarks by stating that "each of us has the greatest sympathy for people who are disabled and who are in need. No one wants to make their lives any harder. But we must also consider the needs of the workers who support the disabled population and the retired population."

Very few Americans will quarrel with Mr. Parker's comments that disability income is a sound social need. The question that now must be asked is whether this program can be controlled and whether it really belongs inside a retirement plan.

As far as the immediate future is concerned, the new Social Security law that took effect in 1977, for those who apply in 1979 or later, will result in lower disability-benefit checks. One change will reduce benefits for younger workers, since under the old law the method of calculating survivor and disability benefits discriminated in favor of the younger workers, giving them much higher benefits than older workers, even though older workers had paid more into the system.

Another change in the law made by the 1977 amendments was an attempt to slow down the rush to early retirement—and the consequent outflow of cash to people who, if they could be

192

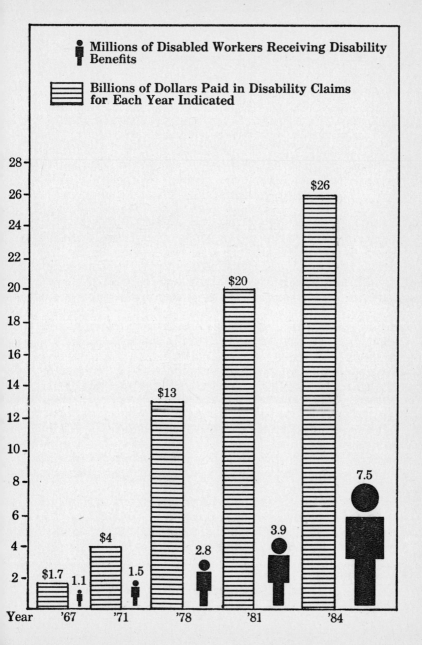

Millions of Disabled Workers Receiving Disability Benefits

Billions of Dollars Paid in Disability Claims for Each Year Indicated

| Year | '67 | '71 | '78 | '81 | '84 |

$1.7   1.1 $4   1.5 $13   2.8 $20   3.9 $26   7.5

convinced to stay on the job, would be pumping money into the system instead of drawing it out.

Since the turn of the century there has been a steady pressure toward earlier and earlier retirement. In 1890 fully sixty-eight percent of all men age sixty-five and over worked; by 1950 only forty-two percent did so. By 1975, only twenty-five years later, the number of men age sixty-five and over still working nosedived to twenty-one percent, with a projection from the United States Bureau of Labor Statistics that by 1990 only sixteen percent of the men over age sixty-five would still be in the labor force. Despite the fact that the benefits are lower for early retirement, millions of Americans cannot wait to break out of the job market, costing the system billions of dollars each year.

Many workers are beginning to realize that by taking eighty percent of the benefits at age sixty-two, they can then draw three years' worth of retirement checks before reaching age sixty-five. No small amount when you consider that a worker with a dependent spouse could receive as much as $20,000 in tax-free income between now and 1983. At age sixty-five a retiree with a dependent spouse would need at least twelve years simply to "catch up" in terms of Social Security payments.

One of the provisions of the new law has the effect of cutting the increase in the cost-of-living adjustments by twenty percent for those who retire at age sixty-two. This is probably one of the first steps toward raising the "normal" retirement age to something over age sixty-five. Social Security would like to move in that direction, and increasing pressure will be put on Congress to move the normal retirement date to at least age sixty-eight. Congress recently raised the mandatory retirement age from sixty-five up to age seventy.

The new law has yet another amazing feature to encourage continued employment after age sixty-five. Starting in 1983 the retirement benefits will be increased an amazing one fourth of one percent for each month of work after age sixty-five. This works out to be a three percent increase in benefits for each year up to age seventy-two.

Assume a worker is tempted to retire at age sixty-five on a monthly benefit of $500. If he stayed on the job another year he could earn an increase of $15 per month. But, in Social Security's madcap world of make-believe, what would it really cost to continue to work that extra year? For a worker and a dependent spouse the trade-off is the loss of about $10,000 of tax-free income from the system. But then the worker would still have to pay Social Security payroll taxes on his earnings of, say, $25,000, which would amount to about $1,675. Added to this would be the personal income taxes of somewhere around $5,000, for a total of $16,675—in order to increase his future retirement income $15 per month!

Today many Americans are finding that a retirement delayed is a retirement lost. The Social Security system has been forced into a no-win situation. On the one hand it cannot buck the trends of early retirement and avoid paying out all that cash. On the other hand it badly needs older workers to continue to pay money into the system. A logical conclusion is that in the future either taxes will have to be raised, or, more likely, the normal retirement age moved up to something like age sixty-eight.

Women in Social Security

It is beginning to occur to an increasing number of older women that they as a group are not being treated fairly under the present Social Security system.

In 1977, of the twenty-eight million adults drawing benefits, sixty percent were women. Eight million women received benefits based solely on their husbands' wage records. On the other hand, only thirty thousand men received benefits as dependents or survivors of women workers, and over eleven million men received benefits on their own wage records.

These figures reflect the social realities of the past, when men were primarily wage earners and women were, for the most part, homemakers. They also confirm that whereas the Social Security Act provides women automatic protection as dependents and survivors, it has begun providing this coverage to men only recently and only if, it appears, they were supported by their wives prior to their wives' death or retirement.

Among the problems facing Social Security today is the change in the American life-style. An increasing number of women are working; divorce and multiple marriages are becoming commonplace.

The basic design of Social Security was fixed in 1939, when married women made up only fourteen percent of the labor force. The benefit formula worked out at that time was based on the archaic assumption that women are always homemakers, that men provide the sole economic support for the family, and that marriages last for life. Today women make up almost half of the total labor force. More important, married women have surged into the work force, increasing from only fourteen percent back in 1939 to forty-seven percent by 1979.

With only fourteen percent of the married women working, there appeared no question back in 1939 that income insurance for married women had to be based primarily on the loss of their husbands' wages. When a married woman worked, she, of course, paid her own Social Security taxes, but it was reasoned that the payment of full benefits based on the wife's earnings would be unnecessary and unduly expensive.

The solution, which now has working women up in arms over the loss of paid-for benefits, was considered a creative way out at the time. Married women were to be considered dependent on their husbands' earnings and the working wife's earned benefit would be paid only to the extent that it exceeded the benefit she would have received as a nonworking wife.

Let's use an example of the husband and wife retiring at age sixty-five. The husband's benefit is $450 per month and the nonworking wife's benefit is $225 per month, for a total of $675 per month. If the wife had worked and contributed to Social Security, she would have earned a retirement benefit in her own right. If that earned benefit was less than $225 per month, she would receive nothing extra for her Social Security contributions. If it exceeded $225 per month, she would receive only the difference.

The magic of the Social Security benefit formula has prompted women all over America to ask a basic question: If I had protection as a wife before and now I go to work and pay Social Security taxes, what do I get in addition to what I had before? The answer today is very little, if anything. In fact, many women who work today will get benefits no higher than those they would have received if they had never worked and never paid a penny in Social Security taxes!

Under the long-standing formula, if both the husband and wife work, the benefits can actually be lower than if only the husband were employed. For example, if the husband had average lifetime earnings of $12,000 with a nonworking wife, the couple's benefit could be $636 per month. If, on the other hand, the husband and wife each had lifetime earnings of $6,000— total $12,000—the couple's benefit would be reduced by $108 per month, or about seventeen percent. In other words, under the absurd retirement benefit formula, if two couples pay in the same taxes, the couple with only one worker gets far more for its Social Security investment. Even worse, retirement benefits for a widow who was employed can be less than for a nonworking widow, even though the couple had the same average lifetime earnings.

Women also face yet another hazard as they head toward retirement. Under the present system, wives are protected only so long as they remain married, and if they are divorced before ten years of marriage have elapsed (before the 1977 act it was twenty years) they lose all protection for the work they contributed to the marriage. But even if the nonworking wife can qualify on her ex-husband's account, she must wait until he decides to retire before she is eligible to collect any benefits.

Now adrift in a lifeboat, the divorcee soon discovers that she will receive only fifty percent as large a benefit as her former husband, since the law was established to provide benefits for a couple living together, not for the support of two single individuals.

The divorce rate in America has zoomed since Social Security's inception. In 1935 the rate was only 1.7 divorces per 1,000 population, but by 1977 it had gone up to 5.1 divorces per 1,000 population and the rate is still climbing. For one thing, divorce has now become more accepted in our society, and, for another, most states have now adopted no-fault divorce laws. Yet another reason is that women are entering the labor force in increased numbers, enabling them to become economically self-sufficient and better able to manage a divorce than someone who is dependent on another person. Whatever the reason, the rising divorce rate is forcing many women into battle with a forty-year-old benefit system, and up to this point they are clearly losing.

Back in 1978 a task force on the treatment of women under Social Security was appointed by then Secretary Joseph A. Califano, Jr., of the Department of Health, Education and Welfare. The special task-force report found at least nine ways the system discriminates chiefly against women. The report also found that the lack of benefits was a particular hardship on widows, disabled homemakers, and divorced women.

The HEW task force did not try to come up with answers, but it did point out again the inequities in our Social Security system. The situation is that the problems of women in the system are so complex that eliminating the inequities will not be easy. From Social Security's standpoint, the future changes could be very costly, requiring more rules, more exceptions, more record-keeping—such as a central file on marital status —and, of course, more money for liberalized benefits.

Last year Lynda Johnson Robb told the House Committee on Aging task force that women face "severe and crippling inequities" in Social Security benefits. "The discrimination that exists is based on archaic notions of the different value that is placed on work done by men and work done by women."

After all the task force reports and public outcry, the major problems still remain. The system was originally designed to provide a married man with one and one half times the earned benefit; the single man with only the basic earned benefit. Women were considered dependent on their husbands, and the additional half benefits were intended to offset this retirement expense.

Now, over forty years later, the single workers are unhappy since they receive far fewer benefits for the same tax contributions than do married men. Women are unhappy since they no longer are all married or dependent on husbands, and they also receive benefits that do not reflect their changing role in America's society.

The only one who still gets an equitable deal from the system is the married man, the original primary beneficiary of the program.

Who Is in the System?

The Social Security system is not universally mandatory, despite what many of us may believe. Universal coverage has been merely a desirable goal of the system. Over ten percent of the workers in America are not paying Social Security taxes at all, with federal, state, and city employees accounting for about seventy-two percent of that total.

When Social Security was first set up, public employees, by and large, already had their own retirement plan. And state and city employees now make up the largest group of those not participating in the system, even though only thirty percent are not covered and seventy percent currently pay into Social Security through "voluntary" agreements between the federal government and the states.

The crux of the matter is that all state, city, and local government agencies can voluntarily enter and withdraw (with two years notice and ten years in the program). If Social Security is to fulfill its objective of universal coverage, steps must now be taken to plug the loophole of voluntary withdrawal.

One of the reasons that withdrawal has become so attractive is that public-employee retirement plans have become much more generous than anything Social Security—or for that matter most private plans—can offer.

Many state and local plans allow employees to retire with full benefits as early as age fifty-five. The benefits are often much higher because the retirement pay is based on the last year's, or even the highest single year's, salary, not on Social Security's lifetime averaging system.

San Jose, California, which in 1975 was ranked as the twenty-first largest city in America in population, is a good example of voluntary withdrawal from the system. After a majority of city employees voted to bail out of Social Security, the withdrawal became effective in July 1975. The employees voted for a "new and improved" retirement system. The cost to the employee was about the same under either plan, but the benefits were substantially greater under the city's own system, reflecting the generous public retirement benefits available today.

The city's withdrawal from the system created nationwide

publicity not only because of San Jose's size, but also because of its ability actually to withdraw smoothly from America's "mandatory" retirement plan. A flood of inquiries descended on City Hall, seeking information on the "how to do it" procedures for voluntary withdrawal.

Even as I write this book, Social Security has received yet another jolt. Alaska has become the first state to make a wholesale withdrawal from the system. The changeover was set to occur January 1, 1980.

Bill Hudson, commissioner of administration, looking toward the future, said, "I think this signals to the federal government that there is a concern about taxation, and I wouldn't be surprised if this begins to happen nationwide."

In a sense the future has arrived. Today 98 government bodies in sixteen states say they want out by 1980. Roughly another 147 local governments now plan to withdraw in 1981. The real concern for all of us who support the Social Security system is the pace of the withdrawal movement. Over the last two years the number of public workers leaving the system has jumped fivefold.

The opportunity for a "new and improved" retirement system on a do-it-yourself basis may have become a tide too strong for Social Security to stop without congressional help. In any event, the flood of workers going out the back door must be closed if the system is going to continue to be a truly equitable one for all Americans.

The next largest group remaining outside Social Security is the civilian employees of the federal government. For the almost 2.8 million federal workers there is no choice of withdrawal, for they have never been covered under the system. Congress has tried repeatedly to cover federal employees but without success. As late as 1977 the House Ways and Means Committee reported a bill to the House of Representatives which would have covered all federal employees on a compulsory basis. Like all of the previous attempts, the bill failed under the press of more "urgent" business and never became law.

Commenting on the escape of federal employees from the system in a 1978 *Forbes* magazine article, Mr. E. T. Collinsworth, Jr., President of Bliss and Laughlin Industries, a critic of Social Security, said, "You know government employees have a great pension program. Congress had the opportunity to make Social Security apply to them, but they had the good sense not to do it. They're not stupid."

Exclusion of federal employees has been allowed to continue largely because of the unions' fear of a possible reduction in the very liberal civil-service retirement benefits. After only five years on the job, a federal worker picks up a generous retirement plan which also includes many of Social Security's important features such as disability and survivorship protection. On top of that, with thirty years of coverage, full benefits are payable as early as age fifty-five.

But most of all, federal employees would like to continue their unique opportunity for "double-dipping." This new term, now rapidly moving into our vocabulary, has become the symbol of one of the greatest scams ever to hit America's retirement planning. Double-dipping allows retired workers to draw benefits at the same time they are working in another private industry job and earning yet another retirement benefit.

For federal employees (as well as many state and city workers) picking up Social Security benefits is not all that difficult. They can qualify for a second pension with comparatively large benefits by taking a job in private industry and paying Social Security taxes for a relatively brief time. By contrast, most Americans generally pay the burden of Social Security taxes over their entire working lives before receiving any benefit checks.

Currently seventy percent of all retired federal government employees age sixty-five and over who are collecting a government pension are also drawing Social Security benefits. For those American workers lucky enough to have escaped the lifetime clutches of Social Security, double-dipping has become a way of life.

The system has clearly gone very wrong when it allows one group of workers to escape the heavy burden of lifetime payroll taxes yet still collect a handsome pension from that same system at bargain rates. But what about the millions of workers forced into Social Security, you ask? They have become the all-time losers. They help provide these bargain pensions for workers outside the system, but at the expense of their own labor and their own savings.

If all this seems very strange and unfair to you, it is. The federal government requires that everyone in private employment be covered under Social Security, yet that same federal government has contrived, completely outside of Social Security, generous retirement plans for its own employees.

Nor is that all. Consider the people who designed the mess and make the rules for millions of Americans covered under Social Security. The 535 members of Congress have created "special provisions" to apply in their case. Not covered by Social Security, they were free to design their own retirement plan. Their benefits are determined by the average pay of their three highest years. No lifetime averaging for them. Their own benefits are even more generous than those of other federal employees covered under the civil-service retirement plan.

But the most blatant offender of all must be the federal judiciary. Its retirement plan is so incredibly magnanimous that participants retire on full pay and, in most instances, receive Social Security benefits as well.

After forty-three years of tinkering with the system, Social Security now resembles an organized sport. Congress has become the club owner, making up the rules on how the sport is played and who is allowed to come to bat. The Social Security Administration supplies the players and will determine, after consulting its marvelously intricate rule book, whether a covered worker will or will not receive benefits. The judiciary provides the officials, who are becoming increasingly important for keeping the game from grinding to a halt. And the American workers, having paid the price of admission each year in spiraling ticket prices, are the spectators. There has been little to cheer about over the last few years, and from the look of the way the game is being played, there'll be even less in the future. Somehow it seems only fitting that over in the corner, laughing his head off, is old Charlie Ponzi.

Collecting the Benefits

Now for the payoff. You've moved out of the grandstand and come up to bat. If you have the idea that collecting Social Security benefits is automatic and painless, forget it. You will now be competing with the more than twenty-five million people already collecting benefits who flood the local offices each day.

You can avoid some of the most common pitfalls during your first year of collecting Social Security benefits by recognizing from the start that you will be dealing with an overworked and unresponsive bureaucracy, basically controlled by one giant computer—which periodically seems to come unplugged.

The Social Security Administration regulations—which read like new-car warranties written in Greek—can easily result in your spending frustrating hours in the local office or wasting days trying to get information you could obtain with a simple postcard.

So what can be done? You might consider the following tips when you actually attack the system in earnest.

Tip One. Stay away from the local office on Monday, the busiest day of the week. Also avoid the third and fourth of each month, since that's when retirees who failed to receive their checks will descend on the office *en masse* to register complaints.

Tip Two. Use the telephone. It beats standing in line since a surprising amount of contact with the local office can be made over the phone. In many cases your claim application can be completed over the phone and mailed to you for your signature. You can also find out exactly what documents you will need once you get to the local office.

Tip Three. Don't shop around for higher benefits. The amount you can receive will be calculated in Baltimore by one of the world's largest computers. In fact you can have access to the computer on the same basis your local office does. All you need do is mail a postcard, available at any Social Security office, to the Social Security Administrator, P.O. Box 57, Baltimore, Maryland 21203. Except for the cost of the stamp, the request for information about the status of your account is free. It is a good idea to use the card periodically over the years to determine the progress of your account, as well as to learn what to do when you are about to file for benefits. If you are going to retire soon, you might also write "include retirement benefit estimate" along the bottom of the card. This is a new service and one that will allow you to double-check the local office regarding your own benefits.

While these cards can provide a look inside the computer, they are only an estimate. Your actual benefits can vary depending on your exact month of retirement and the earnings for your last year of work.

Tip Four. If you are collecting benefits that are being paid on the basis of another person's earning record, such as that of a spouse, then your Social Security card number is different from your claim number. If you try to find your account with your own card number, the computer may report back that you do not exist. To find your account, you must use the Social Security number of the person on whose earnings your benefits are based.

Tip Five. After retirement, you may earn up to $5,000 (1980) per year without loss of benefits. But don't forget that anything you earned before you retired will not count as income earned in the first year of retirement. You can, therefore, still collect the full benefits as well as all the money earned in previous years.

Tip Six. Now that you have filed your claim and the hassle is over, you relax and confidently expect to find the first Social Security check in your mailbox on the third of the month. By the sixth of the month, with the mailbox still empty, you begin to panic. At this point, call the local office and ask to file a lost-claim report. Computer malfunction or not, the longer you wait to trace your own money, the longer you will usually have to wait for your check.

The last tip might be to talk with someone who has just been through the process of threading the needle by successfully filing and collecting Social Security benefits.

Social Security procedures frequently change. This up-to-the-minute information can often be very helpful.

So if you are about to apply for benefits, good hunting!

10 Two on a Hang Glider

Almost six centuries ago, there lived a man named Leonardo da Vinci. Unlike the other learned men of his day, Leonardo thought he knew how birds managed to fly through the air. But when he tried to put a man in the air, weight overtook gravity and man remained firmly planted on the ground for another four hundred years. We can only speculate on how the world would have changed if, with some scraps of wood, string, and some cloth, Leonardo had succeeded in assembling a hang glider on the Florentine hills.

To watch a hang glider in flight is to watch beauty in motion. The human body and the glider seem to become one as they alternately soar and dip through the air currents. The glider owes its success to the large, flexible wings that not only provide a support from which the rider can hang, but also allow him to become a part of the glider: The craft is turned in flight by twisting the body, with the arms literally becoming an extension of the wings.

But their grace and motion belie their danger; forgiveness for an error in judgment is rare.

Dual hang gliders are even more dangerous, for on them two persons must move together as if they are one with the glider. While they are in the air, each is utterly dependent on the other for his own safety. If one loses control from fear of soaring at great heights, or from inexperience in working with another in a smooth flow of body rhythm, the hang glider can easily crash. Dual hang gliders are a classic example of two separate components working smoothly together: Each serves the other, and if one fails, they both do.

It is also not far from the truth to say that America's Social Security system must also become a giant dual hang glider. Both the American public and the government will be forced to work together in a totally new era of trust and confidence if the overburdened system is to remain in the air.

Ironically, over the last five years each group on the dual hang glider has been moving apart from the other, placing all of us in imminent danger of a crash. But Americans will be able, as they would not in the case of a hang glider crash, to walk away from the wreckage of Social Security. For good reason, too, the crash will not result in bankruptcy. The major benefits may be slashed, leaving those who have already paid the bills empty-handed, but bankruptcy simply can't happen.

Social Security is a U.S. government program. Its benefit payment checks come directly from the U.S. Treasury. And who stands behind the Treasury? We all do. Social Security has been with us for more than forty years. Today it is serving such a wide range of socially oriented welfare programs that its loss would be felt by every segment of our society.

The real question facing Americans now is, how can Social Security survive in a way that is fair to both current workers and retired beneficiaries? The bad management of the system over the past four decades has finally come home to roost. The money collected by the system for a host of welfare and retirement programs has been so minuscule that bankruptcy has been avoided only because it can't occur. In fact, any American who has worked over the past forty years—from its start to January 1, 1977—could only have paid a maximum tax of $7,710.

The average retirement benefit alone has already reached twice the average amount paid each year, *each month!* And that includes millions of workers who paid in much less than the maximum tax each year. A race-track tout, even at his most confident, could not match that payout.

Most Americans today have finally come to realize that the Social Security pork barrel has been utterly drained. Punctured like a sieve, it has been leaking money in too many places to count. Not only Social Security, but Social Security's overseer, the Department of Health, Education and Welfare itself, has been in trouble. By one report HEW's "uncontrollable" costs alone are a gigantic ninety-four percent of the Department's annual budget.

As a result of the emptiness of the barrel, a growing disillusion with Social Security has sprung up throughout America. The start of the 1980s will be a stark reversal from that which characterized the beginning of the 1970s when public opinion polls indicated widespread distrust of the private pension system. In 1979 the previously mentioned Lou Harris poll on American attitudes toward pensions and retirement pointed up the depressing news that fully eighty percent of American workers lack confidence in the Social Security system, many doubting that full benefits will continue to be paid in the future. But worse yet, Social Security has now become so distrusted by the average workingman that forty-two percent of those surveyed had "hardly any confidence at all" in it. In fact the survey reports that over one third of both employees and employers who have already made extended payments into the system would, if given a choice, get out altogether.

Other attitudes toward Social Security began to emerge as Harris surveyed the 1,330 full-time employees, 397 retired individuals, and 212 top business and financial executives who work in the pension and retirement field.

One of the most interesting findings from the survey is that current employees and retirees want Social Security to work as originally intended. In fact, seventy-six percent said the program should return to its basic plan of providing a minimum level of retirement income that will supplement other retirement-income sources.

In spite of the fact that most of the people contacted by the survey said they had lost confidence in the system, Harris found that a majority of current and retired employees generally agree that, if necessary, more money should be collected from working people to maintain the Social Security program and keep benefits up with inflation. In fact, the survey dealing with Social Security is replete with contradictions. Even though a whopping eighty-seven percent of today's employees expect to receive Social Security benefits when they retire, nearly half of the respondents (forty-nine percent) have hardly any confidence in the government's ability to run a program in which all retirement income would be distributed through the federal government and funded by taxes.

On who is to pay for Social Security in the future, the current employees have a sharply different view from that of their employers. For the first time the payroll tax, as the sole support of the system, has moved out of favor. Now forty-seven percent of current employees and retirees feel that at least part of the money should come from sources other than payroll taxes. The employers, however, feel, by an overwhelming margin of seventy-nine percent, that all Social Security benefits should be paid from Social Security taxes.

The overall conclusions of the survey are directly related to the changes in the Social Security program—its transformation from a retirement benefit plan into a welfare-oriented plan. Because of the surging costs of the welfare benefits paid to the poor, the sick, and the the disabled, there is now a crisis of confidence among the American working public.

Fully four out of every five workers doubt that Social Security will pay their benefits when they retire. The lack of confidence is further reinforced in the minds of the public by the widespread belief that future generations will simply be unwilling to pay the higher payroll taxes required to support the expanded welfare-oriented program.

Today's Social Security taxes have no direct correlation with the benefits received, illustrating that such benefits are actually "welfare" rather than a form of "earned" benefits. As a result the American workers have not only lost confidence in the system, they have lost the vital ingredient of self-interest.

In short, Congress has asked each worker to accept a massive payroll-tax increase to provide benefits for those already in retirement, with the admission that even that bundle of cash will not be enough to pay all the bills coming due over the next twenty years.

Unless the system is thrown into reverse, the continued decline in the birthrate could, as we have noted before, compel a shriveling work force to pay escalating Social Security taxes in order to support increasing benefits to a growing number of beneficiaries.

At this rate the unthinkable may become thinkable. A day could come when wages at the disposal of a worker, after Social Security taxes have been paid, could be less than the total benefits received by a retiree.

Millions of workers now perceive Social Security not as a retirement plan but as a government-created monster, reaching directly into their own pockets for the cash to finance public welfare. To restore confidence one of the first things we must do is recognize Social Security for exactly that: a system for dispensing welfare benefits. What's more, unlike any other form of public, tax-supported welfare, it has become a unique experiment in American politics.

The state of the Social Security system inspires the asking of the basic question: How much longer will the American worker, as a gesture of goodwill and generosity to the disabled, the sick, and the needy, hand over a large part of his hard-earned paycheck, over and above all the other taxes which must be paid? Apparently, if the Harris survey is accurate, not much longer. A majority of Americans these days believe that the heavily burdened taxpayer can no longer be all things to all people. In a word, the willingness to be fleeced has given way to self-interest.

William Simon, in his book *A Time for Truth*, puts his finger on one of the major problems plaguing America and, more important in this case, the Social Security system, when he observes, "The more one achieves, the less one is rewarded, the less one achieves, the more one is rewarded. The goal is not to enhance individual achievement; it is to level it."

From this point on the future can no longer be laced with rude surprises brought on the system in time-release fashion by congressional giveaways. It is a time for honesty, both to the worker, whom Congress has forced to carry the crushing tax burden, and the beneficiaries, who must realize that, by and large, their current benefits will greatly exceed their investments in the system.

If the current Social Security program is to be retained as a going concern, leaving alone for the moment any attempts to correct the massive inequities that lace the system, Congress must now apply a "quick fix" in four major areas.

(1) Resist any temptation to roll back the already inadequate payroll taxes. Supplementing the payroll tax with a European-style value added tax (VAT) is a shift to nothing more than a national sales tax. As long as Social Security remains basically a welfare-oriented program, it does not make much sense to collect the revenues through a sales tax, which would be regressive, and hit the poor harder than anyone else.

As for dipping into general revenue, this will probably come sometime in the 1980s, if the system remains unchanged.

(2) Require universal coverage. This would make the system more equitable and restore some measure of fairness.

(3) Reduce the rate of future growth of benefits and reduce or eliminate those socially oriented benefits which are already available elsewhere in our society.

For the foreseeable future, Congress and the American public must accept the bad news that skyrocketing benefits cannot continue to be paid from an empty purse. Looking at the arithmetic, there is just no way Congress can push up the payroll taxes enough to even cover the benefits already scheduled to be paid, much less the horde of new benefits that could flow out of Washington if the brakes are not applied in time.

(4) Tighten the rules that apply to early retirement and minimum benefits. The system can no longer afford the luxury of retirement at age sixty-two. It is simply too expensive. By shifting all retirement to age sixty-five, the system might avoid having gradually to hike the normal retirement age up to sixty-eight.

Eligibility for the minimum Social Security retirement benefit also should be tightened. This could prevent workers already retired from other plans from working just long enough to qualify for yet another retirement check from Social Security. Currently these so-called "double-dippers" pay next to nothing into the system, yet they collect the minimum retirement benefit anyway. Not a few—a whopping seventy percent of the retired federal workers now pick up Social Security checks each month.

Whether Congress has the courage to make these suggested major repairs to the system is very much in doubt.

In any event the loss of confidence in Social Security is

already so massive that it probably cannot be reversed unless the American worker can see his own self-interest being served. To restore to the system that direct appeal to self-interest, it may be time to return to the old-fashioned principles of 1935, which encouraged personal interest in the success of the program: back to a time when a person felt he was building his very own retirement nest egg.

Perhaps it is time to revert to a "work requirement" that motivates people to stay on the job in order to contribute toward their personal retirement. It may be time to go for a program that can at least hold out the hope of a fully earned benefit. Perhaps a program in which the equivalent of the present Social Security tax could be contributed to a separate individual account instead of into the Social Security system. Maybe we will even see a time when both the government and the worker can ride together on the same hang glider.

The Future of Social Security

This author's proposal for the future of Social Security is based on the assumption that financing part or all of the system with general tax revenues is inevitable. The cost for the current retirement and welfare program is simply too great a burden to continue to be supported by employee-employer taxes alone.

An equitable arrangement might be for Congress to recognize finally that Social Security is basically two programs in one. The elimination of the various welfare benefits from the Social Security program would allow these payments to be made from general tax revenues. Since general tax revenues have been used for years to fund general welfare benefits, this is not a new course for American government.

In fact, the use of general tax revenues for welfare programs dates back to the First Advisory Council on Social Security in 1938. The council then advised, "Since the nation as a whole will derive a benefit from the program, it is appropriate that there be federal financial participation by means of revenues derived from sources other than payroll taxes." Further, many of the other roughly one hundred countries with some form of Social Security now use general tax revenues to support their programs.

The proposed program would allow a basic survivor and

retirement-income benefit, with all welfare payments now made by Social Security to be paid from general tax revenues, since all Americans, regardless of their contributions to Social Security, deserve a minimum level of benefits in order to satisfy a psychological need for dignity and a reasonable standard of living. The federal government would be required to set a base for the poverty level and adjust the minimum benefit according to the concept of social adequacy.

The Social Security system could then return to its original purpose of providing old-age (retirement) and survivors benefits, which would continue to be funded by payroll taxes. The benefits from Social Security would then be based proportionally on past contributions.

If they are to be tolerated at all, Social Security taxes should be based on the principle of benefit *from* taxation.

The Harris survey has shown that most Americans cling to the belief that the future is worth protecting. They desperately want the security that comes from an insurance arrangement in which their rights to benefits are earned, not received as a grant from the government.

This new Social Security system would then be in a position to correct many of the inequities that have sprung up over the last forty years. Since all benefit payments could now be revised, provisions could be made by Congress to allow contributions from each worker, whether married or not, to relate directly to future retirement benefits. The original concept of "earned and paid for" benefits would then apply to each wage earner. This would return equity to a family with two spousal incomes and insure equal treatment for each worker.

The dependent spouse, in recognition of his or her vital contribution to American society and the family, would also have his or her own separate benefit. The actual retirement figure would continue to be based on the working spouse's contribution. Since the working spouse's actual benefit could now be higher, the couple could receive a three-tier benefit structure: a larger benefit during the life of the working spouse; a smaller benefit at his/her death; and in the event of a divorce, an increase in the separate benefit of the dependent spouse, partly at the expense of the benefit payable to the working spouse. This would return equitable treatment to an area that has been conveniently ignored by the current program, where, through a divorce, a dependent spouse must continue to remain subject to his/her ex-spouse's benefit payments.

This new Social Security system would then allow for other needed changes to reflect the reality of the 1980s.

The major goal for any retirement-income plan should be to maintain a standard of living roughly comparable to that earned while working. Unless inflation is offset by continually increasing benefits, the entire program becomes a sham.

Only now, as the nation confronts double-digit inflation, is it beginning to dawn on pension planners how incredibly expensive the future will become. Our present system, sinking billions of dollars into welfare payments, simply can't supply the tremendous amounts of cash that would be necessary to fund constantly increasing cost-of-living benefits.

Referring again to the Lou Harris survey, both current and retired workers felt strongly that Social Security benefits should be increased with the cost of living. In fact, eighty-six percent felt that Social Security benefits should increase at least as fast as the cost of living over the next five years. Currently, to raise benefits to match the increase in the cost of living simply means increasing the payroll tax for those workers yet to retire. But many students of the Social Security system have maintained for years that contributions into the system are entitled to earn market interest rates. This view is based in part on the fact that private plans allow each contribution to earn interest until retirement.

This would be a logical and fair way to use general tax revenues to support what would then be a separate Social Security system. After all, our government is already borrowing billions of dollars each month from well-heeled investors, so why not tap the American worker, who is also seeking a fair return to help protect his retirement income against inflation?

As another major step in restoring public confidence, Congress should be encouraged to establish a separate government corporation for the new Social Security retirement plan. This would allow the operations of Social Security to be kept separate from other government revenues and expenditures. Actually, Social Security's income and benefit payments were maintained separately from general revenue and expenses until

1969. Today they are buried in the national budget, raising questions as to just what part Social Security really plays in relation to other government programs.

The board of directors of the new corporation, which could be composed of nationally recognized leaders from labor, education, government, and business, would report directly to the American people. This frank and open approach could do much to dispel the growing lack of confidence within the American work force.

Again, this is not new ground to explore. Social Security was first administered by a separate board reporting directly to the President. Then in 1939 Social Security was dumped into what has now become the Department of Health and Human Services. Now, forty years later, with expenditures well over $100 billion a year, the program has grown to such a degree that it dominates most other Washington departments and agencies. By any means of judging the bureaucracy, Social Security as a separate identity has finally come of age.

By emphasizing that Social Security is now a separate corporation responsible for retirement and survivors' benefits, major reforms can be effected in the way we operate the program. No longer will American workers be forced to submit to a maze of regulations on funding and benefit payment; the system can now be simple to understand, fair and equitable to all who contribute to the program.

For starters, contributions into Social Security for those working after age sixty-five would be at the option of the wage earner, but not required. It seems incredible that our system could include rules that require a worker who has paid for retirement benefits virtually his entire working life to continue to pay into the system simply because he is financially unable to retire.

You can, in this connection, take the following as a classic example of Social Security's "unbelievable situations": If you and I reach age sixty-five, and you are a millionaire and I am broke, you receive the full retirement benefit tax-free while I continue to work and receive nothing. But that's not all. Broke as I am, I must, cruel as it may seem, continue to pay substantial taxes on my wages in order to finance the benefits I am not receiving.

The new Social Security system would also provide the incentive for a retired person to continue working by substantially increasing the amount that can be earned from wages. This limit might possibly be $25,000 per year before there is a reduction in retirement benefits.

As things stand now, the "unbelievable situation" arises again: Income earned from other sources than work is presently permitted, whereas work income is discouraged because it can sharply reduce the retirement check.

Once reformed, the financing of Social Security would again reflect a more equitable relationship between the workers and their government. Currently Social Security retirement benefits are received free of income tax. From the government's point of view, however, it would seem only fair that approximately half the retirement benefits received by the retiree should be considered taxable. (This is based on the theory, covered in Chapter 9, that contributions made by the employer, which are not taxable to the employee when made, are taxable upon receipt of the benefits.)

Since all private retirement plans must follow this principle of delayed taxation, it should also apply to the new Social Security program.

Under the present arrangement the employer takes a tax deduction for his contributions to the system and the retiree, in effect, takes another deduction when he collects the tax-free benefit checks. Critics of the program have charged that Social Security is unfair to workers covered under a private plan and to the tax collector, for what they have termed a "back-door raid on the Treasury."

Our proposed change should not affect low-income beneficiaries, since they probably won't pay taxes even if the Social Security benefits are included as taxable income. For the majority of retirees, delayed taxation has big advantages since lower tax rates have been typical during retirement years.

The elimination of welfare payments from Social Security would also allow Congress to take a fresh look at the supporting payroll taxes.

The worker's tax has increased from 1 percent on the first $3,000 of wages in 1937 to 6.13 percent on the first $25,900 of wages in 1980. This represents an incredible jump of 5,192 percent over the last forty-three years. To put this mind-boggling number in better perspective, let's assume that a worker was indeed earning $3,000 per year in 1937. If wages had increased at the same rate as the payroll tax over the last forty-three years, the worker would now earn an annual salary of $155,760.

Obviously the cost of living, or for that matter our own salaries, have not jumped nearly as fast as the payroll tax over this same period. Currently the payroll tax of 6.13 percent breaks down as follows: the retirement benefit (Old Age and Survivors Insurance—OASI) is about 4.43 percent. The additional payroll tax is for runaway disability insurance, about .65 percent, and hospital insurance (Medicare), 1.05 percent.

The Social Security Advisory Council has already proposed that Medicare should be paid for out of general revenue funds instead of Social Security taxes. Removing Medicare from the System, the Council report states, would allow the Social Security payroll tax rate to be cut from the current 6.13 percent to 5.6 percent in 1980. The Council recommends that this rate be frozen for the next 25 years, in spite of the fact that payroll taxes are scheduled to climb to 6.65 percent in 1981.

For a worker earning $20,000 per year, the Advisory Council's proposal to remove Medicare from the System would mean a tax savings of $106 in 1980 and $210 in 1981.

The Social Security program is expected to collect about $115 billion in 1980. If, in fact, the system only provides OASI benefits, then income could fall to about $83 billion, leaving some $32 billion to be paid from general tax revenues.

The sum of $32 billion is immense, so that any abrupt shift to general tax revenues should be avoided. Hence Congress may want to phase in the program over, say, the next five years. With a federal budget well in excess of $500 billion, the difficulties of phasing in welfare payments from Social Security should not prove to be insurmountable. The change could provide a realistic, feasible way to head off a complete breakdown of the current loose conglomerate arrangement.

More important, the proposed change would stabilize the nation's retirement planning. Over the past few years deep concern has spread among retirement planners that unless Social Security's costs are checked they could even seriously impair the growth of personal savings and private retirement plans.

Social Security has already created a massive strain on employers' labor costs. A firm's contribution for each worker, for example, could easily be as much as $2,271 by 1983. Small private pension plans inevitably tend to be squeezed by these mounting tax increases, to such an extent that some thirty-five thousand companies have scrapped their plans since 1975. Moreover, employers are now drilling loopholes in the dark in a desperate effort to cut the mounting federal payroll tax they must pay.

The Social Security Act allows employers to contribute your share of the payroll tax as well as their own. The Act even encourages this step by permitting your share of the tax, if paid by the employer, to be exempt from additional taxation. In other words, there would be no payroll tax on the payroll tax.

Let's see what would happen with this loophole if, for example, you earned $20,000 in 1979. If you remained outside the loophole you would have paid $1,226 in Social Security taxes. If, however, your employer reduced your salary by the amount of the Social Security tax, or to $18,774, you would still have the same gross income. So far so good.

Now the fun and games begin. Since the Internal Revenue Service still considers your Social Security payroll taxes as income, your total taxable income falls by only $75. (The difference between the Social Security payroll tax you would have paid, and that now paid by your employer based on your lower salary.) But this loophole in the way Social Security taxes are collected can bring a much bigger benefit to your employer. By paying both employee-employer contributions, the boss can save over $150. What's more, as the planned sharp rise in payroll taxes occurs, the savings can become dramatic. By 1987 the company's potential yearly savings could be over $450 with a corresponding drop in personal taxable income for the worker.

Included in the original statutes in the 1930s, this optional method of paying Social Security taxes was seldom used. Today, with payroll taxes scheduled to explode over just the next few years, scores of workers and their employers are taking advantage of this loophole to save millions of dollars each year.

Last year J. J. Pickle (D-Texas), Chairman of the Social Security Subcommittee of the House Committee on Ways and Means, began public hearings on the problems the system is encountering on this increasingly popular way to "beat the system."

Another loophole that is receiving wide notice is a part of the act which permits your employer yet another way out of the tax burden. The act states that Social Security taxes do not need to be withheld from your wages when you are paid under a sick-pay plan.

The odds are that because of the tax burden forced on business owners, many of them today can be found staring glassy-eyed in a search for yet another loophole, at the yards of fine print written into the Social Security Act. When one is discovered, however, it is usually closed by Congress.

The spiraling payroll taxes, unfortunately, will remain. Each year these tax increases will force more and more companies either to cut back or eliminate altogether their private retirement plans. This trend has been clear for some time; as our entire private retirement system races toward a dead-end street, Social Security emerges as *the* pension. Rather than by insuring that both the private and public retirement systems survive, then HEW Secretary Califano, in the spring of 1978, said the nation's future retirement benefits might be enhanced by scrapping the private pension system.

In responding to Mr. Califano's remarks, William D. Jones, Jr., senior vice-president and chief investment officer of the First National Bank of Atlanta, said in a 1978 issue of *Pensions and Investments* that "almost every citizen that can read or hear is aware that the Social Security system is in a shambles. Its funding has become a major national issue and some elected officials are finding that increasing Social Security taxes may cost some of them their jobs. The public is becoming restless, angry, and rebellious over the constantly escalating costs of maintaining the Social Security system.

"In my opinion, scrapping the private pension system and expanding Social Security coverage should not even be considered by a rational human being. It would be like putting Willie Sutton in charge of bank security or appointing Attila the Hun director of the Humane Society. Rather than scrapping private pensions for an expanded Social Security system, the reverse should be considered. It is interesting to note that most government employees are not covered by Social Security and choose overwhelmingly to remain that way. The burden of proof, I think, is on the government to justify the continuance of the Social Security system, rather than the other way around."

With a trillion-dollar credibility gap, the response of the author of this book to Mr. Califano's statement is plain shock. How anyone could conceive of replacing the private-pension system, under tight government control, with bloated Social Security completely out of government control, is a mystery whose solution is known only to Mr. Califano. In fact, as I have previously observed, the system is cluttered with so many empty money sacks that it is estimated that at least $4 trillion is currently unfunded. If this were a private plan, the government's own rules would require the debt to be amortized at a rate of about $25 billion each year.

When Congress passes legislation, it usually exempts itself and the government's own operations from the effects of the new law. Since Social Security was not forced to comply with the same federal pension laws as private-pension plans, the fools in Washington have behaved like race-car drivers who have lost their brakes. Veering out of control, they have managed to create yet another truly classic "unbelievable situation."

If we can assume for the moment that the federal pension regulations do make sense as they apply to our private pension plans, then let's look at what changes would occur if, in fact, Social Security now complied with the law.

First, we need to know just how staggering a $4 trillion debt would be for those paying taxes to support the system. Follow this arithmetic: If every person between the ages of twenty and sixty-five were to walk up to the teller's counter and plunk down enough cash to pay only their individual share of the past debt, they would each need $33,188.

The good news is that the law does not require that this enormous pile of cash be amassed at once. The bad news, for those Americans who work for a living while holding Social Security's empty bag, is that an extended payment plan is not much better. To comply with the federal law, so that the bag will gradually fill up with cash, the maximum payroll tax for 1981 would have to increase from $3,950 to somewhere around $5,000. This would require that both employee and employer pay into Social Security, at the maximum level, an incredible seventeen percent of the wage earner's salary.

But that's only the beginning. To raise this kind of hard cash Congress would be forced to hike the worker's 1982 maximum payroll tax to somewhere around $5,400. The bottom line is that our current Social Security system can't be used as any sound financial basis for a massive governmental solution to our public and private retirement problems.

Social Security is not now, nor should it ever be, considered more than a supplementary pension benefit. Any hope Americans have for a realistic retirement income in the future must be based on the traditional triad: Social Security, personal savings, and private employer retirement plans.

Even as Social Security slides toward disaster the passage of the author's proposed Social Security program could provoke some serious opposition. An enlightened Congress, however, could seize this opportunity to ignore the massive campaign that is sure to be launched by a multitude of special-interest groups. The retirement-income security of the American public demands a coherent approach, which will cover all groups equally.

The strength of the proposed Social Security program is that it offers a comprehensive approach, one that has long been sought by Congress. All previous attempts to clean up the system have been labeled "piecemeal" by congressional leaders who say they must look at the big picture before the legislative wheels can turn. To illustrate this all-or-nothing approach, we only need look at part of President Carter's proposed budget for fiscal 1980, which contained about a dozen ways to cut unnecessary or overly generous benefits as a first step in shoring up the financial integrity of the system.

One request was to get rid of the lump-sum death benefit of $225 that is paid to all survivors of Social Security recipients. The money was originally intended to defray funeral costs.

Today it would hardly defray anything. What's more, these costs could be paid from various other welfare-oriented programs to those who really need the money. The annual saving for what has become an unnecessary benefit was expected to be about $200 million.

Another planned saving would come from eliminating the College Student Benefit given to children of Social Security recipients. This money has continued to be paid, regardless of need, when the funds are also available for those who really need help from federal student-assistance programs. This suggested cut, it was estimated, would save about $162 million each year.

These are only two examples of the proposed cuts in benefits that found their way to the House Ways and Means Committee. Once there, these reasonable and modest cuts proposed by the President were quickly sidetracked to oblivion. Piecemeal attempts to bandage a leaky balloon, scoffed committee members, who again declared that progress could only be made after they studied the "big" picture. In 1979 the Social Security Advisory Council, in an attempt to grapple with the big picture, endorsed several changes in the system. Since these represent a "Band-Aid" approach similar to that already derided in the President's proposal, the new changes will probably not fare any better with Congress than did those earlier ones.

The creative changes proposed by the council are to: (1) reduce the current payroll tax about twenty percent up to the year 2005 and slow the rise of the taxable wage base; (2) bring in all newly hired federal, state, and local employees; (3) increase benefit levels for the poorest workers; and (4) experiment with splitting Social Security credits between husbands and wives in case of divorce after ten years of marriage.

But this Congress is no more willing than the last to cut even a few minor benefits proposed by the President from an already bloated program; nor will they seriously consider the expanded benefits sought by the advisory council.

The heart of the matter is that the Social Security system has become so huge, with so many promises made along the way, that any change in benefits, no matter how reasonable, can result in an avalanche of angry mail on Capitol Hill.

The author's proposal is based on the political realities

that cutting present benefits may be too large a task for congressional leaders to grapple with. They have already learned that restructuring a forty-year-old benefit program as immense as Social Security is not easy. What's more, leaving massive welfare-oriented benefits inside the retirement plan has not worked and, in fact, has become a primary factor in payroll taxes escalating out of control.

As the 1980 elections approach, Congress may have finally become concerned about the future of Social Security. In fact, deep concern has already been expressed on the Hill that taxes supporting the system have gone too high, that despite the higher taxes the Social Security trust fund could still go broke, and that some way must be found to reduce the escalating benefits before the cash runs out.

In attacking these problems Congress must recognize that Social Security can no longer serve as a national source of massive welfare-oriented payments. The basic concept of social adequacy should continue to be based on need. If no need exists, benefits should not be paid. If a need exists, then these essentially welfare benefits should be paid from general tax revenues.

Such radical moves are not easily made, but now time has forced the move. The continued use of the "pay now and retire later" method of funding Social Security has the American worker demanding more than promises from a near-cash-empty system.

The widely held belief that Social Security benefits are an earned right based on past work and contributions becomes meaningless if the system is about to go broke.

A separate Social Security program providing the nation's basic retirement benefits would go a long way toward restoring confidence in the principle of an earned retirement benefit. Social Security has been America's most successful experiment with social reform. It has transformed millions of lives from poverty and want to relative security.

Now, forty years later, with the costs soaring beyond the reach of the American worker, the question remains: How much Social Security is enough?

In the final analysis Americans are inherently productive and self-respecting, and they hope not only to pay into Social

Security but to benefit from it. Any positive approach to the country's future must also include a practical approach to the future of Social Security. Many Americans today hope and pray that Congress will act before the dream of financial security after retirement is gone forever.

11 Horns Blowing in Our Ears

During my tour of duty with the Second Marine Air Wing, I was constantly amazed by the complexity of the then modern warplanes. The cockpit resembled a large organ with rows and rows of buttons and gauges. Flying a warplane is today a science to be practiced only by professional pilots who have undergone long and extensive training in the art of keeping the plane in the air.

During World War II, however, the training of pilots resembled an assembly line. They had to learn quickly how to fly. The first step was to learn how to take off and land. Some genius had discovered that if the wheels could come up during the flight, the plane could increase its airspeed substantially. The trouble was that with retractable landing gear, the pilots sometimes landed with their wheels up. So the experts on the ground installed many safety devices. A light in the cockpit would flash if the wheels were up, while a man in the control tower would give a warning over the radio. But still the trainees would skid to a halt with their wheels tucked up inside their plane. Then they tried a warning via a red signal light just in case the pilot happened to be looking out of the plane. Nothing seemed to work. Finally the experts who designed the

plane came up with the idea of installing a horn in every cockpit. This horn would sound in the ear of the pilot every time the
throttle was closed while the landing gear was up.

One day a pilot came in for a landing. It was the same old
story—his wheels were up. The light was flashing in the cockpit, the tower was trying to contact him on the radio, while
another person tried the red signal light, but to no avail. The
result was another wheels-up landing and a badly damaged
plane. As the cadet pilot climbed out of the smashed aircraft,
the officer in charge rushed up to him in exasperation.

"What the hell went wrong this time?" he asked.

The nervous cadet, perspiring under the hot sun, was si-
lent.

"Was it possible," the officer inquired, "that the warning
light in your cockpit wasn't working? Or is it possible that you
didn't see the red signal light? Your radio was working, we
know that much. Why didn't you respond to the warning from
the radio tower?"

The flustered cadet finally replied, "I couldn't understand
what the tower was trying to tell me because there was a horn
blowing in my ear."

That story illustrates the condition of much of our retirement planning today. As I have shown, we have contrived a
financial system with all kinds of safety devices designed and
engineered to make our dollar safe and our retirement living
more meaningful and enjoyable. Yet our entire pension system
is crashing to the ground, weighted down by an inflation that
has left our retirement plans—both public and private—nearly
empty of cash. By some estimates the red ink is as much as $10
trillion, and growing every year.

The result seems to be just so many horns blowing in our
ears.

This presents the specter—so disconcerting that our leaders have thus far chosen to suppress awareness of it—that we
may all in the end be forced to rely on a near-bankrupt Social
Security System.

Even as I write this book, Americans are turning away
from personal savings. They have little incentive to do otherwise. In Chapter 5, I reported that Americans save only 5.2
percent of their disposable income. Before I had even finished
the chapter, I received a report that the rate had plunged to

only 4.5 percent. The latest figure, according to the Savings and Loan Foundation, is only 4.1 percent.

Just as you cannot produce economic growth without investments, you cannot produce financial independence at retirement without personal savings. Abraham Lincoln may have said it best when he advised, "You cannot bring prosperity by discouraging thrift."

Take a recent article on big spending appearing in *The Wall Street Journal*. A thirty-seven-year-old Miami lawyer, living it up beyond his $42,000-a-year income, was quoted as saying, "I might as well spend my money now. What good is it going to do me when I'm sixty-two?"

If we are to save our retirement system as a meaningful source of financial security, we must act like a mature and responsible nation. Above all, we must persist in our battle against inflation. No other course will do much to protect the real value of pensions. Ending the runaway inflation we now face is necessary for any number of reasons, but surely the protection of pensions is one of the best reasons of all. If we can lick inflation, our retirement system will fall into place. If we cannot, maybe nothing else matters.

Inflation comes like a "thief in the night"; its effects are usually hidden. One example is the overtaxation of personal income, which adds the insult of unwarranted tax bite to the injury of lost purchasing power. As inflation pushes up our nominal income, we are simultaneously shoved into the higher tax brackets, though this effect certainly was never intended when our graduated income tax was adopted. This "bracket creep" occurs even though our real income—dollars adjusted for inflation—has not increased at all. Our federal tax system —essentially unchanged for decades—should have a horn blowing in its ear. Unless our entire method of collecting income tax is changed—our tax tables indexed for the effects of inflation— the overpayment of taxes will continue to lower our standard of living by removing from our hands money we would ordinarily have saved.

The effects of inflation on the income-tax rates become apparent when you compare the money the average taxpayer has handed over to Uncle Sam since 1964.

In 1964 the average taxpayer paid a little over twelve percent of earnings to the IRS in federal taxes. Today the rate is closer to eighteen percent, or higher than the 1964 average by a whopping fifty percent. The tax grab has been growing at this unfair clip in spite of income-tax cuts in 1964 and 1965, the average cut for these two years being twenty-five percent. The top rate tumbled from ninety-one percent to seventy percent and the bottom rate fell from twenty percent to only fourteen percent. Subsequently personal exemptions increased to $1,000, further softening the tax blow if only inflation could be avoided.

But despite this congressional tax juggling, falling nominal tax rates have been overtaken by accelerating inflation, creating a steep rise in actual rates of taxation and the proportion paid out of income.

For example, a congressional study revealed that a family earning an expected median income of $25,717 in 1983 (the Social Security wage base for that year will be $33,900) would pay a top federal tax rate of twenty-four percent. But, in terms of the dollar's 1979 value, the purchasing power of the 1983 income would be $1,561 less than a comparable wage earner and his family realized in 1964.

The most alarming aspect of our inflation-wracked income-tax code is the finding that a ten percent increase in our income tends to raise a family's federal income taxes by about sixteen percent. Such a result, as already pointed out, was never intended by those who devised our graduated income tax.

Recognizing that the income-tax rules work against them, and squeezed by inflation and government spending, as many as twenty million Americans are cutting the government out of hundreds of billions of dollars in untaxed income. There are estimates that as much as twenty-five percent of taxable income escapes taxation, resulting in a loss of perhaps $75 billion of tax revenue each year.

This "underground" economy is dominated by the self-employed—from doctors, accountants, and lawyers to barmaids, window washers, and truck drivers—of whom the IRS claims as many as sixty percent report less than their earnings to the government.

The underground economy thrives on what the "smart" operators call "off the books" income.

In England, where the income-tax rates are a great deal higher, starting at a basic rate of thirty-three percent for low-income workers and increasing up to an incredible eighty-three percent, it is called "working on the fiddle."

Whatever it's called, the underground cash economy, well established overseas, is rapidly expanding in this country. With our government seemingly powerless to put the brakes on their defection, millions of Americans are opting out of the formal income-tax system. They have adopted in its place the "cash for service" system in which, by not withholding any taxes, and by not paying any contributions to Social Security or unemployment insurance, as required by law, both the worker and the employer can avoid the blizzard of government paperwork.

Many small businesses, for their part, offer work at "considerably less" than first quoted, if the payment is in cash without the need for a receipt.

The barter economy has also emerged as a sizable source of untaxed income. Trading or swapping services among businesses has become commonplace. A lawyer sums it up best when he acknowledges that he no longer feels guilty about the barter system. "I trade my legal work for car upkeep and repair. I've worked out the guy's divorce," he goes on, "and he's given me tune-ups and a totally rebuilt car."

With the banks facing unprecedented demands for hundred-dollar bills, the cash swirling through our underground economy has now reached, by some estimates, $100 billion. With roughly one hundred million workers in the U.S., that amounts to $1,000 in cash on hand for each worker—far more than most workers, or their families, for that matter, ever have at one time.

Back in 1976 the Internal Revenue Service made an estimate of the size of the underground economy. The figures, adjusted for 1979 dollars, amounted to $184 billion a year in untaxed income. For reference, that's about the size of the entire Canadian economy of $196 billion reported last year.

In the final analysis our outdated income-tax code has not only brought our retirement saving plans into serious question, but it has also allowed to remain unquestioned the methods used to fund our retirement plans through payroll-related contributions. Worse yet, millions of Americans no longer feel guilty about ripping off Uncle Sam; the government seems to be ripping them off first.

"Now I think in terms of economic survival," states a self-employed man moving in and out of the underground economy. "Taxation has become legalized theft."

From the human angle, if you are part of the mangled middle class, you probably feel worse off than people do living at the so-called poverty level.

Dr. Avraham Shama, a consumer psychologist at City University of New York, recently released a survey on the emotional factors that have prompted middle-class taxpayer revolts in a number of states. The survey shows a growing reluctance on the part of those who form the backbone of American society to foot the bill for the increasing multitude of programs that are intended to benefit the poor.

Frustrated at the way prices keep going up, and mindful of the way the feds hike tax rates on purely inflationary (rather than real) income, almost ninety percent of Dr. Shama's respondents say it's hard to make economic plans for the future.

Shama believes that "having gotten used to rapidly improved standards of living, families suddenly face a halt to upward social and economic mobility. The importance of 'being in control,' a strong middle- and upper-class value, has been challenged because of stagflation [inflation coupled with slow real economic growth]. The middle class, perhaps more than any other group, believed they controlled their lives. They felt they could manipulate their environment to their own advantage. But because of the uncertainty associated with stagflation, planning by members of the middle class has become much harder, if not impossible. The ability to control one's own life is also lessened, leaving people shaken and confused."

The shock to millions of middle-class taxpayers is that the old virtue of hard work is no longer rewarded by a steadily improving standard of living.

On the practical side, unless steps are taken to control the income-tax bite, expressed as a percentage of our real income, a serious question will emerge about the value of our retirement plans. It can't be overemphasized, let me add, that deferring taxes on contributions to our retirement plans has always been based on a solid expectation: that the income-tax rate would be markedly lower at retirement because our income would be less than the income we received while still on the job.

But if inflation continues anywhere near the recent rate, the monstrous tax swindle being perpetrated by the federal government on working people could have the result that a worker's retirement-dollar income will actually exceed the dollar income he earned during much of his working life.

For example, if today's thirty-five-year-old worker earning $15,000 receives a ten percent annual pay raise, as a result of our inflationary government policies, until age sixty-five, his final salary at retirement would be a staggering $262,000. If the worker retired under today's income-tax rules, he'd be in a much higher tax bracket than he had been in during many on-the-job years.

The irony of the whole income-tax muddle is that dollars set aside earlier to defer taxes *until* low-tax-rate retirement years are likely to be taxed more heavily *in* retirement.

If this fraud on the American worker is allowed to continue in a time of seemingly out-of-control inflation, everything I have covered in this book may turn out to be academic. Retirement systems as we know them, without at least the illusion of substantial tax savings, may themselves be a casualty in our raging inflationary world.

This not-so-hidden tax or "taxflation" is a little-known way our government finances its spending. Since the government regularly runs budget deficits and controls the creation of money, the feds in effect print money out of thin air. The result is that the government remains unaffected by inflation; we do not. The feds can spend the money they create; we suffer a loss of purchasing power.

If we compare the size of government spending to national income, we can see what has happened to this bundle of inflation-begotten cash that continues to roll into Washington. In 1949 total government spending was 28 percent of national income. By 1976 it had reached 42 percent. This federal part of the increase was not due to defense spending; that was 8 percent of national income in 1949 and only 6.6 percent in 1976. The bulk of the increased government outlay has gone for domestic spending, reaching thirty-five percent of national income by 1976.

You and I as taxpayers ultimately pay for all government spending. We pay explicitly in the form of taxes, and indirectly via inflation. We also pay in reduced economic growth, since taxes depress the very personal savings that make possible greater investment.

Then there is the ballooning national debt. During the last decade the politically painless way to pay interest on the debt has been simply to print more money. We are now reaping the depressing harvest of the high levels of government spending by way of taxflation.

Inflation, then, is our number one problem; it hits us not only during our day-to-day lives, as we build up credits toward retirement, but strikes an even more devastating blow during our retirement.

If our nation's pension system is to survive, and I am beginning to believe that our leaders are not convinced that it should, we cannot tolerate either prolonged double-digit inflation or the shameful advantage our government takes of it in despoiling the people of their earnings and their savings. Like the Miami lawyer, millions of us, with federal horns blowing in our ears, could "spend money now; what good is it going to do us when we are sixty-two?" Ending up in poverty at retirement, the public may never know what really hit them. For the people at large are innocent. All the while the temptation of most in Congress seemingly is to do nothing.

One political figure, however, is active. Al Ullman (D-Oregon), Chairman of the Committee on Ways and Means of the House of Representatives, announced hearings on the proposed Tax Restructuring Act of 1979. The announcement read, "The purpose of these hearings is to reexamine the basic federal tax structure in light of the imperative need to face up to the critical problems of persistently escalating inflation, to encourage capital formation, and to increase savings, investment, and productivity in the private sector, and to provide important tax relief for individuals and businesses."

To be productive in our fight to save our retirement security, the hearings must come to grips with the gross mistreatment of savers, and especially small savers. Sobering is the fact that federal income-tax rates today are as high as seventy percent on token savings interest. Such token interest, with grotesque injustice, is officially viewed as "unearned" income. Also, the American public should no longer tolerate the way disgraceful federal regulations limit the nominal interest rate paid to millions of small savers, to less than half the rate of inflation. Big savers can get the inflation rate. Why not the small as well?

For unless something is done in these two areas of interest ceilings and taxation of savings, and done soon, saving for retirement will become next to meaningless. The nation's savings rate compared to our disposable income will continue to fall below the already alarming four percent. And for good reason Our wonders in Washington cannot continue to believe every one in America just got off the hay wagon.

For reasons partly connected with the foregoing, many Americans are facing a bleak financial future. Take the findings of pollster Lou Harris, who is widely regarded as one of the best in the business. "The people without pensions are really hurting in this time of inflation. Among the retired who have no pension benefits, fifty-three percent report that they are in desperate shape, with their standard of living perilously reduced." Harris is talking about the probability that only one in four of the private work force will be lucky enough to receive a pension and thus escape the indicated desperation.

For the overwhelming majority of Americans facing retirement, it is little comfort to learn that Social Security benefits alone are not enough to live on—and were never intended to be. Social Security was expected to provide a "base" or "floor" on which a realistic poverty-escaping retirement income might be built. This floor was to have superimposed on it income from personal savings and private pensions. But inflation has drastically changed the way this retirement structure was expected to work. People are understandably scared. They are deeply troubled by runaway, out-of-control, all-consuming, double-digit inflation. According to the Harris poll, "Fully eighty-four percent of all retired people feel that inflation is reducing their standard of living. An even higher eighty-eight percent of currently employed people share the same view."

When both our government and our nation's workers live beyond their means, a day of financial reckoning is inevitable. By pressuring our government for programs that we believe are free, when in fact we cannot afford them, and by letting our government expand the money supply artificially through gross excesses of the Federal Reserve, we have allowed inflation to rob us of much of what we have saved.

A chorus of "I told you so" would not be inappropriate.

After arriving at the airport, I hailed a cab. En route to the hotel, I struck up a conversation with the driver. As the meter clicked away and the tab for the brief taxi ride escalated out of sight, inflation again became present and visible. The cabbie, as it turned out, was facing some serious medical bills and all hell broke loose when I stated that maybe a nationally mandated health plan along the lines of England's national health scheme would be a financial disaster.

Weaving between cars as we raced back to the hotel, the driver said, "Maybe I don't understand the whole health-care issue. But I've got a wife and four kids, and I can't afford the doctor bills any more. We need some kind of government program, and it's got to be *free.*"

What my cabbie—and so many others—do not yet realize is that *nothing* is free. As a nation we must begin to realize that there is no such thing as a free lunch. We can no longer borrow money to pay for it. We can no longer print the money to pay for it. In fact, reliance on free-lunch governmental programs to solve all our problems has, in reality, reduced the purchasing power of our money so badly that we can, in many cases, no longer buy the "free" lunch.

But that's not the end of it. With the American auto industry running on empty, major corporations are rattling the begging bowl in Washington. We are now asked to guarantee the free lunch once again.

Many Americans may not be aware of the fact that their government has been guaranteeing wobbly loans for some time. In fact, during the fiscal year ending September 30, 1980, the federal government and its sponsored enterprises will make new loans and guarantees of as much as $200 billion. But —and get this for understanding your government's operations —only about $2.8 billion will show up in the budget totals that appear in the newspaper. The economic and fiscal effects of these off-budget programs have largely been ignored by Congress when it comes time to make the annual budget.

"The American people and their representatives are not being properly informed as to the extent of the government's impact on total credit flows," warns Nancy Teeters, a governor of the Federal Reserve Board.

Chrysler, the nation's third largest automaker, employing over 125,000 workers, and supporting as many as two hundred thousand jobs when you consider all the suppliers, is on the verge of bankruptcy. The 1979 loss is expected to exceed $1 billion, marking the first time any American corporation has lost that much money in a single year. But even if Chrysler received the controversial transfusion of a $1.5 billion federal loan guarantee, there is little hope for the future. Wall Street auto analysts have publicly stated that the company is doomed.

"For all practical purposes, they are bankrupt at this point," said one analyst. "Anybody who looks at the financial ratios has to come to the conclusion that this company hasn't much life in it."

The Carter administration seems willing to take the risk of allowing government's loan guarantees to prevent outright bankruptcy at Chrysler because it is politically expedient, and because it is the nation's tenth largest industrial corporation.

President Carter may well point to the fact that federal loan guarantees did not start with troubled Chrysler. In fact, the federal bailout did not start with the near bankruptcy of Lockheed, or of New York City, or even of the struggling Wheeling-Pittsburgh Steel Company. They started many years ago. With an increasing number of government agencies and private companies picking up federal loans and loan guarantees, the total of direct and indirect government loans has tripled since 1970. For 1979 and 1980, they are expected to increase by twelve percent each year! Not all the federal loan guarantees go to private business. As individuals, we are at the head of the line as home buyers, farmers, and veterans, accounting for half of the total outstanding guarantees.

In 1980, according to the Office of Management and Budget, all federal loans and loan guarantees will amount to a colossal $554 billion. In fact the $1.5 billion loan guarantee sought by Chrysler hardly makes a ripple compared to the congressional bailout and loan guarantees already granted other private companies.

The shipbuilding industry got $5.2 billion, five steel companies picked up a total of $365 million. On and on the list goes.

But the classic example of what can happen when federal loan guarantees permit a never-empty purse has to be the Washington, D.C., subway. Now labeled the "solid-gold Cadillac of mass transit," the Washington Metro has left the nation's taxpayers holding the bag for a nightmare of financial irresponsibility. Back in 1972 the government was asked to guarantee $1.2 billion in bonds to help build the subway. The argument was that, with federal guarantees, the bonds could offer a lower interest rate and it would not cost the taxpayers a cent.

The subway was begun in 1969 at an estimated cost of $2.5 billion, and is now almost complete. Stretching for 101 miles, it represents about forty percent of the 261 miles of all new U.S. subway construction for the cities of Atlanta, San Francisco, Baltimore, Buffalo, and Miami. Its $7.2 billion price tag is over a half billion dollars more than the combined cost of all five new subways listed above!

But what about you and me as taxpayers, we who were assured by Congress that the subway would not cost a cent? Congress has already guaranteed that we will pay the bill.

One of the reasons the Washington area ended up with a glaringly disproportionate share of federal mass-transit money was because it remained outside of federal transportation policy. With a federal giveaway tucked in its pocket, it never had to compete with the rest of the country for federal money. Congress was able to stick the nation with the price of a solid-gold mass transit system.

But federal guarantees, in addition to assuring constant munificence, continue to mask a deeper problem faced by virtually all failing companies—the pension scandal.

For Chrysler is also shaping up as an ominous harbinger of the pension woes that could be awaiting America's major corporations in the mid-1980s. In fact, in the rush to save Chrysler, almost nothing has been said publicly about its unfunded vested pension debt—estimated in 1978 to be at least $1.1 billion. Unfunded vested pension benefits are current legal obligations of the pension plan, and of the company itself. They must be paid eventually, even though the employee leaves the company or the plan is terminated at bankruptcy. The Chrysler bailout is, in fact, steeped in irony. Whatever the merits of the government loan guarantee, the company's chances of survival are bleak while the pension debt continues to soar out of control.

Saving Chrysler from collapse may only postpone the next bailout—that of the pension debt. With inflation pushing up salaries, this billion-plus pension debt could surge tremendously over just the next few years, far surpassing anything Chrysler could be expected to earn—if, in fact, it earns a profit at all.

In our rush to save Chrysler, we may have overlooked the most important asset the company has—its workers. If the company survives, will their retirement security slide into default?

How can we turn our financial security at retirement right side up? Much of what has to be done requires an awareness on the part of the American public that many of the changes need to start in Congress. Federal regulations have so evolved that we, as workers, are, for the most part, effectively prevented from ever receiving a realistic private pension. We are also, as savers, similarly prevented by our own government from earning a realistic net return on any money we may save individually toward our retirement.

We now turn, at last, to the more constructive side of the picture.

What in heaven's name can be done in the 1980s to support rather than discourage the retirement income security of our nation's workers? Bear in mind, taking a look at the future is always risky.

Like the stranger who came into the restaurant and said to the waiter, "I need a bowl of soup and a few kind words." Silently the waiter brought a bowl of soup and set it before the stranger. Looking up at the waiter, he said, "And now for a few kind words?" The waiter leaned over and whispered, "Don't eat that soup."

But if the future seems risky, let's concentrate on our past mistakes. You don't have to be terribly smart to identify the federal legislation that threatens to tumble our financial security down around our feet.

Much of what I will recommend has already been alluded to in this book in a more specialized context. Let me sum up the areas where constructive change is essential if we are to have any reasonable hope of providing financial security in a world of galloping inflation.

First, we need to give individual savers a long-overdue break. As we have already seen, under today's inflation, we need to earn an interest rate of twenty-two percent just to stay even with the purchasing power of our dollar. An interest rate this high is clearly incompatible with the smooth operation of our economy. But Congress could do what other countries have done. It could exempt interest income, at least to the extent that prevails in—say—Germany (where a family of four can earn $4,400 in tax-free interest). It becomes almost absurd when you think about our current federal policy. We are required to pay personal income tax—up to an astonishing rate of seventy percent because interest is classified as "unearned" income—on money placed in our savings account while the funds suffer a rapid decline in purchasing power.

Congress could also provide the average American the same opportunities open to wealthy individuals when it comes to earning realistic interest rates. It seems incredible that federal policy allows a person with ten thousand dollars to invest to realize over twice the interest rate that can be earned by a person with less than ten thousand dollars to invest.

"The little guy is being taken for a ride every time he saves some money," a banker told me. "Hell, the government-rigged interest rates are currently set so low that after the saver pays even minimal taxes on his interest income, he's way in the hole! In fact, the passbook saving rate, after taxes, now allows him less than a four percent net gain on his money before inflation. With inflation running at about fourteen percent, our government has embarrassed the hell out of the little guy who has maybe two or three thousand dollars to save."

"The message seems to be getting through," I said. "Americans as a whole are not saving money."

"That's right," my banker friend continued. "The government needs to really encourage savings. They need to open up the IRA to all workers. Give them the chance to save for their retirement on the same tax-favored basis as their employers."

In fact, my friend is right. The belated legislation by Congress allowing workers to open their own individual retirement accounts has turned out to be complicated and grossly unfair. Besides excluding millions of Americans, Congress has allowed the remaining eligible workers a ridiculously low limit of savings under the IRA. Congress has been content with this unfair limit during the past six years of galloping inflation, the immoral excuse being that the feds need the revenue to maintain spending programs all over the map. In fact, the original IRA limit of fifteen hundred dollars, set back in 1974, has probably been *reduced* to less than a thousand dollars in today's purchasing power. Only the prodigies in Washington can apparently understand how this pittance of an annual limit on IRA's actually encourages saving for retirement; the cold fact is that it has not done so.

If the IRA program is to offer any reasonable incentive for the American working public, it must be flexibly based on the individual's age, income level, and family responsibility. For individual saving for retirement is really a personal matter, not one that lends itself to bureaucratic red tape and complex federal laws.

Now let's look at another area where Congress has to act, and rather quickly. This is in the sprawling terrain of Social Security. As I proposed in a previous chapter, a strong case can be made for confining Social Security to the retirement sector alone—which, as we have seen, was the original goal of the system when it was sold to the American people.

The Social Security program of today, in effect, is a disaster looking for a place to happen. Congress might be willing to insure against a catastrophe if some way could be found to assure Americans that their contributions are being accounted for in a reasonable manner in their own retirement accounts.

A new, separate Social Security system could provide the answer in a way most Americans might find acceptable in spite of the increasing payroll taxes that are sure to come.

Social Security Commissioner Stanford G. Ross, who resigned late last year, fired off a parting shot at the system when he said that people must, when it comes to contributing to their own retirement, forget the "myths" that have built up over the years. They must, he went on, recognize today's payroll tax for what it is—a tax to support not just the elderly, but also the disabled, sick, and their dependents.

"The myth that Social Security was an individual contribution, not a tax, proved valuable in the early days of the program, but . . . is helping to confuse the debate over Social Security today."

The problem, as Ross explained, is that workers don't understand the way Social Security works and how it has evolved on an ad hoc basis into a broad social—instead of retirement—program. In fact, the runaway cost prompted Ross to admit that if today's workers really want "every piece of the currently legislated benefit package . . . then the corollary is the mandating, without their consent, of ever-higher tax payments by tomorrow's workers."

Commissioner Ross pointed out that the graying of America in the early twenty-first century will cause vast changes in the Social Security system. "The real issue," he said, "is whether the taxpaying public accepts the government's exactions—whether in the form of payroll taxes, income taxes, or other kinds of taxes—because of civic responsibility."

But the system is now teetering on the verge of financial collapse, confronted with hopelessly unfulfillable current obligations. Hence the continued payment, in the name of "civic responsibility," of those climbing payroll taxes has become increasingly difficult to sell to the average American worker, especially those a long way from retirement.

Commissioner Ross, in a burst of unusual candor for a public official, stated that younger workers must be given at least an honest explanation of Social Security. This writer would add, now that payroll taxes are really pinching, that workers for the first time must be given a chance to express themselves. Specifically, it's about time they are allowed to decide what benefits they are willing to support with their heavy payroll taxes.

Nothing like a proposal of this sort has ever been advanced before. Since its inception, Social Security has operated as if it were on an isolated island. It has relied on its separately collected payroll taxes. It has been able to avoid routine yearly scrutiny by Congress. Thus it has effectively been able to fend off questions about its truly sprawling operations.

Highly respected academic specialists are also concerned about the problem. Take Michael J. Boskin, a professor of economics at Stanford University. Writing in *The Wall Street Journal,* he concluded that Social Security has become "a political system which is heavily biased toward dispensing current benefits without worrying about future costs."

As we have already seen in Chapter 9, we face the grim prospect of a seventy percent increase in the ratio of retirees to workers, who will be living longer and collecting greater numbers of benefit checks. This raises another question about the future of Social Security. A major problem facing the system, often overlooked by the public, is the crippling effect the lengthening retirement period has on the cost of doing business. Actuaries have estimated that a single year added to life expectancy or subtracted for early retirement could increase the long-term Social Security liability by more than one third!

As a result, even the steeply increasing payroll taxes now set by Congress can't begin to cover the expected long-term liability. The system's huge obligation to pay simply reflects the fact that Social Security as presently constituted attempts to combine an earned entitlement or retirement program and a welfare arrangement for poor elderly people. But, as has already been suggested, there's no need to combine the two programs.

If the retirement and welfare programs are separated, we could finance welfare out of general revenues. Then such welfare programs would compete openly with other government programs so that Congress could have a better chance of allocating the nation's scarce resources in a more rational way.

Another issue Congress must face, after years of patched-up legislation, is the makeup of a realistic national retirement policy. What is a person entitled to for a lifetime of work? Right now the United States, partly because the feds have drifted into an inflationary morass, has no overall retirement philosophy to provide an answer.

The passage of ERISA, including pension insurance offered

by the PBGC, has not brought the average worker the protection necessary in today's inflationary economy. Steps must be taken to insure that all pension plans are adequately funded, not just insured for a loss that has already occurred. Public pension plans must also be brought under control with the passage of PERISA so that the nation, for the first time, can understand the massive financial morass underlying much of our public retirement system. There is no reason for public pension funds to be exempt from the same types of safeguards that we have enacted for the private retirement system.

Most pressing of all may be the need for a national compulsory private employer-sponsored pension system, as outlined in Chapter 7.

Under the current pension rules, most workers, moving from job to job, will fall between the cracks of the vesting schedules and leave most of their earned retirement benefits behind. Our private pension system cries out for portability of *earned* pension credits. A national compulsory private pension system would recognize at last that a realistic pension was, indeed, a legitimate payroll cost; that it was a form of deferred compensation; and, in short, that it has become a necessary cost of doing business.

For a clear grasp of what's going on in America today, take a gander at the accompanying chart.

I have constructed this device for illustrative purposes, conveniently rounding the total number of workers in the private sector to 100 million. The chart is not intended as a textbook reference, but merely as a graphic illustration of the extent to which our private pension system has failed to meet the nation's needs for a supplementary pension income over and above the "floor" of benefits provided by Social Security.

With the private pension system estimated to cover only one tenth of those people now retiring and/or already retired, and less than one in four American workers soon to retire, this is a crisis that touches us all now, or at the very least will touch us in the near future. It is a crisis we ourselves have helped to create by allowing the people who dominate federal retirement planning to be responsible to no one—the ideal prized by every bureaucracy.

The fragmented federal approach to retirement policy-

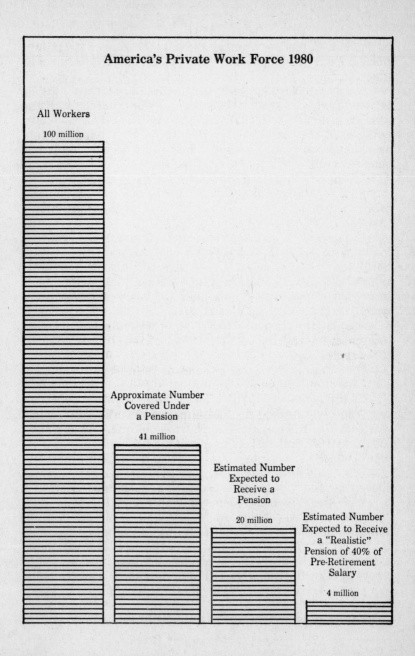

America's Private Work Force 1980

All Workers

100 million

Approximate Number
Covered Under
a Pension

41 million

Estimated Number
Expected to
Receive a
Pension

20 million

Estimated Number
Expected to Receive
a "Realistic"
Pension of 40% of
Pre-Retirement
Salary

4 million

making now subjects our private and public pension plans to as many as thirty-six laws administered by no fewer than nineteen federal agencies!

Like it or not, it is in Washington that the pension laws are Scotch-taped together. The average citizen has neither the time nor the money to be there; he wouldn't understand what they were saying anyway; and without the special-interest groups to apply the pressure on Congress, no one is going to do it for him.

As a result the American worker has been left "twisting in the wind," faced with a near-empty purse at retirement—a purse that can be quickly exhausted by government-created inflation and taxes.

Moreover, the aging process is no longer a gradual, lifetime affair. Our aging begins with retirement from a lifetime of work. For most Americans, retirement does not constitute the best years of their lives. Our gloomy attitude toward the state of being old, clouded by the concerns of aging, and the fear of death itself, make this a subject most active workers tend to avoid.

All the warnings about poverty in retirement seem years away—until we turn sixty. But these days the graying of America is moving many more millions of people relentlessly toward the magical Otto von Bismarck age of retirement.

Forced to rely on a combination of outright welfare and welfare-oriented Social Security, few retirees seem able to provide for themselves against the cruelties of crippling inflation.

Just for openers, income from savings and investments currently amounts to only about fifteen percent of the total income received by retired individuals over age sixty-five. What was once expected to provide future travel and adventure in retirement has been taxed away and stolen by inflation.

In effect, without serviceable overall federal policy on retirement, our nation has allowed many of its more mature citizens, both the retired and those facing retirement, to slide below the poverty line.

And the retirement mess will get worse. A growing number of young Americans are marching to a different drummer. They simply don't want to be parents. In fact, twice as many twenty- to thirty-year-old women are childless now as in 1960. Recent estimates indicate that as many as twenty-five percent of women now in their twenties will never have children, compared to only ten percent of all women who are childless.

Like it or not, the graying of America has arrived. It has been pushed on top of the already overburdened retirement system by an American birthrate that has virtually skidded to a halt, falling to its lowest level of the twentieth century, even falling below the paltry levels reached during the Depression years.

In the earlier chapters we discussed what amounts to a national disaster affecting our entire pension system. Today the frightening fact is that no one knows how to pay for most of the private and public retirement benefits already promised when the cost explodes into the trillions of dollars, as it will in the decades ahead. The Social Security tax bite—for worker and employer—could soar beyond twenty-five percent of payroll and well over thirty percent of take-home pay. The federal bill to support the elderly could jump from the current $200 billion to $6 trillion in just the next fifty years. Finding money to pay today's mushrooming benefits will pale by comparison to the nightmare that awaits the American worker in the early part of the next century.

Unless we as a nation pull together and fully understand how perilous the future can become for the aging, we may be forced to abandon the idea of meaningful financial security in retirement.

In a world where our daily lives resemble a bicycle ride—all of us pumping furiously to avoid falling off—Congress must help by restoring prudence in government and by encouraging, through tax laws and regulations, long-term personal savings. Equally important, we as individuals must learn to make ourselves primarily responsible for our own well-being.

A top priority must be to abolish poverty among older Americans. In a nation as wealthy as our own, no one should be forced into such a marginal existence after a lifetime of working. An adequately financed system of Social Security retirement benefits, combined with dependable and fully funded pension plans, must be the basis for this transformation.

For knowledge is power. With widely dispersed knowledge, the system can be changed for the better. The present generation of political activists has challenged the institutions that